World Civilization Since 1770

Margaret L. Inglehart

GMI Engineering & Management Institute
Flint, Michigan

Maps prepared by
William Henderson

KENDALL/HUNT
PUBLISHING COMPANY
Dubuque, Iowa

This edition has been printed directly from the author's manuscript copy.

B   403088   01

PREFACE

This book is a very short and highly condensed account of world history from about 1770 to the present. It is written for the student who is not a liberal arts major, and who wishes to get the main thrust of such a course in less time than a full semester. I have attempted to provide at least a rudimentary account of all key events which have happened since the mid-18th century. Thus the reader of this book will not miss any important development. What he or she will miss is the thorough analysis usually found in conventional textbooks for freshmen history courses. Such textbooks are marvels of facts, and some, such as the venerable History of Western Civilization by Christopher, Brinton and Wolfe (which I cite more than once) have trained more than a generation of undergraduate history majors. It was that specific book and that specific course, called in ancient times "Western Civ", that made a historian out of me when I was a freshman. It is still one of the best books on the subject, and I heartily recommend it to any student who wishes to learn more about any given topic I discuss in the pages which follow. I also include a perfunctary bibliography at the end of each chapter. These bibliographies are by no means complete; they are intended to be only a starting point for the advanced student.

In condensing so much material into such a short space, I was obliged to make numerous difficult decisions about what to include and what to leave out in my discussion. For example, I say very little about the Third World before the mid-19th century, and focus throughout the book on the advanced industrialized western countries. The reason for this is that the changes during this period which were important enough to affect the whole world, such as the Industrial Revolution, the world wars, and imperialism, all emanated from Western Europe or the United States. We tend to study the countries which are the movers and shakers, whether what they move and what they shake is good or bad.

Another caveat to the reader is that many of the events discussed in these pages are still being hotly disputed. Was the Industrial Revolution good or bad? Was Napoleon a villain or a great man? Could anything have prevented Hitler's rise to power? Was Franklin Roosevelt a genius or a demagogue? Some of the issues such as the Vietnam War and the crisis of the Middle East are particularly volatile. The student should bear in mind that most authors of textbooks try particularly hard to be objective about such matters, or at least to describe alternative points of view; but no author can completely succeed in objectivity. Thus the sensible student should begin to question my analysis on page one, and continue a critical attitude to the end of the book.

iii

I should like to thank my friends and colleagues who have encouraged me in this enterprise, particularly Linda Walker, Jerry Ailes and Bruce Boss. My special thanks go to William Henderson, who prepared my maps and gave much good advice, and to Harry Hendrickson, my indefatigable editor and fellow historian. Carrie Wagner gave me much valuable and cheerful assistance during the early stages. The heroine of the piece is above all Lorraine Martin, who performed heroic feats in helping me put the book together.

Margaret L. Inglehart
Ph.D., University of Chicago
Associate Professor of History
GMI Engineering and Management Institute

TABLE OF CONTENTS

MAPS

CHAPTER 1 - REVOLUTION: THE FIRST WAVE

Part I

Background: The Enlightenment

The Enlightenment was a period of intellectual awakening in Europe and America in the 18th century which saw great contributions in all the arts and sciences and new philosophical attitudes about the role of man and his place in the world. The buoyant confidence, the optimism and the emphasis on democratic concepts contributed markedly to the American and French Revolutions which followed. Some of the concepts defining the rights of man, introduced at that time, have since become the accepted creeds of democratic countries of the world.

The Enlightenment was characterized by a feeling of confidence about man's ability to solve problems. The German philosopher Leibnitz epitomized the prevailing attitude when he described ours as the best of all possible worlds. The world was a clock, created and set in motion by God, with a mechanism intelligible to all. Man had only to observe its laws to see how the works functioned and if it had broken down, to repair it. The French writer Voltaire later satirized this complacency in his novel, Candide, but for most of the century optimism prevailed. Confidence in the perfectibility of man combined with the assurance that he was bright enough to bring this perfection about himself. Many accepted the logic of another French philosopher, René Descartes. Descartes felt that to arrive at truth one must first doubt everything. In particular, emotions and impressions gained by sensory perceptions were not to be trusted. The only certain thing, he thought, was that he existed: "I think, therefore I am." ("Cogito, ergo sum.") From that step he applied the use of reason to arrive at knowledge, and convinced several generations of followers that reason was indeed the key to the universe.

Brilliant new discoveries fueled this confidence. Leibnitz and the British mathematician, Sir Isaac Newton, arrived at calculus at the same moment. Intellectual triumphs proceeded apace in fields as diverse as chemistry (Antoine Lavoisier discovered oxygen) and economics (François Quesnay founded the Physiocrats, who believed in the rule of nature, and said land is the only source of wealth.) Carolus Linneaus epitimized much of the prevailing attitude in his research ascribing an ascending order of "perfection" to plants and animals, a significant step contributing to the theory of Evolution a hundred years later. This concept was espoused by Condorcet, and by historians Giovanni Vico and the Johann Herder, who at the end of the 18th century perceived all of history as a continuous spiral moving upward toward perfection. Rationalism was triumphant. The mind was supreme. Scrupulous attention to the laws of mathematics and logic would bring all conceivable rewards. "Reason, natural law, progress"--This was the essence of the Enlightenment.

Among the real contributions of the century were reforms undertaken in areas where inefficiency or injustice was perceived. Adam Smith attacked the

1

nationalistic trading policy of mercantilism which involved government controls and regulations of the economy. In contrast he advocated laissez-faire, or free trade, and free competition among private entrepreneurs as the only real way to increase wealth. Casare Beccaria of Italy called for reform of law codes, so that punishments might no longer be cruel and arbitrary, but made to fit the crime. In education numerous attacks were made on the rigid attitude and educational discipline of the old order, the most remarkable of which was Emile, by the Swiss philosopher, Jean-Jacques Rousseau. Summing up the work of the entire movement, Denis Diderot put together a massive encyclopedia of contributions from all the leading thinkers in pursuit of reason and progress.

In literature and the arts the Baroque style from the previous century continued to be important, while neoclassicism became a major influence. Like the Enlightenment as a whole, neoclassicism was characterized by an emphasis on reason, or clear thinking and precise rules. It included a genuine reverence for Greece and Rome, which was given new vigor by the discovery of Pompeii in 1748. In keeping with this mood, one of the major works of the century was The Decline and Fall of the Roman Empire by Edward Gibbon. In architecture, both of these influences were apparent: many important buildings were done in a refinement of Baroque called rococo, which was lighter, airier and more charming: in churches from that time one sees a great deal of gold and white decoration, the ceiling done like a pale blue sky, with complacent pink cherubs gambolling about white cotton clouds. Neoclassicism was more austere and tended to strip buildings of such frivolous decor and take them back to logical proportions. Late in the century all manners of buildings began to appear which were replicas of Greek temples; some of them masterpieces in their own right, such as Monticello, designed by Thomas Jefferson.

In painting it was a century of great portraits, particularly the English school of Sir Joshua Reynolds, Lawrence, Gainsborough and Romney. At the end of the century neoclassicism appeared in painting, as in the portraits done by Jacques David during the French Revolution and the Napoleonic era. The colors are muted, the action restrained, with Greek buildings often in the background, and the subjects frequently dressed in classical clothes. Yet another school was that of William Hogarth who did realistic and satirical studies of common life. Hogarth's fascination with the sordid aspects of life was also a theme of literature in the 18th century. The novel became the most popular literary device, but it tended to be earthy and realistic and had little in common with the refined and austere mood of classicism. Daniel Defoe wrote Robinson Crusoe and Moll Flanders in this vein, and Henry Fielding wrote the first truly great social novel, Tom Jones.

With both Bach and Beethoven, the 18th century was one of the great periods of music of all time. The Baroque techniques of the previous century were continued and mastered. Johann Sebastian Bach was a genius at the organ and harpsichord, who developed the fugue to a state of perfection, and awed his contemporaries with his mastery of counterpoint. Bach was most closely identified with the most brilliant of German Protestant music. His contemporary, George Frederic Handel, also a Baroque musician (they were both born in 1685), was more of a theatrical court composer. Handel loved opera, and even his oratorios were Italian operas in disguise; his Messiah is one of the most popular musical works ever written. Other geniuses of the time were Scarlatti, Hayda and Wolfgang Mozart. Mozart, a child prodigy who died penniless at thirty-five, epitomized the later part of the century: he was the master of Viennese classicism, and also the first musical romantic. His operas <u>Don Giovanni</u> and <u>The Marriage of Figaro</u> were masterpieces of both melancholy and charming melodies, and heralded much of the work done in the 19th century.

Political Theory

One reason why the Enlightenment period was so important was that it constituted a revolution in ideas, a break with many of the religious and political convictions accepted by the western world up until that time. In religion there were two developments which were important: the first was the success of the new point of view known as Deism; the second was the continued impact upon the world of some of the innovative contributions of Protestantism.

Deism was the belief of a radical wing of skeptics who were ready to dismiss virtually all Christian doctrine and keep only a very rudimentary belief in God. The world was a giant clock; God had made it and set it ticking; but now it was on its own and God could not or would not intervene. Deists tended to be virulent attackers of the Catholic Church and what they considered to be its heresies. The most famous of them all was François Marie Arouet de Voltaire, the witty Frenchman, who hated intolerance and injustice. Voltaire said that if God did not exist, it would be necessary to invent him. However, he abhorred the intolerance of the Catholic Church in France at that time. He defended the innocence of a Huguenot named Jean Calas in a famous murder case and although unable to save Calas from execution, furthered the cause of religious toleration. The actual number of Deists was rather small. In the mainstream of ideas some of the concepts of Protestantism as a whole were probably more important.

The real revolution in religion, the Protestant Reformation, had already occurred two hundred years earlier. Martin Luther, John Calvin and John Knox were the leaders in an attack upon the abuses of the Catholic Church. Their "protests" led to fierce hatreds, bloody wars, economic upheaval, and ultimately to the creation of a new kind of non-Catholic Christianity. The Protestants discarded the hierarchy of the Catholic Church, the rule of a Pope, and the rites of confession; and presented a radically different point of view: every man was responsible for his own salvation through faith in a merciful God. He could interpret the Bible himself and no one could claim to intervene between man and God. One immediate result of this heretical view was that differences of opinion on how to interpret the Bible sprang up immediately and within a generation there were dozens of varieties of Protestant churches. One of the main controversies which divided Protestants was the argument of Predestination versus Freewill. John Calvin espoused the harsh doctrine of Predestination, which stated that most of mankind was doomed to burn forever in Hell. A small number of people in every generation were saved, known as the "elect"--not because of anything they had done, but because their fate had been preordained. Calvin's view became the creed of the Puritans and was brought to the New World in 1609. There they played a role in creating a new nation quite out of proportion to their numbers.

Puritanism has had a continuing legacy in American thought and behavior. Some writers, including the brilliant German economist, Max Weber, also think it had a decisive impact in helping create the Industrial Revolution, as we shall see in due course.

One striking concept which gained credence among the Puritans was the idea that if the average man bore the responsibility of the hereafter on his own two shoulders, it was because his forefathers had signed a compact with God. This concept of contract or compact was taken from the Bible (newly translated in 1609 at the auspices of King James I) and became a cornerstone of Puritanism. The Mayflower Compact, signed on board ship as the Puritans sailed for the New World, was a concrete realization of the idea; the passengers agreed to live a Godly life in their new country and God would protect them. This doctrine of mutual responsibility appeared virtually simultaneously in the fields of religion, economics, law, and government. Half of the Christain world henceforth began to conduct their daily lives as if they were fulfilling half of a bargain: their hard work, sense of duty, godliness, and personal responsibility became identified with certain groups of people--the compulsive Germans, the tough, independent Yankees of New England, the Huguenots of France. In economics the concept was carried forth literally in the form of contracts creating companies, soon called joint stock companies, whereby numerous individuals shared both the hazards and the profits from voyages to the New World or the Far East. The British East India Company and the British West India Company were both created in this way; and both also became instruments of government in India and America.

While contracts actually became a basis for government in a few specific instances, as on the Mayflower, they also became the framework for important political theories written from the 17th century on. The Spaniard, Juan de Mariana, who died around 1623, was one of the first to argue cogently that even tyrants had obligations to the people they ruled and if they failed, the people could turn against them. Thomas Hobbes (1588-1679) refined this in his famous work, The Leviathan. Hobbes conceived of man as basically evil and unruly and argued that originally he had lived in a state of nature, in anarchy, where life was "nasty, brutish and short." Hobbes envisaged a contract at the beginning of time between a basically evil and unruly people and a strong ruler, an absolute king, who would govern and protect them for life. However, the power derived from the people, and if the sovereign failed to protect them, they had an implicit right to overthrow him. In the same century when the divine right of kings led to the awesome power of a man like Louis XIV of France, Hobbes was already challenging the source of the king's power.

John Locke (1632-1704) continued to emphasize the idea of a contract between the ruler and the people, but in his case he flatly diasgreed with Hobbes on the state of nature: man was not evil but good, and in the state of nature, life was happy and tolerant. The contract creating government was designed to protect man against anyone living outside the state of nature and disobeying its laws; if the ruler failed to fulfill the contract, man had not only a right, but an obligation, to rebel.

Jean-Jacques Rousseau (1712-1778), a native of Geneva, Switzerland, a musician, a mathematician, and author of many books, was the leading figure of the Enlightenment and one of the most influential writers of all time. He expanded the ideas of John Locke, and challenged the old order on virtually every point. He celebrated primitive life; he deplored the evils of "civilization." Rousseau described the evils of cities, governments, property, and traditional education. He sang the virtues of man in a "state of nature," a "noble savage", good and virtuous until the day that private property began to destroy his innocence. This concept led to the glorification of American Indians as the embodiment of happiness and justice. Americans, who knew Indians better than most people, enthusiastically romanticized them in verse and prose ("Hiawatha," The Last of the Mohicans). After Indians, Rousseau's followers next idealized the farmer--the noble tiller of the soil. Farmers were no longer considered illiterate and uncouth, but repositories of hard work, virtue and wisdom. Rousseau also glorified nature and felt that a true education could be acquired merely by studying nature and nature's laws. In Emile, he advises society to bring up its children with tutors showing them the woods and fields and all of nature's ways, and eschewing all books until at least the age of sixteen.

Rousseau had importance for political theory in virtually everything he wrote. His ideas were often distorted beyond recognition, but for better or for worse he has influenced practically every political theory developed since that time. He asserted the value of the common man, and the idea of a contract among all members of society agreeing to submit to their general will--that which is best and right for the entire community. Ideally, government would be merely an extension of the community and would "force" all to be free. Practically, Rousseau recognized the necessity of retaining traditional figures of monarchy or aristocracy for large nations, with direct democracy only for small and poor societies. The right to overthrow governments violating the social contract, however, would never be relinquished. He praised the simple life, the life of the farmer in the country as opposed to the evils of the city and all of civilization. He advocated a break with traditional elitist education and proposed a kind of education available to all, with no need of institutions. There was a definite implication that books, scholarship and accumulated knowledge were all worthless and that the simple Indian or farmer gained greater wisdom from communion with nature. Put in rougher terms, this was essentially the creed of Andrew Jackson, the popular American President, elected in 1828. Jackson may have been the one president ever elected in the United States who embodied most of Rousseau's beliefs: a simple and rather crude frontiersman, he hated cities, the "East," and "book-learning," and idealized the values of frontier living (although he parted company with Rousseau and other romantics on the question of Indians).

As Rousseau and Locke laid the foundations for a revolutionary new way of looking at ordinary people (Rousseau wrote, "Man is born free but is everywhere in chains."), other writers in the Enlightenment challenged traditional ideas about law and government. Montesquieu attempted to link political theory and geography, not very successfully. He thought climate should determine what kind of government a people had--that is, a small, barren country might be a republic; a vast empire had to be a despotism. More useful was his concept of separation of powers as a way of limiting excessive authority. This concept was brilliantly applied by Thomas Jefferson, James Madison and other American forefathers when they designed the government of the United States. Checks and balances means that the three branches of government, executive, legislative and judicial, are independent, a practice which has served to limit abuses of power.

The writers of the Enlightenment were critical of government and society then prevalent, angry about religious intoleration, criminal injustice, and abuses of power. But many of them were optimistic about man's ability to reform. In their own day a number of European monarchs, "enlightened despots," undertook to put some of their ideas in practice. Frederick the Great of Prussia was so intellectual that he corresponded with Voltaire and even entertained him in person (although he offended him when he compared him to an orange.) He also improved life in Prussia with many reforms, such as the reduction of torture, and ending corruption in the courts. Catherine the Great of Russia invited Diderot to come and manage her library, and in other ways tried without much success (for she was a genuine despot) to pass herself off as "enlightened." Joseph II of Austria, who tried to free the serfs, reform the education and combat the bureaucracy of his empire, was easily the most sincere of these rulers, but not much more effective. Ironically, his own enthusiasm for liberal causes was premature and upon his death a reaction set in, so that much of his program was abolished.

Most of the philosophes were French. Most of the Enlightenment focused on France, where Paris was the cultural and intellectual capital of the world. But no government was more critical of the Enlightenment than the French rulers of the House of Bourbon. It is no accident that a catastrophic revolution erupted there in 1789. However, before that happened, the first actual fruits of the period were being plucked in America.

Part II

The American Revolution

The American Revolution gave birth to a new country which was the largest republic then in existence, the first ever designed on paper, and the first whose government was inscribed in a constitution. It was also the first step of a 20th century phenomenon, decolonization. England had just acquired India, and would soon acquire colonies in Africa and the Middle East in the 19th century, but just as England was getting used to being the world's greatest and grandest empire, the Americans demanded the right to leave it.

The causes of the Revolution are numerous. The colonials lived three thousand miles from the mother country at a time when transportation was still primitive and communication took many months. They had already experimented in numerous ways with self-government, beginning with the New England town meetings. England had created royal colonies with royal governors beginning in the late 1600's but their efforts were in vain to control their unruly offspring. The Americans evolved democratic forms of legislatures, with two houses, in every colony. The lower houses popularly elected. Because of the distances involved and because of economic woes, Britain had allowed these legislatures to control the governors' salaries, a practice which delivered them into the hands of the people they were governing.

England fought a number of wars in the 1700's which had drained their treasury. The most picturesque, probably, was the War of Jenkins' Ear--a war over rival world trading rights (1739). The appendage in question was delivered to an English courtroom, still wrapped in a bloody handkerchief, after it had been lopped off by a Spanish pirate. But the most important war was the Seven Years War (1756-1763), known in America as the French and Indian War. This conflict, fought in Europe, the Far East, and America, was in actuality a world war. The French lost their holding in both India and Canada, and England emerged as the greatest power in the world. But English jubilation was short-lived, for the conflict led directly to the American Revolution. Hitherto, the American colonies had been threatened on many occasions by the French, who had often armed the Indians and incited such conflicts as the Deerfield Massacre 50 years before. Now the French were gone and the frontiersmen were buoyant. But at the same moment that the Americans felt safe in the assumption that their primary enemy was defeated, the British changed their course.

During the wars, England had pursued a policy known as "salutory neglect" of the colonies. Busy at home and on the continent, they had allowed the colonials to run their own show. Now they were faced with the great cost of the French and Indian War; with the problem that if the French were gone, the Indians were still hostile (Pontiac launched a new revolt in the Ohio Valley in 1763); and with new Canadian provinces which had to be assimilated. The British also had to come to terms with a straggling colonial outpost many times larger than their own country, thousands of miles away, inhabited by an unruly people of whom now 40% were not even British. They failed. They initiated a two-pronged solution to their crisis and impaled themselves on both prongs: First, the British tried to raise money from the Americans by imposing duties on various products; and secondly, they attempted to close the frontier beyond Appalachia to American settlers, a policy they followed for ten years before they formally established it in the Quebec Act of 1774.

The Quebec Act attacked one of the most important and cherished features of life in America: it attempted to close the frontier to the adventurous, restless, independent and proud young settler. Many years later (around 1900), the historian Frederick Jackson Turner conceived of a theory to explain much of American national behavior. He argued that the frontier had exerted a magnetic influence upon the American people, luring them ever westward, acting like a safety-valve upon those who were frustrated or poor. Americans originally came to the New World because they were dissatisfied with conditions in Europe. Some set out for religious reasons; others as younger sons of aristocrats; still others to seek their fortune. Aside from the African slaves (the only ones brought by force), the colonists were characterized at the outset by an extraordinary feeling of enterprise and independence. They had already defied persecution, unjust laws and economic stagnation by coming here. They were adventurous. They or their grandparents had defied fate, chucked overboard a civilized, orderly life in Europe and traveled thousands of miles in the most alarming circumstances to live in a raw new settlement. To close down all future settlements beyond Appalachia was a serious threat. The English had at least two reasons to do this: first, they did not have the manpower necessary to keep peace in the area between the settlers and the Indians; second, and most important, they wanted to keep the colonists confined to a small area so that they could control them better.

In accord with the first of these two reasons, the British tried to raise money in America to pay for American defense--not an unreasonable act, in their opinion. In 1764, the English Parliament, at the behest of Lord Grenville (1712-1770), passed the Sugar Act; in 1765 they decided to tax newspapers and legal documents through the Stamp Act. The sums of money were negligible, but the Americans were outraged. They said their land was the property of the king, as evidenced by their royal governors. They did not belong to Parliament, and even if Parliament did have the right to tax them, it could not do so unless Americans were represented there, which they were not. King George III was determined to assert his sovereignty over the colonies and Parliament was equally determined to persist. The taxes did not seem unreasonable in view of the much higher taxes the English paid; and as for representation--the English were not properly represented in Parliament either (not until after the Reform Bill of 1832). But colonial opposition was successful. In 1766 in the Declaratory Act, Parliament asserted its right to legislate for the colonies--but it repealed the Stamp Act. This set a pattern: like a doting parent who is at the same moment affectionate, cross and confused, the British government made one grand declaration after the other, only to change their minds. In 1767 Parliament was persuaded by Charles Townshend, Chancellor of the Exchequer, to pass a series of acts levying duties on imports such as paper, paint, glass, and tea. Again the Americans protested. Customs agents arrived to collect the duties, then British troops to protect the customs agents. In March, 1770, hot tempers and tension erupted in the Boston Massacre, when a milling crowd bated the troops and the troops fired, killing five citizens. (Like the storming of the Bastille, the Peterloo Massacre, and many other notorious events, the heinous nature of the crime was slightly exaggerated.) Parliament, aghast, repealed all the duties except the one on tea. But this also would not do, and in 1773 an intrepid group of citizens painted their faces, boarded a ship in Boston Harbor and heaved the tea overboard. Now England resumed the attack, this time directed by Lord North. In 1774 Parliament passed the Intolerable Acts: they closed the port of Boston, quartered troops in private homes and reorganized the government of Massachusetts. Bad as this was, it affected only the citizens of Massachusetts, although other Americans were sympathetic. The Quebec Act, passed the same year, threatened to stop the flow of settlers into the Ohio Valley and potentially alienated every man in the country.

Angry citizens created committees of correspondence to complain of British injustice and keep everyone informed. From these evolved the First Continental Congress in Philadelphia in September 1774, an attempt to persuade Parliament to restore to them their self-government. In April of 1775, shots were fired at Lexington and Concord, and in June at the Battle of Bunker Hill. Determined peacemakers convened the Second Continental Congress in May of 1775, but by the end of the summer, the king of England declared America to be in rebellion. Thomas Paine in his pamphlet, Common Sense, urged independence--at that stage still a shocking point of view; but a colonial army and navy were hastily assembled. Loathe to break completely from the mother country and in almost every case wanting only to live peacefully and be properly represented, the Americans adopted the Declaration of Independence on

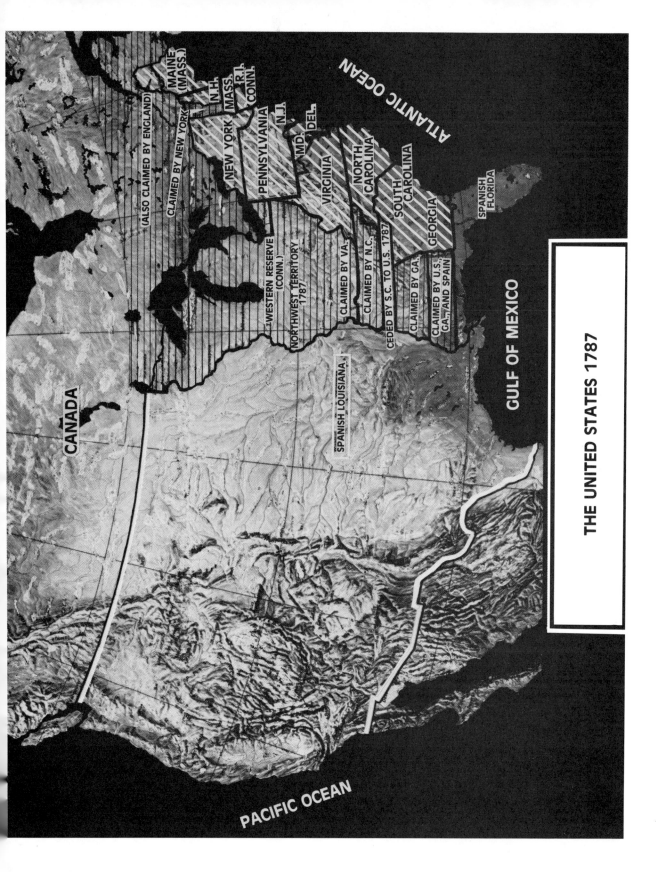

THE UNITED STATES 1787

July 4, 1776. A brilliant statement in the lucid prose of Thomas Jefferson, it summed up two generations of Enlightenment philosophy by claiming through the right of nature and "Nature's God" that Americans are to be free and independent.

The struggle lasted until 1781 with scenes familiar to every American school child--Washington crossing the Delaware, Washington and his ragged troops on Christmas Eve, Lafayette gallantly coming to his aid. With a French army fighting to aid the Americans, and German Hessians less successfully assisting the British, once again a colonial conflict broadened to worldwide dimensions. Spain and Holland entered the war and it became the struggle of a powerful coalition of France, Spain and Holland with Russia, Sweden and Denmark neutral, against a desperate England fighting alone to save her empire. England lost the United States, but kept her empire. The struggle ended with the Peace of Paris in 1783.

As the war was coming to a close, the Americans created a federal government in 1781 called the Articles of Confederation. This government was only a loose arrangement between the thirteen colonies, without any powers sufficient to function as an effective central government: each colony had the right to its own stamps, tariffs, weights and measures, and virtual sovereign power. The Confederation passed a Northwest Ordinance in 1787, which was a formula for settling the northwest territories: all the land which subsequently included the states of Wisconsin, Indiana, Illinois, Michigan, and Ohio was forbidden to slavery, given instructions for entering the union, and guaranteed civil rights then not even guaranteed to all the citizens of the original colonies. That remarkable document if allowed to prevail in spirit and by example, could have avoided the Civil War, and saved the future nation from intolerable grief. It was the only important legacy of the Articles. With their hopelessly weak central government, the Articles were dismissed as a failure in 1787; and a new Constitution was drawn up at Philadelphia.

The Constitution of the United States of America represented a good efforts of some of the brightest men ever to convene in one spot for a worthy purpose. Thomas Jefferson, James Madison, John Adams, and Benjamin Franklin, to name only a few, agreed to create a federal republic which they hoped would govern the population equitably, without ever amassing too much power. Guided by a number of principles emphasized during the Enlightenment, they incorporated separation of powers by creating an executive, legislature and judiciary which were independent from each other. Interested above all things in limiting power, the forefathers devised a complicated way to pass legislation. Through checks and balances, they hoped each branch of the government would oversee the other two branches and cancel out any outburst of despotism, however tentative. Congress passed legislation by itself, without any obligation to the President (which distinguishes the U.S. government from many other constitutional governments of the world today, including that of Great Britain and Germany, where the executive depends on the legislature. Even this first step is difficult, however, for the identical process must be followed in two separate houses before a bill is complete. It then goes to the President who may or may not sign it. If he vetoes it (a step which took about a generation of presidents to establish), the bill may be passed over his veto by the legislature. Once it becomes law, there are still ways to contravene the measure, one of which is a failure to "execute" it properly. Or the third branch of government, the Supreme Court, may exercise its own prerogative of declaring the act unconstitutional. This step was not clearly specified in the Constitution, and was taken only with great hesitation. However, in a landmark decision in 1803, <u>Marbury v. Madison</u>, the Supreme Court declared an act of Congress unconstitutional, an epic move which is now firmly established practice.

The government with the addition of the Bill of Rights, ten amendments guaranteeing basic human freedoms, which were affixed to it in order to persuade the thirteen colonies to ratify it, was operative by 1789.

Part III

The French Revolution

When the king of France went to the aid of the United States during the American Revolution, it was certainly not out of love for republics or rebellious populations seeking liberty, but to avenge their own loss to England during the Seven Years' War. Had he foreseen the consequences for his own throne, he would have been aghast. In point of fact, much of the intellectual fodder for the revolutionary movement did come from France in the first place. Jefferson and his peers were guided by the principles of the Enlightenment throughout their conflict with Great Britain and also afterwards when they created the new American government with built-in deterrants against despotism.

The revolution in America had been shocking, but as revolutions go, it was remarkably mild. There was no class hatred, no slaughter of helpless citizens (like the French Terror), and no period of dictatorship, as later there were in both France and Russia. The American elite was admirable. George Washington, everyone's idea of a genuine hero, proved that he truly was heroic by steadfastly resisting the lure of power. He turned down a title and a crown and refused to be president for more than two terms. While he served, he used his power on the most minimal level. With such restraint in America, there were few people about who could have predicted the bloody consequences as the revolutionary virus spread. The 1789 revolution which broke out in France engulfed all of Europe eventually in a war which lasted for an entire generation. It spread to Latin America and after thirty more years of bloodshed, the Spanish Empire was destroyed. The revolutionary fervor came to encompass much of the western world and wave after wave of it broke over the European continent in the 19th century.

The American Revolution led to the French Revolution, first, for it set an example of a people challenging authority, and winning; secondly, it had drawn the French government into the American conflict. The French built up a massive debt. An economic crisis resulted. By a dismal coincidence, crops failed throughout France at the same time, so that the people did not get enough to eat.

11

France in 1789 was the richest, most populous and still most powerful country in Europe. Its people were the most elegant and its culture the most envied. France was supposedly an absolute monarchy, with a king enjoying total power, but in reality its nobles had a stranglehold on the court and country. There were about 250,000 French noblemen at that time, all of them enjoying certain exclusive privileges, immunities and exemptions from the law, including above all, exemption from taxation. Apart from the nobles, there were some wealthy members of a tiny middle class. But the vast majority of the population of 30 million consisted of peasants and small farmers. These people were taxed in every conceivable way the government could devise: there was a tax on salt (the gabelle), a tax on windows, even a tax exacting labor on roads and ditches (the corvée). With the common people taxed to the limit, the most obvious way to raise additional revenue was to tap the wealth of the nobles. There was no way to do this without stirring up a hornet's nest, so the king's finance ministers (there were several in a row--Narbonne, Calonne and Necker, who tried, and failed, to solve the problem) decided to call the Estates General for May of 1789. This was a representative body dating back several hundred years, which had not met since 1614. It consisted of three houses: the first estate was clergy, the second, nobles, and the third, commoners. The government hoped to convey that they were having a genuine crisis, and thereby persuade the nobles to submit to taxation. But calling the Estates General was a mistake. The nobility, in the first place, were far from entertaining generous ideas about permitting themselves to be taxed. Secondly and more serious, the government was so vague about its aims that a widespread feeling of confusion developed about the real purpose of calling the Estates General. The middle classes thought this was their opportunity to acquire representative government or equality before the law, inspired, no doubt, by the American Revolution. Yet this was the last thing on the king's mind.

It would be a mistake to think that the Revolution occurred because conditions were worse in France than elsewhere, that the people there were particularly oppressed. On the contrary, peasants in the Austrian Empire, for example, or in Russia, were still in a state of serfdom. It is a truism widely acknowledged that revolutions generally do not occur in those countries where the people are the poorest off. Rather, they are a phenomenon of rising expectations--the situation where a population is actually better off than before and has come to expect even better things of the future. A population has to believe itself capable of changing things before it does something so radical as taking to the barricades. In the France of 1789, this was the case. It would also be a mistake to think that the population of France acted as one at any point in the war which followed, or that different segments of it ever shared a common goal. Their motives were confused at the best of times. Certainly, no one expected to destroy the monarchy or turn the government into a republic at the beginning. And as events moved more or less inexorably in that direction, more and more of the French people were alienated and eventually horrified; and many of governments of Europe shared their horror, so that the crisis in France set off a series of wars unprecedented in their political ramifications.

The Estates General convened on May 5, 1789. Many of the delegates arrived there in a fine state of euphoria, expecting great things to happen. A crisis erupted during which the middle class representatives of the Third

Estate demanded that they sit as one body--for they did not want to be outvoted by the other two estates acting against them. After all, the first and second estates, combined, made up only about five percent of the population of France, yet, their representatives numbered roughly fifty percent of the delegates convened. Louis XVI acted in much the same way that George III and the English Parliament had when confronted by the defiance in America: instead of taking a firm stand at the outset, he vacillated, and then overcompensated by acting ruthless. On June 27 he granted the request that the three estates meet together as a National Assembly. However, a few days later he changed his mind and called in troops. Meanwhile, the working classes of Paris were responding to the food crisis and the general sense of unrest in the country. They took to stirring about the streets with pitchforks, threatening bakers who had run out of bread. On July 14th, after several days of rabble-rousing in the vicinity, they attacked the citadel of despotism--the Bastille--a stone dungeon with ten-foot walls. Notorious as a torture-chamber of political prisoners, in fact there were only seven inmates inside at the time--all petty criminals of one sort or another (The Marquis de Sade had been with them until the day before). The governor of the Bastille was dispatched on the spot and his grisly head, impaled on a spike, was carried about Paris by the mob in the days that followed.

From that point onward, events proceeded on several levels at once: the middle class lawyers and writers (like the Abbe Siéyés) who dominated the new National Assembly (which replaced the Estates General), undertook various political actions in what they presumed was a legal way, while the masses of Paris and the peasants in the country became increasingly violent and began to attack the upper classes and the symbols of authority. From the very start, the French Revolution was a class revolt in a way which differed totally from the American Revolution.

On August 4, 1789, the National Constituent Assembly (still another body, elected to write a constitution) performed a minor revolution: in a spontaneous gesture inspired partly by fearsome tales of violence out in the country, the nobles one after the other stood up and renounced their titles. Soon after, they issued a Declaration of the Rights of Man and of the Citizen, which was a document inspired by similar declarations in America (especially that of Virginia, then the most liberal of all the colonies). Echoing Rousseau and Locke and Jefferson, Frenchmen were told that all men were born free and equal in rights. They had rights to "liberty," "property" and "resistence to oppression." All citizens were equal before the law. When the king was presented with these two occurrences, he refused to accept them. In October a large crowd gathered out at Versailles, the royal palace, and milling about in a threatening manner, they so intimidated the king and his advisor, Lafayette, that the royal family voluntarily returned with the crowd to Paris. They were kept under a version of house arrest from that time forth.

In 1791, after a number of relatively calm months, the National Constituent Assembly announced a Constitution reorganizing the government into a constitutional monarchy with a unicameral legislature. Had they restricted their political innovations to this, they might have transformed France into such a government with only moderate difficulty. But during the same period of time, since many of them were Deists because of the Englightenment, they also squared off against the Catholic Church. In a document called the Civil

Constitution of the Clergy, they tried to transform the French branch of the Catholic Church into a secular part of the state: all clergymen henceforth were to be salaried employees of the state and to take an oath to support this. At one momemt the assembly alienated more than half of France. Until then, many clergymen had been on their side against the oppression of the king. Afterward, all but the most radical priests became enemies of the revolution and as they turned against it, they took with them the devout members of their congregation.

With each successive development more people in and out of France were alienated from the revolution. Large numbers of aristocrats called emigrés fled for their lives (including, eventually, Lafayette himself) for refuge in courts of other kings. Louis XVI and his family tried to flee themselves, in disguise, in June of 1791. Dressed as servants, they travelled as far as Varennes; but there they were recognized, and with a jeering crowd running alongside, they were returned to Paris. Their days were numbered and many people were beginning to see it. Because of this insult to a reigning monarch and fear for his life, and because of pressure from the emigrés, in August 1791, the rulers of Austria and Prussia issued a threatening statement known as the Declaration of Pillnitz. It was not a declaration of war, but it was read as one in France, where it unleashed a new wave of violence. A radical group of deputies emerged during this time known as the Jacobins. The Jacobins were republicans and unlike the vast majority of the French population, they wished to abolish the monarchy. One wing of this group, known as the Girondins, came to dominate the government for the next year. The Girondins were particularly nationalistic and when a threatening new ruler, Francis II, came to the throne of Austria in April 1792, they pushed the French assembly to declare war. The queen, Marie Antoinette, was Austrian and part of the lust for war was occasioned by a resentment which had built up against her foreign ways. Prussia joined Austria in the conflict.

By the summer of 1792, a new dimension had been added to the mounting hysteria of the French people: in addition to violence in town and country, lack of food and the uncertainty about the government, there was fear of invasion. When Prussian troops entered France in September, the hysteria gave way to unprecedented violence known as the September massacres. Mobs of frenzied Parisians roamed the streets and raided the prisons for traitors, giving summary trials and killing over one thousand people. All these horrors were to be repeated a many times over when the Terror got underway a few months later, except that the executions then became more systematic and, with the invention of the guillotine, quicker.

The various factions of the Jacobins battled for supremacy and the more moderate Girondins were finally defeated and ousted from power. The turning point was January 21, 1793; on that day Louis XVI was decapitated. The new leader in the assembly was Maximilien Robespierre (1758-1794). Immaculate and well-dressed, Robespierre was a political fanatic who wanted France to be a republic with a strong centralized government, embodying all the good things Rousseau had described in his Social Contract. One of the greatest anomalies was Robespierre's claim that to establish the ideal democracy, they must first wage war on tyranny, which is to say, that all the enemies of his point of view were to be put to death. Although the first republican form of government for France began with the newly elected National Convention in

August-September 1792, a new formal constitution did not emerge until almost a year later. Even then, its implementation was postponed. For a time the actual government of France was an institution known as the Committee of Public Safety, a twelve-man cabinet (including Robespierre) which oversaw all important matters in the country. Under their supervision France again became centralized, and more than 20,000 people were murdered. In the ruthless way by which the leaders of the Terror demanded allegiance to their radical point of view, and execution of all dissidents, as well as the efficient way in which the government was centralized and the executions carried out, one is reminded of 20th century totalitarianism. The fact that their goal was a country guaranteeing freedom, equality and democracy, very commendable, makes their technique for establishing those things all the more chilling.

One of the more salient observations of the French Revolution was that it had a way of devouring its own children. The leaders of the Girondin, who held power for many months, were almost all killed during the Terror which followed; and in a moment of supreme irony, Robespierre and his fanatical cohorts were themselves guillotined in July of 1794 (a month they had relabelled Thermidor). From that turning point, the pendulum swung slowly back in the other direction, inaugurating now a period of reaction against the radical excesses which had occurred.

The counter-revolutionary phase also produced violence and excesses, but by 1795 these were mostly spent and with a new constitution (the third since the Revolution began), the country received still another government, this one called the Directory. The Directory, so named because the executive of the country was in the hands of five men known as Directors, was a distinctly middle class government, one which had drawn back from the rabid democracy of Robespierre to a more limited and conservative concept. Confronted with war abroad, economic crises at home, and the difficulty of steering a straight course between the fanatical Jacobin point of view on the one hand and the monarchist on the other, the Directory struggled with moderate success until it was overthrown in 1799. After ten years of turmoil and strife, France was now launched on yet another adventure; this time at the hands of Napoleon Bonaparte.

Part IV

Napoleon

The French Revolution was a political and social revolution in which the lower class revolted against the elite, threw them out, and temporarily gained control of France. At the peak of its excesses, the government was extremely democratic, and liberty, equality and fraternity were widely touted as the credo of the new order. Yet France is nothing if not a paradox. Robespierre, the most radically democratic of the revolutionaries, behaved with authoritarian intolerance toward his opponents, and guillotined thousands of them. In the same vein, less than ten years later the country of democracy and equality welcomed an emperor who created a new aristocracy, supported a secret police, and was bent on conquering Europe.

15

Napoleon Bonaparte was born to a large Italian family on the island of Corsica in 1769. By an accident of history, Corsica had just been acquired by France. Thus when the French Revolution broke out, this bright young man, who might otherwise have spent his life absorbed in the petty intrigues of Corsican politics, was thrown into the biggest maelstrom Europe had seen in several centuries. He was twenty-four when he gained instant fame by his prominent role in the recapture of the French port of Toulon from the British. He skirted the most dangerous outbursts of the Terror, survived a brief imprisonment himself, and in 1796 was the brilliant commander who swept through northern Italy. His victories there were stunning; he swept out the Austrians, created two new republics, and began spreading the doctrine of the French Revolution--promising liberty, freedom and constitutions, a process he was to repeat many times in his campaigns. Back in France, and glowing with success, he next embarked on a grandiose scheme to disrupt the British control of India by seizing the Middle East, specifically, Egypt. His goals were not strictly military.

More than any enlightened despot in Europe, Napoleon embodied some of the best hopes and values of the Enlightenment. His favorite author was Rousseau and he embraced (at least intelectually) the political implications of the French Revolution. He also sought, in true enlightenment fashion, to encourage science and to expand the knowledge of antiquity. He took with him to Egypt over one hundred scholars and scientists, and whatever the military repercussions of that expedition, the contributions to knowledge were monumental. The single most extraordinary feat was the accidental discovery of the Rosetta Stone, a priceless stone carved out with the same message in Greek, Coptic and hieroglyphics. When Champollion finally deciphered the hieroglyphics twenty years later, he lifted the curtain for the first time into the mind of the ancient Egyptian.

However, the Egyptian expedition was an ill-fated adventure in every other way. The French troops established their supremacy over the poorly armed Egyptians with little trouble, and then carved their way eastward in search of further victories. But they were less successful in Palestine, and the army was beset with illness and poor morale. Worse, the French fleet was defeated by Admiral Nelson in the Battle of the Nile, and the British managed to capture the Rosetta Stone and transport it to the British Museum in London, where it reposes to this day. Napoleon at this point left his army behind him and secretly sailed back to France.

Napoleon was a military genius and a charismatic leader. One of the remarkable traits which set him towering above his fellow men was his ability to turn defeat into victory. Like all political geniuses of the modern age, he was a master of propaganda. At this juncture, he rufused to allow his career to be ruined by the dismal situation in Egypt and the loss of the fleet, not to mention his desertion of a wretched army in an advanced state of disease and malaise. On his return to Paris, Napoleon implied that the Egyptian campaign had been a success. He arrived home in early September 1799, and on November 10, he overthrew the Directory. The new government was known as the Consulate, a triumvirate of three men--Napoleon, the first consul, Abbé Siéyés of revolutionary fame, and Roger-Ducos. Napoleon assumed greater and greater power as the months passed--first in overshadowing his two colleagues and becoming the only consul, then in becoming consul for life (in 1802), and finally, in crowning himself emperor (in 1804).

In his reign as emperor, Napoleon's achievements must be divided into two rather different subjects: his continuation of the revolution in France; and his foreign policy, which was military conquest. Within France, Napoleon enacted changes of every description, touching in some way or other virtually every educational, religious, scientific, legal and political institution in the country. Most of his reforms brought significant improvements to French life. To do this, he resorted to tactics alien to all modern liberal societies: censorship of the press, a secret police (under Fouché), and the execution of at least one famous man, the Duc d'Enghien, for reasons of state.

One of his most important changes was in law. French law under the old regime had been a hodgepodge of differing customs, codes and privileges. The emperor changed all that with the Code Napoleon (1804-1810), which established the same law from one end of the country to the other, and for all ranks of society. Many aspects of the Code were enlightened: it established equality before the law, and it established divorce. But like much that Napoleon did, the law code was a mixed blessing at best, for it incorporated much of old Roman Law into France, which meant that it favored the state over the individual. It also favored men over women, and stripped women and children of many of the rights they had acquired during the revolution. It even restored slavery to the French colonies.

In the field of religion, Napoleon brought peace to the nation's Catholics by signing a Concordat with the Pope (1801). This settlement ended the rancor created by the Civil Constitution of the Clergy. It established the Catholic Church as the majority religion of France while at the same time guaranteeing religious toleration. It gave the government a great deal of control over the church, for it continued to pay church salaries and it had the right to circumscribe church activities. Anticlerical sons of the Revolution were angered by the Concordat, but Napoleon knew what he was doing. He won over the vast majority of French Catholics by this deed. Personally, he was an agnostic, and when Pope Pius VII later defied him, the emperor had him imprisoned.

Napoleon also created the Bank of France and the Legion of Honor. He encouraged science and the arts, and began an extensive reform of higher education. He established the "Ecole Polytechnique" which could be described as the first exclusively engineering school. Politically he made lasting reforms by sweeping away the debris of centuries of long rule and centralizing the government. He encouraged science and the arts. He left a permanent impression upon France. But if he is still revered today as the greatest Frenchman in all history, it is probably due more to his military exploits than to his reforms.

At the peak of his power Napoleon was one of the most dramatic personnages who ever lived. He was five feet, six inches, in height, short though robust, with a handsome, brooding face. He was at all times bursting with energy and exhausting to all those around him. He slept only a few hours a night, insisting that servants or military officers camp outside his door so that whenever he arose he could demand immediate service. He personally oversaw the most trivial details of the management of his empire, and his brain was so crammed with figures and statistics that he could easily leap from one complicated subject to the next, often dictating to several secretaries at once on totally diverse topics. He was a master of manipulation, and absolutely charming when he wished. But he also had a famous temper, and would burst out in a frenzy of abuse at whoever crossed him. Unfortunately, his outbursts were not always justified, and his judgment was not always good. There was a dreadful scene with the French Admiral Bruix in 1804, when Napoleon decided to review the fleet at Boulogne just before a storm. Bruix categorically refused to call out the ships because of the weather. Napoleon called him insolent, fired him on the spot, and replaced him with Magon. This story is worth telling in part because the entire fleet was lost a few months later at Trafalgar; who knows, perhaps Bruix might have won that battle.

Through a policy of allying with certain European rulers against others, Napoleon created an empire that at one time or another included most of Italy, Austria, Prussia and the rest of the German Confederation, the Netherlands, Belgium, Poland, Spain and Switzerland. His victories were legion. His military genius seemed flawless, master as he was of the lightening transport of his troops, brilliant insight, and propaganda which inspired his soldiers to deeds never before seen. He made a few monumental errors, however, which cost him all his glory. When he tried to take Spain in 1807-1808, he sent his brother Joseph to be king there, yet refused to heed Joseph's astute advice. Joseph warned him that the Spanish were very resentful and must be won over

Napoleon at the Battle of Eylau, 1807. Artist: Antoine Jean Gros. (The Granger Collection)

carefully. He was right. The Spanish people rose up in rebellion against the French occupation on May 2, 1808, immortalized by Goya in a magnificent painting. The British general, the Duke of Wellington, raced to the spot with English troops, and the Penisular War, as it was called, plagued the French from that day forward.

Another mistake Napolean made was due to his Italian notions of marriage and family. He was a young man of twenty-six when he married the coquettish widow, Josephine de Beauharnais, and flew into Italian rages of jealousy over her Parisian behavior. He divorced Josephine in 1809 and married Marie Louise of Austria in 1810, who gave him a son. In both of these marriages he endulged in his family to extremes; he not only placed his own brothers and sisters on every available throne in Europe, but also his stepson, Eugène de Beauharnais. However, his most serious error was to assume that Francis II of Hapsburg, his new father-in-law, felt the same family loyalty that expatriated Corsicans did. After 1810 Napoleon took Austria's allegiance for granted. But Francis II felt no ties toward him to speak of, and helped create the Grand Coalition which finally defeated him once and for all. As a dying man in exile, Napolean cited this as his worst single mistake.

Yet his most famous mistake was his tragic decision to invade Russia in 1812. It was impossible to follow his usual policy of having his army live off the land, as the Russians burned their fields and cities; and although he took Moscow, the city of two hundred churches, that city caught on fire, and while he watched in anger and chagrin, burned to the ground before his eyes.

The Third of May, by Goya. (The Granger Collection)

The campaign destroyed Napolean's army; of the 500,000 men who crossed the Russian border in July, only about 50,000 returned in December. The European coalition was victorious against him in 1813 in the Battle of the Nations, in Leipzig, Germany, and Napolean was soon totally defeated and exiled to the island of Elba. The French brought back a Bourbon as king, Louis XVIII, but the new monarch had hardly started the satisfying task of getting revenge for the revolution when on March 1, 1815, Napoleon astounded the world by escaping from the island. He returned to France and gathering soldiers as he went, made his way up to Paris. As he and his mostly assortment of troops approached Grenoble, according to one account, he was told that the royalists holding Grenoble had the entire garrison laid out awaiting them. Napoleon left his men behind and proceeded alone to face the enemy. When he got within striking distance he called out, "Here I am, shoot me if you must". The garrison threw down their weapons and cried in one voice, "Vive Napoleon!"

For one hundred days Napoleon was restored to his throne. But on June 18, 1815, he was again faced by a coalition of all his enemies, led by the Duke of Wellington, and was defeated definitively at Waterloo. He threw himself upon the mercy of the English, and that government exiled him once again, this time to a more remote island with no chance of escape, St. Helena. He died there in 1821, of arsenic poisoning. But whether his death was an accident due to the routine use of arsenic in medical remedies at that time, or whether he was put to death on purpose, has never been completely discovered.

The Legacy of Napoleon

After Napoleon's final defeat, there was a period of disenchantment with him in France which lasted about twenty years. Then there was a change of heart in France and his remains were returned there to be reinterred in a magnificient tomb in the center of Paris, the Invalides, where tourists still cluster daily in reverent silence before his marbelized memory. But Napoleon had not needed a marble tomb to leave his mark on the world; he had already done so. Sometimes with calculation, sometimes unwittingly, he changed the map of Europe and the ideas of many of its people.

He helped form the two great waves of political enthusiasm which swept through Europe in the 19th century--nationalism and liberalism. The first was a passionate arousal of interest in one's homeland; the second a novel attitude that the people should participate in the goverment. Both were new concepts. Hitherto there had been little Nationalism. Separate languages and cultures had not been politically important, for rulers had seized land in war and acquired vast territories through marriage, but generally never created political divisions at the request of the people who actually lived in the areas. The French Revolution changed this. It was a mass uprising of people from all classes and regions of France. When war broke out with the rest of Europe, the French people shared a vague but emotional feeling that they were exporting their revolution; the army put in the field against the Prussians and Austrians was a people's army. Ordinary men fought for France, instead of professional soldiers as in the past. As this army tried to export the liberalism of the Revolution, they unwittingly exported their other fever also--nationalism.

The Spanish had been united in one country since 1479, but the political superstructure scarcely impinged at all on the regional variations--the differing dialects, the local concerns--of the people of Catalonia or Galicia or Castille. This changed when the French occupied Spain in 1807. When their muddle-headed, vacillating and rather1y cowardly king, Charles IV, surrendered to French demands and voluntarily went off to live in Biarritz, the populace became upset. On May 2, 1808, the royal children were also being packed off to Biarritz, but as a murmuring crowd of people watched through the palace gates, the little prince (who wasn't even the king's son, but the son of a royal lover named Godoy) threw a scene and refused to enter the carriage. In the sort of misunderstanding which all romantic impulses feed on, the people took his tantrum to be a patriotic stand against surrendering to French demands. They pressed against the gates, first muttering, then shouting, and began to riot. The riot was the beginning of the Peninsular War, for the French never did take Spain.

But even when the population rebelled against Napoleon, as they did in Spain, their brief contact with him was sufficient to spread both nationalism and liberalism. The nationalism fueled the uprising against him. The liberalism became evident in a small but determined group of Spaniards who wrote the Constitution of 1812, in imitation of France, and tried to turn their country into a constitutional monarchy. The Spanish attempt at reforming their government was given a setback when their King Ferdinand VII was restored to power in 1815, along with other Bourbon Kings in France and Naples. As with many other countries in Europe at that time, the Spanish liberals were sadly premature in their efforts. In their case they would not have a viable democratic government for another hundred and fifty years.

As these events were happening in Spain, the joint causes of liberalism and nationalism ignited another series of wars in the Spanish Empire. From 1810 until the 1820's the revolutionary fervor swept from Mexico to the Tierra del Fuego, until the whole of Latin America except Cuba got its independence.

But Napolean did more than stir up revolutions. In central Europe there had existed a large conglomerations of states, plagued by a great weight of historical traditions, local privileges, petty jealousies and political confusion. This was the Holy Roman Empire, which Voltaire had said was neither holy, nor Roman, nor an empire. The empire had been ruled from Vienna by the House of Hapsburg for five hundred years, with territories stretching from The Netherlands to Italy. Included in the empire were large portions of German-speaking lands, as well as the homelands of such varied ethnic groups as Czechs, Poles, Serbs, Croats and Hungarians. With one stroke Napoleon moved this loose and badly governed federation of petty principalities from the middle ages into the Nineteenth Centry; he abolished the Holy Roman Empire, and replaced it with two different states, a much smaller body called the Austrian Empire, still ruled from Vienna by the Hapsburgs; and the Confederation of the Rhine, which included every German state except Austria and Prussia. The Confederation of the Rhine included some 300 of the old petty principalities and Germanic duchies of the past, but now redrawn on the map and consolidated first into about thirty new states; and at the Congress of Vienna, in 1815, consolidated still more into some fifteen states. As this was happening, some Germans were immensely enthusiastic about Napolean. One was Ludwig Von Beethoven (b.Bonn, 1770-1827), who wrote his third symphony, the Eroica, in Napoleon's honor. He and others were pleased as French armies hacked away medieval boundaries and borders like so many petrified cobwebs. French decrees abolished serfdom, feudal laws and other traditional inequities. Yet many Germans, instead of thanking France for the abrupt transition into a modern age, came to resent French arrogance, and grew convinced of their own unique superiority in language, history and culture--a process typical of every nationality group feeling the first heady surges of nationalism. At this time the brothers Grimm collected their fairy stories, old German tales which had been passed down orally for hundreds of years, a monument to the German past. The philosopher Fichte, the administrator Baron Von Stein, the poet Goethe, and many other Germans fueled an admiration for the German language and German ways. The University of Berlin, founded in 1810, became a center of nationalistic professors and students who endorsed the movement, and for the next half of century plotted both openly and secretly to unite all Germans into one great fatherland.

Two countries not affected by Napoleon's impact were England and Russia. England, already united for seven centuries, was not particularly affected by the rising wave of nationalism. And as the most liberal country in Europe, with a constitutional monarchy and a parliament responsive--however slowly--to the wishes of their people, England also had no need for revolution in the name of liberalism. Russia was at the other extreme. They had experienced a nationalistic response when the French invaded them in 1812; but as a large and ancient nation had no need for revolutions to unite themselves. On the other hand, due to their abandonment of Moscow and their scorched earth policy, they had almost no contact at all with French revolutionary concepts. With serfdom intact, with an absolute emperor in power, Russia remained an anachronism for the next century. When they finally had their revolution, it was considerably more radical than anything since the French Revolution. Looking at Russia is perhaps the most useful way to assess Napolean's legacy: The one major country where he had no impact at all, is the one which had the most bloody revolution a hundred years later.

QUESTIONS FOR REFLECTION

After every chapter in this volume, you will find a short list of questions for your consideration. Many of the questions have no correct answer; they are merely intended to challenge your thinking. In some cases, if there is a correct answer you will not find it in this book, which is extremely condensed, but will have to do additional probing on your own. The purpose of the questions in every case is to encourage you to look upon the material you have learned in a number of different ways. Above all, approach this book and everything in it with a questioning mind. Did things really happen in that way? Was a given policy really the correct one? What would have happened if Napoleon (or Hitler, or whoever) had won in the end? How would the course of human experience have differed?

1. The 18th century was a time when men finally began to believe in a theory of progress. Such a view is possible only if one accepts the intrinsic goodness of man. Start a notebook on the subject, and record the attitude

about progress, and about the good or evil nature of man, of Rousseau, the Romantics, Karl Marx, the Puritans (who made up the Protestant Ethic), Nietzsche, Freud, Hitler, Shiite Moslems, Martin Luther King, and Gandhi. Add to this list any other nations or individuals whose views you find to be important in shaping your lives. How do attitudes about progress and the goodness of man affect institutions? (such as schools; prisons)

2. Make a list of historical events as the course proceeds. Try to form your own criteria for evaluating the existence of genuine progress among human beings. How should progress be defined? What is more important, material well-being or happiness?

3. Rousseau said that governments should respond to the "General Will" of the people. How could later authoritarian rulers, including Napoleon, Hitler and Mussolini, claim that they were following the General Will? Do democratic states always follow the General Will? Should they?

4. Was a war between Great Britain and the American colonies inevitable? In what ways were the Americans being unreasonable? Could Britain have avoided the war if they had given in to American demands, or would the war have only been postponed? Were the British right to try and keep the Americans confined to the area east of the Alleghanies?

5. Name as many reasons as you can to explain why the British lost the war.

6. Was the American Revolution really a revolution?

7. Why do you suppose the French Revolution was so much more violent than the American Revolution? Was it more revolutionary in addition to being more violent? At what point could the king have avoided the tragic (for him) outcome--or could he not have avoided it? What was the most serious mistake of the revolutionaries? Were there any justifications for liberal men like Robespierre, claiming to want progress for humanity, using totalitarian methods to gain his ends? What 20th century parallels do you see to Robespierre? Do you accept the thesis that all great revolutionary upheavels move in cyclical fashion, veering first to one extreme, then to another? What other events can you cite which bear this out?

8. Would it have made a big difference to the course of the revolution if France had avoided a foreign war? Would you agree that the fear generated by the foreign war contributed to the violence and terror? How can you explain the difference in terrorist activities in France and the United States during their respective revolutions? Without a foreign war, would France still have gotten a Napoleon?

9. Did Napolean have a permanent affect on Europe? Was he a great man? Had he not lived, would someone else have become dictator of France about that time? Did he accomplish any good or useful things? Would you describe him primarily as a tyrant? If yes, did he use his tyranical powers in any way for the purpose of bettering mankind, or was the good that he did merely coincidental? Do you agree with the line, "The evil that men do lives after them, the good is oft interred with their bones"?

10. Would it have made a difference in the history of the 19th century if Napoleon had not been defeated? What were his biggest mistakes? Could he have conquered Russia if he had planned better, or should he never have tried? If he had remained in power, is it likely he would have stopped his military conquests?

SUGGESTED BIBLIOGRAPHY

J. R. Alden, The American Revolution, 1775 - 1783 (Torchbooks)
P. Amann, ed., The Eighteenth-Century Revolution: French or Western? (Heath)
B. Bailyn, Ideological Origins of the American Revolution (Harvard University Press)
C. Becker, The Declaration of Independence (Vintage)
C. Becker, The Heavenly City of the Eighteenth-Century Philosophers (Yale Univ. Press)
L. I. Bredvold, The Brave New World of the Enlightenment (Univ. of Michigan Press)
C. Brinton, A Decade of Revolution, 1789 - 1799 (Torchbooks)
J. B. Bury, The Idea of Progress (Dover, 1955)
P. Geyl, Napoleon, For and Against (Yale Univ. Press)
L. H. Gibson, The Coming of the Revolution, 1763 - 1775 (Torchbooks)
Peter Gray, The Enlightenment, 2 vols. (Knoph, 1969, Vol. 1, also Vintage)
G. R. Havens, The Age of Ideas: From Reaction to Revolution of Eighteenth-Century France (Free Press)
M. Hutt, Napoleon (Spectrum)
L. Krieger, Kings and Philosophers, 1869 - 1789 (Norton)
G. Lefebure, The French Revolution, 2 vols. (Columbia Univ. Press)
F. Markham, Napoleon and the Awakening of Europe (Collier)
J. Michelet, History of the French Revolution (Galaxy)
J. C. Miller, Origins of the American Revolution (Stanford Univ. Press)
E. S. Morgan, The Birth of the Republic, 1763 - 1789 (Phoenix)
R. R. Palmer, The Age of the Democratic Revolution, 2 Vols. (Princeton University Press)
J. M. Thompson, The French Revolution (Galaxy)
J. M. Thompson, Napoleon Bonaparte: His Rise and Fall (Oxford, 1952)

CHAPTER 2 - REVOLUTION: THE SECOND WAVE

Part I

The Restoration of the Old Order

The Congress of Vienna

As soon as Napoleon was dispatched to Elba in 1814, diplomats from the four countries which defeated him, England, Prussia, Austria, and Russia, assembled in Vienna to work out a peace settlement. The most brilliant statesmen in Europe were there, and the music, banquets, beautiful women, and sumptuous celebrating at that peace congress fascinated Europe for years afterwards. The overriding theme of the assembly was to obliterate the memory of the French Revolution from the face of Europe--to blot out all recollections of mob violence, radical constitutions, and terror; and also to eradicate any vestiges of sympathy for the upstart adventurer from Corsica. It is easy to criticize their naiveté in trying to recreate a world which had disappeared forever; but when one compares their decisions to those made after the next great war, World War I, they acquitted themselves fairly well.

By the Treaty of Chaumont early in 1814, the big powers restored the Bourbon family to the throne of France, and took away the conquests made for France by Napoleon. Austria, Prussia, Russia and England also formed a Quadruple Alliance or concert of Europe. The concert of Europe was an arrangement foreshadowing the ideal principle and function of the Security Council permanent members (the "big powers") in today's collective security mechanisms of the U.N. In 1815 the big powers wanted to keep the peace (the same general goal as today); at Vienna, they specifically wanted to guarantee that neither France nor any other country would dominate Europe. They restored the former royal family and former French boundaries, and they created buffer states to guard against French expansion--The Netherlands (including Belgium) in the north, and Piedmont (including Genoa) in the south. Prussia received territories along the Rhine River, and Austria got northern Italy. Much of what Napoleon had done was left untouched: the Holy Roman Empire was not revived, and most of Germany remained as he had reorganized it. Legitimate monarchs were put to rule in many areas, and the Bourbon Family in particular was restored in France, Spain and the Kingdom of Naples.

On some issues there was serious disagreement--particularly on the subject of Eastern Europe. The country of Poland as we know it did not exist in 1815. Poland, which had been quite a large state in the Middle Ages, had grown weak and vulnerable over the years, and had been partitioned in 1772, 1793, and 1795, between Russia, Prussia and Austria until nothing was left. Napoleon recreated Poland and called it the Grand Duchy of Warsaw. But when Napoleon was defeated, the Poles were again at the mercy of the three countries who had devoured them before, and again they were each jealous of the others. The wily French diplomat, Talleyrand, who had served every French government for the past twenty years, made the compromise. Austria, Prussia and Russia all kept large chunks of Poland; some of Poland was restored as a

EUROPE AFTER THE CONGRESS OF VIENNA 1815

1. CORSICA
2. TUSCANY
3. MODENA
4. PARMA
5. LOMBARDY-VENETIA
6. SWISS CONFED.
7. BADEN
8. WURTEMBERG
9. BAVARIA
10. SAXONY
11. HESS
12. HANOVER
13. MECKLENBURG

AUSTRIAN EMPIRE
PRUSSIA
FRANCE
BOUNDARY OF THE GERMANIC CONFEDERATION

ATLANTIC OCEAN

NORTH SEA

BALTIC SEA

RUSSIAN EMPIRE

GREAT BRITAIN

KINGDOM OF NORWAY AND SWEDEN

KINGDOM OF DENMARK

KINGDOM OF NETHERLANDS

PRUSSIA

POLAND

HUNGARY

AUSTRIAN EMPIRE

BLACK SEA

OTTOMAN EMPIRE

KINGDOM OF FRANCE

ADRIATIC SEA

PAPAL STATES

KINGDOM OF THE TWO SICILIES

KINGDOM OF SARDINA

MEDITERRANEAN SEA

KINGDOM OF SPAIN

KINGDOM OF PORTUGAL

country; and Prussia got half of Saxony--altogether a fairly typical diplomatic compromise, for nobody got much, but everybody got something.

The most powerful man in Europe in 1815 was Prince Clement Metternich (1773-1859), the handsome, dashing, aristocratic foreign minister of Austria. As a young student in Strasbourg he had seen some revolutionary rioting, a spectacle which alarmed him to such extent that he became the leading actor in all efforts to prevent revolution from recurring after 1815. The Austrian Empire, ruled by one of the oldest dynasties in Europe, and including several dozen different nationality groups in its borders, was particularly vulnerable to threats from liberals who wanted to weaken the emperor, and nationalists who wanted their own nation (including the Hungarians and Czechs). After the Treaty of Vienna was drawn up, Metternich dominated the Quadruple Alliance, and had every intention of putting down any revolutionary outburst whenever and wherever it should occur in Europe. Czar Alexander I was in agreement, but also promoted his own Holy Alliance at the same time. The Holy Alliance was another agreement of 1815 which consisted of a harmless but lofty-sounding plan that the major powers would be guided in diplomatic matters by God. Castlereagh, the English minister, called it "a piece of sublime mysticism and nonsense"[1] and refused to join. This was the beginning of a rift between the powers which became increasingly serious, for it was hard to imagine the extremely liberal country of England cooperating for long with three autocracies such as Russia, Prussia and Austria. In fact, trouble broke out almost at once. Revolutions began to sputter and crackle all over Europe within five years of the treaty. This angered Metternich, and he and his fellow conservatives tried fiercely to put them down. In this effort, the British were obliged to disagree. They had cooperated at the peace conference, but they could not bring themselves to support the idea of sending in armies every time an oppressed population asked for a few elementary political rights. In this regard, the Congress of Vienna failed, and the Quadruple Alliance was ineffective. The effort to restore absolute monarchy was chimerical at best. An entire generation had been hearing about the rights of man, and in every hamlet and farflung corner of Europe there seemed to be at least one idealistic soul who wanted to do something about it.

Part II

The Revolutions of 1820 - 1830

In 1815 most of the population of Europe was relieved and satisfied to have a familiar government back again. Kings returned to thrones, and aristocrats resumed their superior place in society. Only the tiniest group of rabble-rousers dissented with the new order (which was the old order); but few as they were, they were scattered about in every country on the European continent, and as they began to revolt one after the other they frightened Metternich and other conservatives.

----

[1] Quoted by Crane Brinton, John B. Christopher and Robert Lu Wolf, A History of Civilization, 1715 to the Present (N.J.: Prentice Hall, 1976, II), p. 541

27

The first wave of revolution occurred in Spain in 1820. After the Spanish King Ferdinand VII was restored to power he attempted to suppress all memory of the Constitution of 1812, and he tried also to put down the revolutions which had broken out in the Spanish Empire. In 1820 he ordered 20,000 men to the port of Cadiz to sail for America, but a mutiny broke out, and the discontent spread to other cities and became a demand for the restoration of the Constitution. Ferdinand VII may have been long of nose, but he was short of courage. He gave in at once. Metternich then hastily summoned his allies to Troppau, and Prussia and Russia agreed with the idea of immediate intervention. They agreed to send a French army across the Pyrenes, which killed large numbers of Spanish revolutionaries, and restored Ferdinand VII once again to his throne. England had refused to go along, partly because she suspected Metternich of having plans to put down the South American revolutions. England was decidedly leery of having European governments (other than her own) interfering in that part of the world, and proposed to the United States that they issue a joint communiqué warning them off in some fashion. The United States refused. But in December, 1823, President Monroe issued the Monroe Doctrine, which amounted to the same thing, though an exclusively American statement. The United States warned other powers not to meddle in the affairs of Latin America, at the risk of incurring American wrath. The European powers did not exactly quail before this threat, but they also did not intervene. As a result the United States took great pride in the Monroe Doctrine, assuming it had been responsible for keeping malfactors away. Since the American navy in those days was nicknamed the mosquito fleet, with only five or six ships, it is altogether possible that it was the giant British fleet, the most powerful in the world, which protected Latin America from intervention.

The revolt in Spain was only the first. Others broke out in fairly short order, some successful, some not. The success of the revolutionaries was in direct correlation to the degree of threat they represented to Austria and her possessions, or Prussia or Russia and their possessions. Thus, a revolt in Portugal was allowed to continue, but a revolt in Naples, which directly menaced Austrian holdings in Italy, was crushed. A revolt in the Netherlands was allowed to continue, and led to the creation of a new country, Belgium; while a revolt in Russia proper, the Decembrist Revolt (1825), was put down.

Throughout the 19th centry the Balkans was to be one of the most unsettling and unsettled areas in Europe. Three major powers--Austria, Russia and Turkey had covetted the area for centuries. Turkey, or the Ottoman Empire, as it was called, had once been a great and powerful empire and still held lands which stretched across half the Middle East. Now in a state of decay (hence their nickname, "the sick man of Europe"), Turkey was withering. Some national groups in the Empire were laying plans for independence, and both Austria and Russia were hovering nearby to take what they could. Russia had always wanted an outlet from the Black Sea, and now saw her opportunity. England, meanwhile, was beginning to see her role of keeping a balance of power in Europe. With the world's greatest empire she did not covet the Turkish possessions; but she was determined not to stand idly by while another European power seized part of Turkey and then threatened European peace. Thus when the Greeks threw themselves into a rebellion against their Turkish overlords in 1821, the ensuing conflict had many implications. The war was fierce, with atrocities committed on both sides. In 1827, Mohammed Ali of

Egypt, a vassal of Turkey, seemed about to take the last Greek stronghold, when Britain, Russia and France decided to intervene to save Greek independence. At Navarino Bay, ships from those three nations sank the Egyptian and Turkish fleets, and the war was over. The peace terms were a compromise, for not all of Greece was freed from Turkey, but most of it was. Russia was rewarded with only a small Turkish province. The struggle in Greece was the most popular romantic event of the day. Not only did it inspire reams of poetry, but with fatal fascination lured the most famous romantic of them all, Lord Byron, who died there. England and France had succeeded in keeping moderation at work, a concern which was to occupy them a generation later when another bigger war broke out on the Black Sea--the Crimean War.

Another conflict erupted in 1825 in Russia, but in the land of the Czars, liberalism was a rare and fragile plant. For some years, the Freemasons, an international secret society of liberals founded in the 18th century, and other secret societies in Russia, especially the Northern society and the Southern Society, planned in various ways to encourage reform. Some wanted to free the serfs, some wanted also to give them land. The Southern Society was the more radical--it called for a republic and the assassination of the Czar. When Alexander I died without direct heirs, the choice fell between his two brothers, Constantine and Nicholas. There was a brief revolt of the Petersburg garrison against Nicholas; but he established himself in power and had the rebels shot or sent to Siberia. The experience thoroughly unnerved him, and Nicholas I, who ruled from 1825-1855, became one of the most autocratic rulers of his day.

As the wave of revolts continued unabated across Europe, in 1830 an important and successful one broke out in Paris against the Bourbon monarch, the charming but inept Charles X (1824-1830). For fifteen years France had been divided into factions who disagreed utterly on government policy. The aristocrats and monarchists wanted to banish revolutionary reforms such as elections; moderate politicians accepted the monarchy, but wanted a legislature which was at least moderately representative. For a few years France was ruled by a charter which allowed religious toleration, some freedom of press, some equality before the law, and a legislature with a lower house based on extremely restricted suffrage (100,000 people out of 30,000,000) The "far right" was very disturbed by these liberal provisions. When the old king's nephew, the Duc de Berri, was assassinated in 1820, the Ultras, who were the most monarchist and conservative faction, led a movement for reaction. They were partially successful. But a crisis occurred in 1830, over Algeria. The Bey of Algiers had offended French honor and national dignity by attacking the French consul with a flyswatter. The Ultra minister, the Prince de Polignac, decided to take an appropriate stand over this matter--war. In July the French captured the city, and thus did they gain Algeria, the first colony of their African empire. Heady with success, Polignac pushed his advantage by issuing the July Ordinances, reactionary measures which would crack down on the press and disenfranchise the middle class. If he thought the French people were so distracted by Algeria that they would casually give up their rights, he was wrong. In the hot summer days in Paris, crowds gathered around the Pantheon and up and down the Boulevard St. Michel to protest. Barricades were thrown up; Notre Dame was seized. Charles X abdicated in alarm, and repaired to England. Several hundred people were

Giuseppe Mazinni.
(The Granger Collection)

killed, but as revolutions go, the 1830 episode in Paris was remarkably tame. The people eventually settled on a new king, Louis Philippe, the Duke of Orleans, a king who acted and looked more like a successful banker. He brought in a constitutional government founded on the principle that France should be governed by a king and the wealthiest top classes of society. He ruled for eighteen years, but was then overthrown himself.

The excitement of the July revolution was contagious, and within a few weeks revolutionaries in various other countries were inspired to try their luck as well. There were shots fired in Poland, Italy, Germany and Belgium, and by Christmas, the Belgians had won their independence from The Netherlands. The Poles were not so lucky. Because they received a constitution in 1815 from Czar Alexander I of Russia when he was in a particularly mellow mood, the Poles had one of the most liberal regimes in Europe. But as a province of Russia they did not have a nation. In 1830, some Warsaw army cadets tried to start a war for Polish national independence, but they were no match for the new Czar, Nicholas I. He fiercely put down the insurrection and turned the liberal Polish regime into a repressive society under martial law.

In Germany and Italy, the revolutionaries did not fare much better. In Italy the rebellion was short-lived, for Austria sent troops to put it down immediately. Close observers of the Italian scene might have picked out an interesting young man in the crowd of hotheads--Napoleon's own nephew, by the name of Louis Napoleon Bonaparte. He would spend the next eighteen years as a revolutionary, he would see the inside of more than one jail, and he would be emperor of France.

In Germany, political agitation had continued unabated for fifteen years, although confined almost entirely to the small but vocal intellectual community around German universities--professors, students and writers. A student organization named the Burschenschaft was the most vocal critic of reaction. In 1817 they had a small riot at the University of Jena, where they insulted the authorities; and in 1819 the Burschenschaft was blamed when a student assassinated a Russian agent named Kotzebue. Metternich used both incidents as reasons to persuade the German Diet to accept the Carlsbad Decrees of 1819, which disbanded the Burschenschaft, cracked down on the press, and curtailed academic activities. During the next few years, student plotting continued, but in secret. Their numbers were impressive, for 30,000 of them gathered at a protest meeting at Hambach in 1832. The next year several dozen students and professors tried to take over Frankfurt, which was the capital of the German Confederation, but they were caught and virtually all imprisoned. Revolutionary zeal died down for a number of years after that.

From 1820 until 1830 there had been a decade of revolutionary activity in Europe, some of it successful; most of it not. Generally speaking, the successes were indirectly related to the determination of Austria, Prussia and Russia to put them down. The formula was simple: if Metternich wanted to stamp out a revolution he could do it. But when five or six took fire at once, he chose to quench the one closest to Austria and let some of the others go.

Part III

The Revolutions of 1848

In 1848 after more than fifteen years of quiet, revolutions broke out with renewed intensity in many different spots on the European Continent. The ideas of liberalism and nationalism continued to attract enthusiasts, and had been fanned by the intellectual ideas then in vogue in the Romantic movement. The Romantics wrote glowingly of emotional committment (as against cold logic), love, honor, and death. Their artists were men like Delacroix, who glorified revolutions on canvas; or poets like Byron, who wrote passionately of love, and who went to Spain and then to Greece to take part himself in the glorious struggle. Liberalism was a movement which grew out of reverence for the common man: it held that all men were basically equal, and even the humblest peasant was as wise or wiser than a sophisticated banker. Governments should serve all these men, and if they did not, every man had the right to fight for freedom.

These are high-sounding words, and embody concepts cherished by all free countries then and now. But they were often antithetic to the notions of other revolutionaires fighting along side them for the totally different cause of nationalism. In many ways nationalism was directly counter to liberalism. Liberalism stressed the universality of man--freedoms deserved by all, rights common to everyone everywhere. Liberals of all countries identified with the noble cause of the Greeks, or the Poles; it was common for idealists of one country to go and fight for the people in another. But nationalism fed on particularism, arrogance and selfishness. Quite contrary to universal belief in basic rights, nationalism stressed that only the people of one particular country or area had such rights. The Poles thought they were superior to all other people; the Italians thought Italians were. The emphasis was necessary in a way, for in order to inspire a population to risk their lives fighting an enemy vastly superior to them, they had to believe that they were <u>better</u>, and could win out of sheer excellence. They also had to believe that the cause was worthwhile; not only could the Poles beat the Russians, but they should beat them--God himself was on their side in that noble struggle. For if the Austrians really were as good as the Czechs, for example, there was no point to the Czechs objecting to their rule. However, if the Czechs felt that they were a unique and special group of people, with a stirring history and a soulful language, with poetry and music, food and customs unique to them, then their reason to fight for their right to have their own country with their own Czech government was morally compelling.

However necessary these concepts were to the first stages of nationalism, they spelt misery for many nations in later years. For if a people were so special that God himself gave them the right (they thought) to fight for independence, then it only followed that they should rule other people as well--that their language should be taught to other children, that unfortunate natives throughout the world should be exposed to their high civilization. The truth of this can be seen in the attitude of the Hungarians, for example: they fought valiantly for their own cause of separation from the Austrians in 1848. And up to a point they won, for a few years later the Hapsburgs split the empire into a dual monarchy, so that henceforth the Austrians ruled one half and the Hungarians the other half. Yet the Hungarians were even worse than the Austrians once they had the right to rule other nationality groups: they forced all the other populations now to learn Hungarian (before it had been German); one couldn't get a job in their government or on the railroads unless one spoke Hungarian. This arrogance was apparent everywhere in the world where one nation won a struggle against another, or conquered a colony.

In 1848, the first signs of revolution once again occurred in France. There, as throughout Europe at that time, there was an economic crisis which caused the initial political crisis. The European economic crisis took the form of an industrial depression in some countries, with layoffs and low wages; and the form of an agricultural depression in others, especially in Germany, Poland and Ireland, where the potato blight and ensuing famine caused incalculable suffering. In France, however, the potato had not become the universal food that it was in a country like Ireland, and the economic woes were industrial. There were legitimate grievances of workers against the factory owners, and there were others who focused more on the government of Louis Philippe, which had been elitist from the beginning. One of the critics of the regime was Adolphe Thiers, who had once been a loyal supporter of Louis Philippe. Cynics felt that Thiers' main criticism was that he had been replaced in office by Francois Guizot; but Thiers himself was a constitutional monarchist who felt that the suffrage should be broadened and the government made more responsive to the middle class. Other critics went much further than that, and called for the right to strike and the right to have unions; still others wanted a republic; still others were outright socialists.

In 1847 moderate republicans and critics like Thiers organized a series of banquets in France to dramatize their opposition. In February 1848, Louis

32

Philippe tried to save his sinking ship by recalling Thiers to office, but riots broke out in which fifty workers, students and radical protestors were killed. Barricades were thrown up, and the masses of Paris poured into the streets for revolution. Louis Philippe followed and took to his heels and overnight France was a republic again, with a provisional government head by Alphonse de Lamartine, a romantic poet (which suited everyone's mood). Complaints and demonstrations continued, and the government moved rapidly to the left. Some revolutionlists went into the government, and there was a semblance of sympathy for the ideas of the most famous of their group, Louis Blanc. Louis Blanc (1811-1882) was an articulate friend of the worker, for years had been calling for a socialized France recognizing the "right to work" (as he called it), and containing national workshops, which would employ workers and pay them state salaries. Blanc was allowed to organize some workshops, but rather than a genuine experiment with socialism, some thought they were really a way of putting the 100,000 unemployed on the dole.

Meanwhile, elections were called for a National Assembly in April, and feelings were running high, in part because it was the first election in European history based on universal manhood suffrage. Eight million Frenchmen voted, and the results confirmed that most of the country was still staunchly conservative, antisocialist, and eager to protect private property. The Paris radicals resented the conservative effect of the countryside in the election, and on May 15 invaded the National Assembly demanding a new government. Tempers flared, violence spread, and within a few days the first authentic class war broke out, known as the June Days. Unemployed workers milled about the streets, shouting and rioting. Middle class shop owners, property owners and farmers with pitchforks poured into Paris, and a bitter struggle ensued. Over 10,000 people were killed before General Cavaignac brought in troops and restored order with bayonets. Some, including Louis Blanc, fled; thousands were arrested, and many of those were deported to Algeria.

The government restored order and firmly insisted on the wishes of the majority in the new constitution it drew up; property was declared inviolable. A new constitution called for a directly elected president and a one-house legislature to be chosen in December of 1848. Of all the candidates running for president, the man chosen for the job, receiving five and a half million votes, was the nephew of Napoleon, Louis Napoleon Bonaparte (1808-1873). Although he had fought in revolutions himself, and had spent time in jail for his politics, Louis Napoleon was a charismatic and machiavellian politician. He spoke French with a German accent (he had been raised in Switzerland), and did not cut much of a figure on a horse, but he passed himself off as a lover of law and order, and he capitalized greatly on his name. Like his uncle, he seized progressively more power, and declared himself emperor in 1852. He threw over his devoted English mistress who had spent all her money to bring him to power, and married a beautiful Spanish aristocrat, of flashing eyes and sweeping hoop skirts, the Empress Eugenia. Thus the second Republic died in infancy, replaced by the Second Empire.

In Italy revolutionaries of various hues had been plotting for years. Most were agreed on one point only--that Italy needed to be free of foreign (Austrian) domination; for great divergence existed on the best kind of government their new country should have. Many conservatives preferred a monarch but were in disagreement over which monarch should rule; some wanted the King of Piedmont to extend his reign over the united Italy. Other conservatives envisaged a united Italy governed from Rome by the Pope; or perhaps the Pope presiding over a federation of states, each with its own king. The third and liberal group was called Young Italy (all members were under forty), and wanted to establish a democratic republic. Giuseppe Mazzini (1805-1872) founded the movement in an attempt to replace an older and unsuccessful secret society, the Carbonari. Mazzini had been plotting for years. In and out of jail, often in exile, he was the embodiment of the Italian nationalist and liberal movements, and his Young Italy became the model for societies elsewhere, Young Germany and Young Poland.

Revolts broke out in 1848 in January in rapid succession in the Two Sicilies, in Tuscany, and in Milan, capital of Lombardy. When news spread that Metternich had been overthrown in Austria, the Italians were exultant. In Venice they created the Republic of St. Mark, and in Rome they created the Republic of Rome, under Mazzini himself. An army under King Charles Albert of Piedmont engaged in a national crusade against the Austrians, and with early successes at every point, optimism soared. Unfortunately, no leader won complete endorsement, and eventually all of the revolutionaries failed because of rivalries among them. Piedmont turned aggressive and annexed Lombardy and two other northern states, thus quenching all enthusiasm other Italians had had for Piedmont leadership in the new united state. In Rome, the Pope made the painful decision that he should be neutral in the war against Austria, thus ending most enthusiasm that he should rule. Austrian troops rallied and finally defeated the Republic of St. Mark, while French troops were brought in to put down the Roman Republic of Mazzini. In all, the results were discouraging. The only permanent result was the success of Piedmont. The people of all the different city states had been disunited and at cross purposes, and unable to unite Italy or agree on a common government. But Piedmont would do it from above, with its army, before many more years had passed.

In Germany, 1848 was the high point of revolutionary efforts for liberalism and nationalism. Violence broke out in all directions, and as in Italy, many of the initial revolts seemed to be succeeding. But in both cases the revolutions failed from lack of decisive leadership. There were too many different factions, too many alternative solutions, and also too much procrastination.

In Germany solid economic groundwork seemed to promise unification. A customs union known as the Zollverein was created in 1818 under the leadership of Prussia, which had as its goal the abolition of internal tariffs in Germany. A number of small states joined the union, and abolished most of their local tolls and taxes, so that for the first time trade could take place among them with relative freedom. In 1848, patriotic Germans were persuaded that political unification was also at hand, and they began to riot simultaneously to that end. In Prussia, hundreds of workingmen took to the streets, milling about and shouting, and killed at least two hundred people. They seized the royal palace, seized the person of the king, Frederick William IV, who was quaking in his boots, and persuaded him that he was more liberal than he thought he was. He hastily called an assembly at Frankfurt to enable the liberals to draw up a constitution, and announced that Prussia and Germany were now one.

STORMING THE ARSENAL, BERLIN.

The Revolution of 1848 in Berlin. (The Granger Collection)

    More than eight hundred delegates were chosen to go to Frankfurt, and
although they represented the cream of German intellectural life, they did not
represent the common people. They were also inexperienced in political
matters, and in disagreement on their goals. The nationalists were divided
into two groups, the Grossdeutsch and the Kleindeutsch. The former called for
unification of all German speaking people in central Europe into one large
country; but the latter expressly omitted Germans in the Austrian empire, and
called for a small cohesive state of Germans from Prussia and the German
Confederation. Since Austria rejected the idea of German unification, the
Kleindeutsch solution was the only one available, and the delegates settled on
that. On the subject of liberalism, the delegates drew up a moderate
consitution for a united Germany, and invited Frederick William of Prussia to
be king of the united country. However, they had alienated the conservatives
by being too liberal, alienated the workers by being too conservative, and
they never did have the confidence of the king. When he rejected the
constitution, most of the delegates began to go home, and the final hangers-on
were eventually dispersed by troops. German efforts from below to unify the
country and to create a liberal government both failed. As in Italy,
unification was eventually imposed from above. Those in power were not
interested in a liberal government, and many thousands of liberals who had
participated in the revolution fled to America. For all practical purposes,
the liberal voice in German was silenced in 1848, and when unification finally
came in 1870, the government which brought it was autocratic.

The events of Italy and Germany in 1848 were repeated with only a few variations in the Austrian Empire. Groups of liberals criticized the repressive Hapsburg government and the reactionary mentality of Metternich, while groups of nationalists sprang up on all sides who wanted to break up the empire so that they could have a homeland. The situation was vastly complicated by the fact that many of the nationality groups heartily detested each other, and actually preferred Hapsburg rule to domination by one of their own--the Hungarians, for example. Czechs, Rumanians, Serbs and Croats all competed for a homeland; but only one minority group actually succeeded in 1848--the Magyars, or Hungarians. Led by Louis Kossuth (1802-1894), a charismatic nationalist, the Hungarians rebelled in March of 1848, and for a time were successful in defying the Hapsburgs. Eventually the imperial army defeated them, aided by troops from Russia, and for a time military rule was established in Hungary. However, some of the changes were permanent. Metternich was gone, and the old emperor abdicated in favor of his nephew, Franz Joseph (1848-1916). Although victorious in 1849, Franz Joseph eventually honored Magyar claims and split the empire with them in the Ausgleich of 1867.

Most of the 1848 outbreaks of revolutionary violence occurred in major cities throughout Europe where industrialization was taking place, fostering increased numbers of exploited (low-paid, often unemployed) workers, who lived in conditions of close communication and mutual stimulation, sparking off revolutionary behavior. The events of 1848 also marked the last great upsurge of romanticism in the cause of human rights and longings for a homeland. Emotion, courage and rhetoric were all very well, but they were no match for hardnosed rulers with superior forces. In many aspects of life after 1848 romanticism gave way to realism. The romantic love and death sagas of literature were replaced by grim novels about lower class wretches by Charles Dickens, or bored members of the middle class by Maupassant. In politics also, realism seemed more sensible.

Part IV

Romanticism

In 1815 Europe was reeling from the devastation of a brutal war which had lasted for a full generation, which had destroyed the old social order, left millions dead, and challenged the most important principles held dear to the old regime. At the Congress of Vienna, the diplomats made a determined effort to mend the broken thrones, and place a new generation of nervous kings in power again over the skittish people. Intellectually also, one can argue that the generation of 1815 tried to ignore the bloody realities of revolutionary and industrial Europe--two separate blights upon the old order--with Romanticism. They tried to escape by a freewheeling flight of fancy to another time and place, a simpler order, a primitive or agricultural existence, a world governed by the heart and not the mind. Some escaped as far as the Middle Ages, and wove inspired fancies about knights and chivalry; while others hearkened back to medieval religion, and found refuge from a disorderly world in the cool persasiveness of the Gothic Cathedral. On the political scene, some people also tried to escape: physically. They drew up plans for perfect states in which the evils of war and industrialization would be avoided forever.

Romanticism was also a reaction against the Enlightenment of the 18th century. The Enlightenment emphasized reason and distrusted emotion; it valued logic, and rules. It found inspiration in the coldly calculated excellence of the classics, and imitated them in art, architecture and poetry. And even before it reached its peak, the rebel destined to lead the western world against it was already writing in Paris. Jean-Jacques Rousseau (1712-1778) was born in Switzerland, and although he ran away to France and established himself there as a genius in many diverse fields, he never completely divested himself of his origins.

Inspired perhaps by the beautiful Swiss landscape of his youth, Rousseau believed that man had once lived in a state of nature, an idyllic time of gambolling in wood and field communing with nature, when all were happy and contented. "Civilization" and all its trappings had been imposed later, after the invention of private property. Laws and governments eventually became necessary, but they are evils to be borne, not blessings. In the Dijon essay and in his other books, including The Social Contract, and his novels, Emile, and La Nouvelle Heloise, Rousseau planted the seeds of Romanticism. Among the ideas which now became popular were the conviction that emotions were more reliable than reason; the enjoyment of nature in all its forms, not only for its beauty but as a source of geniune knowledge and wisdom. Wisdom derived not from books and the trappings of civilization, but from observing nature and nature's laws. Instead of admiring cities as exemplars of civilization, Rousseau admired primitive life, and was especially enraptured with American Indians, whom he called "noble savages". Rousseau believed Indians to be wise, good and happy because of their constant communion with nature. After Indians, he admired farmers or peasants, who lived close to the soil. Cities eventually came to be so denigrated by the romantics that they were condemned as repositories of evil. Since in real life industrialization did play havoc with cities, and created hideous slums worse than anything seen before, much of this seemed incontestably true. If nature was the fount of wisdom, traditional education was also suspect, and in Emile Rousseau described the only kind of education which was really suitable. Emile, the pupil, would be tutored in the woods and fields, and never given a book to read until the age of sixteen. At that point he would receive Robinson Crusoe, which was appropriate, as it was the story of a civilized man who found true happiness and wisdom with a savage on a desert island.

In literature, the Romantic Movement lasted from about 1780 until 1830. It included a fondness for nature, a fondness for children and for simple, primitive man, and for peasants; a fondness for the Middle Ages, for the pageantry of the knights and the beauty and mystery of the Catholic Church. It included a distaste for reason and science as incapable of explaining important truths about existence, and instead a reliance on the emotions and faith. Romantics loved the mysterious, the supernatural, the occult (characteristic of many antiscientific people), and celebrated above all other experiences love and death. One of the first to show a revulsion against science and the ugly beginnings of the Industrial Revolution was William Blake, also famous as an artist. But the first romantic lyrical poet was

William Wardsworth (1770-1850). In one of the poems that particularly summed up romantic sentiments Wardsworth wrote, "My heart leaps up when I behold / A rainbow in the sky"; and some of his most famous lines:

One impulse from a vernal wood
May teach you more of man,
Or moral evil and of good,
Than all the sages can.

Three romantic poets lived their lives in the same romantic spirit in which they wrote, Percy Bysshe Shelly (1792-1822), John Keats (1795-1821), and Lord Byron (1788-1824). All three died young--Keats died of consumption, Shelley of suicide, and Byron while fighting for the Greek Revolution. All three wrote on nature, love and death; both Shelley and Keats were inspired by birds. In Ode to a Skylark Shelley wrote:

Teach me half the gladness
    That the brain must know
Such harmonious madness
    From my lips would flow,
The world should listen then, as I am
    Listening now.

Even happiness, as heard in the rich tones of a singing bird, reminded the melancholy Keats of death, as he said in Ode to a Nightingale:

Now more than ever seems it rich to die,
    To cease upon the midnight with no pain,
While thou art pouring forth thy soul abroad
    In such an ecstasy!

Immortality was to be found in beauty; in nature; Keats said of the nightingale, "Thou was not born for death, immortal Bird!" The song, like beauty and nature itself, lived on forever.

The rich outpouring of poetry during the romantic period suggest that the sentiments held by romantic writers lent themselves especially well to poetry. However, the novel also fared extremely well at that time. One romantic work which is really a short story, but of some importance as the beginning work of a genre, is Mary Shelley's "Frankenstein". Frankenstein was an inherently antiscientific creation, a story of science creating evil, where the monster who come into being is really an innocent victim, and the arrogant scientist is the real evildoer. "It's not nice to fool Mother Nature" is the message here; there are certain mysteries of life and death which human beings should leave unexplored. This truly begins the modern school of science fiction, most of it founded on this same premise; scientists are "mad doctors" who cause eternal evil.

Other romantic novels were La Louvelle Heloise by Rousseau, and The Sorrows of Young Werther by Goethe (1749-1832), both rather sentimental three-handkerchief stories of unrequited love. Goethe's most famous work was Faust, yet another romantic theme of antirationalism and antiknowledge, a parable once again on the dangers of trying to know more than mortals should.

One very important characteristic at the time was a fascination with the Middle Ages. In Sir Walter Scott (Ivanhoe) and Victor Hugo (Notre Dame de Paris) the reader got a good swashbuckling story on a distant time when values were clearer and heroes more heroic. Alexander Dumas, father and son, were among the most popular of all romantic novelists. The father wrote The Three Musketeers and Twenty Years After, wonderful stories of adventure and heroism in 17th century France. The son wrote Lady of the Camelias, which was more in the genre of unrequited love and the romantic preoccupation with death. Based on a true story, it depicted a woman of easy virture who sacrificed herself and finally died for love of a young man, who is left stricken at her grave. The novel was a best-seller at the time; was taken by Verdi as the story of one of the most popular operas of all time, La Traviata; and in the 20th century became one of the most famous films of all time, Camille, starring Greta Garbo.

Romantic music was characterized by a highly spirited quest for freedom, energy and grandeur. Of all the great geniuses of the period, none epitomizes it more than Ludwig von Beethoven, who was born in Bonn in 1770, and died in Vienna in 1827. Beethoven first attracted attention as the most brilliant and astonishing pianist of the age, a "giant", who possessed a technique and imagination "beyond anything which we might have dreamed".[1] Beethoven was short and fierce, with dark and shaggy hair and unkempt clothes, but kept the greatest aristocrats of Vienna and all Europe waiting upon him. His improvisation at the piano was the most brilliant anyone had ever experienced, and often reduced his listeners to tears. His notorious idiosyncracies of behavior were at least partly due to his own personal tragedy: the fact that he began to go deaf early in his career, and never heard his own great masterpieces. E.T.A. Hoffman, a contemporary poet, reviewed Beethoven's Fifth Symphony in 1810 with the words that it "moves the lever of terror, of fear, of shock, of suffering, and it awakens that endless Sehnsucht (longing) which is the essence of romanticism." However, Beethoven was not a complete romantic rebel in his music, but an heir of the 18th century tradition, who had "received the spirit of Mozart from the hands of Haydn". He bridged the two periods, and towered over both of them, with all the logic lucidity of the first, and all the stormy passion of the second. So great was his impact that no musician broke out of his mold for the rest of the century, but endlessly imitated his symphonies.[2]

Other romantics in music were Hector Berlioz, Frederic Chopin, and Franz Liszt. The Frenchman, Berlioz, the oldest of the three, described the qualities of his own music as "passionate expression, inner fire, rhythmic drive and the element of surprise," all characteristics which distinguish romantic music from the logical and orderly classical which preceded it. Berlioz created the romantic Sehnsucht more than any other--the great yearning and anguish which kindled their imagination, especially to be found in his Symphonie fanatastique. A greater genius was Frederic Chopin, an ardent young nationalist from Poland who went to Paris to seek his fortune. There he began a love affair with the lady novelist George Sand, contracted tuberculosis and died. A piano prodigy, he wrote over two hundred works--

[1]Frederic Grunfeld, Music (NY: Newsweek Books, 1974), p. 80
[2]Ibid., p. 82

George Gordon, Lord Byron,
by Richard Westall
(The Granger Collection)

brilliant outpourings to his romantic spirit--scherzos, waltzes, polonaises, and mazurkas. Liszt, a Hungarian, was yet another prodigy, a friend of Chopin but temperamentally quite different. "Chopin carried you with him into a dreamland in which you would have liked to dwell forever; Liszt was all sunshine and dazzling splendor, subjugating his hearers with a power none could withstand."[1] As the reckless revolutionaries who fired the imagination of Europe were defeated and discouraged in 1848, so the romantic movement also began to fade after that; Chopin and Beethoven were dead; and Liszt went on to experiment with the new generation of musicians, which included Wagner, Borodin and Moussorgsky.

In the fine arts the success of romanticism came later and lasted longer than in the fields of literature and music. The spirit of neoclassicism continued to dominate painting and especially architecture well into the 19th century; in architecture, for example, the Greek revival was the single most popular theme. In France it can be seen in the Church of the Madeleine (actually a copy of a Roman temple); in England, in the British Museum. Even the English Houses of Parliament rebuilt in the 1830s and 40s after the fire, which seem to embody the new romantic taste for gothic, are classical in their principles of symmetry and balance. By mid-century, however, gothic did tend to win many adherents with all the accompanying spires, gargoyles and gloomy interiors, as well as spiky, pointy gothic furniture which threatened to impale the unwary visitor at every moment. Railroad stations, churches and libaries throughout Europe and the United States were built in this style,

---

[1]Ibid., pp. 99-101

even late in the century--such as the splendidly medieval American universities, incuding the University of Chicago.

In painting, subdued colors, formal style and classical subject matter were all present in such artists as Jacques Louis David, who even favored Napoleon dressed in Roman togas and olive wreaths. But if his style was classic, in some ways his subject matter was revolutionary and romantic in theme--Napoleon crossing the Alps, and the death of Marat. David was the most popular artist of the revolutionary period. His contemporary, the Spanish genius Goya (1746-1828) in his maturity was much more romantic than David in his brooding, melancholy, even nightmarish depictions of the horrors of the French invasion of Spain. Goya's most famous painting is the Third of May, an execution scene depicting an anonymous group of French soliders killing a frightened group of Spanish patriots. Romantic artists were flamboyant in style and subject, with bright colors and lots of movement. The Frenchman Eugéne Delacroix (1799-1863) broke away from the classical confines of the studio, and embodied the full romantic flair in his painting of Moroccan peasants, political revolution ("Liberty Leading the People"; "The Massacre of Scio") and prancing horses. At its best, romantic art showed a new freedom of movement and livelier sense of color; at its worst it resembled certain novels of that time, with saccherine females, improbable heroes, and a good deal of posing. The tiresome postures of such characters and the languid or overblown melodrama of their behavior inspired the next generation to take a refreshing attempt at showing life as it really was, thus launching a new movement, realism.

QUESTIONS FOR REFLECTION

1. Armchair historians have always loved to point out the mistakes of the past. Traditional wisdom has always had it, for example, that the big mistake of the Congress of Vienna was to try and turn back the clock. Do you agree with this criticism? If so, what should the Congress have done--encouraged representative government? How realistic is this, considering the power still held in every country by the landed aristocracy and monarchies?

2. One of the political passions the Congress of Vienna tried to hold in check was nationalism. Was this a mistake also? Is nationalism a good thing? What purpose has been served by the creation of small countries out of former empires (such as Hungary, Czechoslovakia, Yugoslavia, Lebanon, Syria and others)? If nationalism is so commendable, why has the 20th century seen so many efforts at creating supranational organizations?--the League of Nations, the United Nations, the Common Market, the United Arab Republic?

3. If nationalism never really existed before 1789, is it possible to move on to another supranational phase, or is nationalism here to stay? Are there genuine national differences between people?

4. If you had been in charge of keeping the peace in Europe after defeating Napoleon, how would you have handled the revolutionary aspirations of the people in Europe? Should Metternich have been more lenient? Should he have been tougher in keeping the peace?

5. Why did England help the Greeks get their independence but not the Poles or Italians? What was England's main concern?

6. Was Metternich more alarmed over revolutions in Italy or Belgium? Why the difference? Which revolution alarmed Russia the most?

7. Which revolution failed? Which succeeded?

8. Where did a revolution succeed in 1848? Could it still have been called a success five years later?

9. Why did the German efforts at Frankfort ultimately fail?

10. What happened to Metternich?

11. Which group of people in the Austrian Empire were the most successful in getting their goals?

12. What were the romantic writers and artists reacting against? What were the main characteristics of the movement? What were some of the ideas they thought important? Do you agree with them? Do you see any contemporary artists or writers or filmmakers following in the same path?

13. Generally speaking, what is the best guideline in your opinion in music or painting or writing, the brain or the emotions? What are the shortcomings of each? What advantage does each have over the other?

14. Who were some of the most important romantic names in literature, music and art? In general, have their works stood the test of time?

SUGGESTED BIBLIOGRAPHY

M. S. Anderson, The Eastern Question, 1774-1923 (1966)
I. Babbit, Rousseau and Romanticism (1919)
J. Barzun, Classic, Romantic and Modern (1961)
W. J. Bate, From Classic to Romantic (1946)
R. J. Bezucha, The Lyon Uprising of 1834: Social and Political Conflict in the Early July Monarchy (1974)
C. Brinton, The Lives of Talleyrand (1936)
C. Brinton, The Political Ideas of the English Romanticists (1926)
M. Brock, The Great Reform Act (1973)
G. Bruun, Revolution and Reaction, 1848-1852 (1958)
G. de Bertier de Sauvigny, Metternich and His Timess (1962)
N. Gash, Politics in the Age of Peel (1953)
Frederic V. Grunfeld, Music (N.Y.: Newsweek Books, 1974)
J. B. Halsted, ed., Romanticism (1965)
H. E. Hugo, ed., The Romantic Reader (1957)
H. Nicolson, The Congress of Vienna: A Study in Allied Unity, 1812-1822 (1946)
A. Palmer, Alexander I, Tsar of War and Peace (1974)
J. Plamenatz, The Revolutionary Movements in France, 1815-1871 (1952)

R. Price, ed., Revolution and Reaction: 1848 and the Second French Republic
     (1976)
H. S. Reiss, The Political Thought of the German Romantics (1955)
P. Robertson, Revolutions of 1848: A Social History (1952)
H. G. Schenk, The Aftermath of the Napoleonic Wars: The Concert of Europe
     (1947)
R. H. Soltau, French Political Thought of the Nineteenth Century (1931)
P. N. Stearns, 1848: The Revolutionary Tide in Europe (1974)
C. K. Webster, The Foreign Policy of Castlereagh, 1812-1822, 2 vols. (1931)
C. K. Webster, The Congress of Vienna, 1814-1815 (1934)
C. M. Woodhouse, The Greek War of Independence (1952)

CHAPTER 3 - THE INDUSTRIAL REVOLUTION AND ITS CONSEQUENCES

Part I

The Industrial Revolution

The Industrial Revolution was not a revolution in the political sense. It occurred slowly and without violence, but its impact on the human condition was extraordinary. Like the Italian Renaissance or the Spanish discovery of America, it is a striking fact that this period of great technological breakthrough, happened because in one small corner of Western Europe--in this case, England--a tiny group of people burst upon the world in the 1700's with a sudden spurt of energy and ideas. One might well ask, why did England, and not some other country, begin the world-wide change which would produce a new economic order? There are several reasons for it.

One ingredient necessary for the Industrial Revolution was the accumulation of capital; another was an available work force already embued with necesary attitudes about thrift, hard work and responsibility. The German sociologist Max Weber theorized that these conditions were present in England because of the rise of the Protestant religion. Protestantism challenged the Catholic Church on a number of basic points: Protestants stressed the role of the individual in seeking salvation and flatly contradicted the authoritarian, hierarchical concept of Catholicism. Some specific Protestant churches went even farther than that, and focused on theological points which potentially called for important changes in behavior. Specifically, the Puritans, who were small in number but extremely outspoken, played a strategic role in British life in the early 1600s. They were followers of John Calvin, of Geneva, Switzerland, one of the most austere and uncompromising religious zealots who ever lived. This religious doctrine was not for the faint hearted. Calvin revived some ancient ideas of St. Augustine on predestination, so that the Puritan view of the world was one where the entire human race had been condemned by God to burn forevermore in Hell, with the exception only of one tiny group of people, the Elect, who had been predestined to be saved. How could one tell who was a member of the Elect? In a number of ways: by his religious devotion, his upright life, stern behavior, and also by his success in this world. Because of that conviction, work had a special significance for the Puritans. They worked harder than anyone because only a prosperous estate would satisfy themselves and the Church that they were among the Elect. In contrast to Catholic kindness and toleration, the stern Calvinists were contemptuous of the poor: the poor were not only lazy, they were sinful. This hard work and attention to duty had one result particulary relevant to the Industrial Revolution, for it did tend to lead to success and to the amassing of capital. After his tithe to the church, the ascetic hardnosed Puritan saved his money. Extravagant display of wealth was out of the question. And capital was one of the key ingredients to any society at that point of industrialization.

Max Weber's concept of the Protestant Ethic, like most great hypotheses, has certain inconsistencies and difficulties, but it is also a provocative and useful way to explain why the Industrial Revolution began where it did. There does seem to be a correlation between the Protestant faith and industrialization. Why did the Industrial Revolution begin in Protestant England and not Catholic France, Spain or Portugal? Why did it take hold so vigorously in the Protestant United States? And within a Catholic country like France, why were Protestant subgroups such as the Huguenots the most thrifty, hard working, and industrious group of people?

In addition to the presence of capital and a motivated work force, England undoubtedly had other advantages which assisted its industrialization. One argument is that its decentralized and rather relaxed administrative structure permitted experimentation with new factories, new laws and new products (in contrast to highly rigid, centralized France). Furthermore, her great empire provided raw materials, as well as a free market without tolls, and her magnificent fleet provided the best transportation in the world at that time. When the railroad was invented, again it was England, ahead in all respects, which had the first lines built, and benefited immediately from rapid inland transportation. Britain was politically stable, without oppressive taxation, and her population was mobile. Another difference between England and other West European countries at the time is the attitude in the upper classes toward work. Due to a number of circumstances, aristocrats in countries such as Spain and France, had become persuaded that work was beneath them. For example, after the discovery of America, many Spaniards became rich with the gold and silver brought back by the conquistadores, and the first thing most of them did was purchase titles of nobility with their money. The title meant that neither they nor their heirs would ever work again--a circumstance which helped bring about the decline of Spain two centuries later. In England, in contrast, younger sons who did not inherit land or title often entered commerce and worked hard; many came to sit in the House of Commons.

Some other causes of the revolution had to do with innovation and luck. For example, there had been improvements in the manufacture of woolen goods for a considerable time, but no single breakthrough had ever changed the reams of restrictions, laws, codes, regulations and circumscriptions which had confined that industry since the Middle Ages. With cotton, a new fibre imported from the American colonies, with no existing laws or customs to complicate its manufacture, a change occurred. Within the space of just a few years, the manufacturing process shifted from cottages to factories; home industry variations were replaced by standardization; and individual laborers were replaced increasingly by machines. As with all other manufactured goods, cloth had originally been made in dozens of steps in private cottages, with the raw fibre, or the thread, or the cloth, laboriously worked over by hand and then transported to another place altogether for the next stage of production. All this changed with factories.

The first technological breakthrough came in the 1730's when James Kay invented the flying shuttle, which greatly increased the output of workers spinning thread; a few years later came the spinning jenny of James Hargreaves (in 1765). The large quantity of thread was not much help, however, as long as the time-consuming process of weaving was still done by hand; but this was finally solved as well. The step of moving the spinning from the private home to a factory came from Richard Arkwright (1732-1792), who patented a water frame in 1769, a device which used water power to drive the machinary, and which enabled factories to be built wherever there were streams. Other inventions speeded up production and broadened its uses, such as the power loom of Edmund Cartwright, and the steam engine of James Watt (1769). A great contribution was the cotton gin invented by Eli Whitney in 1793, which separated the raw cotton fibres from the seeds. The finest merican cotton had been so tedious to gin hitherto, that its production had been too costly. The cotton gin invented by Whitney was such a simple device that it was instantly copied all over the world (the patent was useless and he made almost no money from the device), and increased the amount of cotton one man could gin by fifty times. Britain became the greatest single market for raw cotton, and manufactured such vasts quantities of it that by the mid-19th century cotton cloth counted for 50% of all British exports, and employed half a million workers in its manufacture.

Meanwhile, other industries began to flourish, and they in turn created new ones. The steam engine led eventually to the railroad, the manufacture of which called for both coal and steel. Steam was used in coal mines also, to pump out water and ventilate shafts, thereby increasing coal production. Iron smelting was improved by the invention of the blast furnace in 1828; and better yet, a much superior product--steel--became feasible at low cost with the Bessemer converter in 1856. Bessemer was an Englishman; his invention made cheap steel possible. Siemens, a German living in England, went still further with the open-hearth process which increased the amount of iron one could convert. These two men helped raise world steel production by ten times between 1865 and 1880.

As steel production increased, so did the construction of railroads, which revolutionized transportation in the world. The Romans had once had the greatest network of roads in the world--("all roads lead to Rome") never surpassed until the railroad. Napoleon himself could travel about no more quickly, and probably much more slowly, than Julius Caesar, a handicap which would change with astonishing rapidity only twenty years after his death. In 1830, the first train, the "Rocket", of George Stephenson, traveled 12 miles in 53 minutes. Eight years later England had 500 miles of track; by 1870 they had 15,000. Across the Channel, the railroad came somewhat later. The first railroad in France was in 1837, and by 1850 they had about two thousand miles of track. Germany by then had three thousand miles and Austria had one thousand miles. The United States was behind at first, but caught up very rapidly, first with railroads up and down the Atlantic coast, then increasingly into the interior. By 1860 the United States had 30,000 miles of track. Indirectly the cause of the Civil War was a railroad: Stephen Douglas of Illinois wanted to build a vast line out to the Pacific Northwest with Chicago as its terminus; to win Southern support he thought of ways to permit slavery to be allowed in the new territory. After the war, such a railraod was built, with a golden spike nailed down at Promontory Point, Utah, in 1869 symbolizing the link between east and west.

After the initial phases of the Industrial Revolution were over, the construction of the first factories and railroads, and the emphasis on iron with the advent of steel came what is known as the Second Industrial Revolution. Steel made marvelous new inventions possible--the sewing machine, the typewriter, lighter steamships, bicycles and then automobiles. It inspired innovations in architecture, providing a lightweight skeleton for bridges (the Brooklyn Bridge), sky-scrapers, or sky-scratchers, as the French called them. By 1913 the Woolworth Building in New York was the tallest in the world, 792 feet with an elevator also made of steel. Other marvels came from the development of electricity. Michael Faraday made the world's first electric motor. Soon electricity was a major source of power and light, utterly transforming everyday life, through streetlights, streetcars, radios, phonographs, washing machines, and refigerators. The telephone added another touch of wonder to human existence.

Along with new inventions which eased the drugery of human existence, there were less romantic changes which accompanied the industrial revolution, changes in business organization and banking. Many of the most powerful companies, such as Krupp or Carnegie, attained some of their vast success through sheer size, combining all the steps of production under one umbrella. They also conceived of horizontal integration of companies all in the same line of production, in holding companies or trusts, such as Standard Oil of John D. Rockefeller. In banking they changed from industrial to financial capitalism: earlier capital had come from the industrialists themselves, and capital for expansion came out of their own profits. Now the people themselves participated in the funding of companies through joint-stock companies, thanks to the concept of limited liability, which protected small investors from failure. Beginning in Britain in 1825, and moving then to the United States, France and Germany, by 1900 most forms of manufacturing were in joint-stock companies.

Another industry which produced wondrous changes was chemistry. Beginning in Germany, synthetic products (including dye and paint from coal tar) affected the rapid development of photography, the color of clothes, and the cheap manufacturing of paper. As with most changes of the time, however, the bad was as striking as the good. Chemical plants were particularly odious at pollution, spewing out noisome sulphuric fumes over town and country. Some of the leading chemical products were gunpowder and explosives, of the specialities Dupont Company in the United States, and Alfred Nobel in Sweden. Nobel left a vast sum of money to honor men who worked for peace, no doubt because of his own guilt for inventing dynamite in 1867. Thanks to Nobel, by the turn of the century man's ability to kill had multiplied a thousand times, as everyone was to see during World War I.

Part II

The Agricultural Revolution

At about the same time that the invention of power-driven machinery, factories, standardized production, and other components were making up the Industrial Revolution, rapid developments in plant breeding, new kinds of plants, new tools to cultivate plants, and other innovations were producing an agricultural revolution. For most of human history, the majority of the human race had been hungry; and during those times when there was enough to eat, the diet at any given place was apt to be monotonous and unappetizing. For centuries European peasants lived on black bread and cabbage. Each region naturally took to the grain which grew best in that area, and locally grown vegetables. In a poor country such as Scotland, the people ate oats, and

47

their national dish is haggis, a boiled sheep stomach stuffed with spices and oatmeal. Haggis is the culinary marvel of a very poor country; and many other traditional European foods reflect the exigencies of poverty--involving unappetizing parts of the animal, such as tripe (andouillette, the meal eaten every New Year's Day in France), familiar in the American South as chitterlings. Other countries did no better: in Norway they ate lye-treated codfish; in Germany they tucked into great huge pieces of fried fat.

One of the first changes was that traditional grains and vegetables were improved with hybrid varieties of seed, and yields improved through better tillage with crop rotation, better irrigation, and the use of fertilizers. Improvement of the land had been slow to come because of the medieval method of allotting land each year, which was still in practice in most countries (though obviously not in those countries with serfdom). In Britain each community owned most of the land as common land, and each spring would divide it up among all the farmers in the area, so that each farmer would receive a number of unconnected strips of land, chosen by lot, leaving large portions of fallow every year. The system was extremely inefficent, and in every way discouraged innovation and improvement. In the mid 1700s landlords tried to increase production by enclosing the land, consolidating dozens of small strips in largish fields, and reclaiming waste areas. Some of the farmers rioted, as it seemed to disrupt and change forever the British rural community. However, agricultural production became much more efficient and the longterm effects were undoubtedly beneficial. Some people claimed that the farmers were actually routed off the land and chased away to the cities, where they ended their days as factory workers living in slums in the early stages of the industrial revolution. Today some historians challenge this, maintaining that rural population figures did not go down, and in some areas even increased. There is no question, however, that there was both an increase and a displacement of rural populations.

In addition to improved efficiency in the use of the land, crops were also improved with new kinds of fertilizer. The German chemist, Liebig, worked a small revolution in this area in the 1840's when he warned against leaching three basic elements, nitrogen, potassium and phosphorus, from the soil (as was done in Virginia), and advised how to replace them. Liebig recommended using guano from the nests of South American birds, nitrates from Chile and potash from mines. Other agricultural experts focused on different aspects of improving crops, and included such innovators as Jethro Tull (1674-1741) and Charles ("Turnip") Townshend (1674-1738). Tull was a great experimenter, and popularized the idea of constantly striving to improve crops. Townshend not only encouraged people to consume turnips as a new food, he also worked with crop rotation and fertilizer, encouraging larger herds of livestock so that more plentiful manure would then fertilize larger areas of land. Robert Blakewell (1725-1795) improved the quality of livestock, so that the population gained better meat and more milk. There was a spillover effect as the industrial revolution brought forth more and better technology. Hundreds of new inventions appeared to help the farmer, including better plows and reapers. New crops became widely used, first the turnip, but much more popular, the potato. Then industrial innovation provided for rapid transport of foodstuffs all over the world, the railroad inland, and better faster ships over the seas, culminating in the steamboat of Robert Fulton (which took years of development before it was feasible for transatlantic voyages).

In the second half of the century the transportation of wheat and other foodstuffs became an international business: American and Canadian exporting of wheat grew by six times to 150,000 bushels a year by 1880. A lively trade developed in flour, in dairy products within the British empire, in bacon from Denmark. Canning led to many new possibilities: tinned beef from Argentina was shipped all over the world. New products became important, including beet sugar, developed in Germany. Trains had already permitted the rapid shipment of perishables such as oranges and applies; but by World War I the innovation of refrigerator cars opened up vast new possibilities, for lettuce, fresh meat and milk could then be shipped long distances. Everyone benefited from the agricultural revolution: the diet of the average family no longer depended on dried and salted foods in winter, it was no longer so dull and tedious. Even out of season, more and more varieties of food became available to the masses.

Part III

Effects of the Industrial Revolution

The Industrial Revolution brought cheaper clothes, more plentiful food, better housing and longer life, but the good that it brought was always accompanied by bad effects too. At no time were the evil consequences more apparent than in the first generation.

The first immediate result was the springing up of cities overnight to accomodate the factories and their workers, such as Manchester and Liverpool. The factories themselves were poorly lit, poorly heated, and badly ventilated, with workers straining over their tasks for 12-14 hours at a stretch. Primitive machines and inadequate experience in running them accounted for frequent accidents. Years later in The Jungle, Upton Sinclair described the horrors of the meatpacking industry in Chicago, where an occasional rat fell into a vat of meat, or a worker's arm was accidentally lopped off, all of it ground up with the nether regions of pigs to make sausage. In the textile industry accidents abounded as well, so that with the slip of a foot one might find oneself spun into thread or woven into a carpet. The new industrial cities were polluted and foul-smelling, with appalling slums, inadequate drainage, and no running water. Large families struggled to make a home in one or two rooms. The streets were seas of mud and animal offal, with pigs cruising by like mine sweepers. The unpleasant contents of chamber pots were routinely thrown out the windows. Children with dripping noses and ragged clothes gathered to play in the streets, filthy and barefooted in the muck. Typhoid fever, diptheria and tuberculosis were endemic in these city slums, for the open drains and running sewers bred every kind of disease and contagion, and the undernourished tubucular population had no resistence. Life expectancy for a slum boy of Manchester in 1840 was thought to be half that of a country boy. The children got no education, and were often put to work by their parents in the factories, sometimes for nineteen hours a day until they fell asleep at the machinery. Pictures survive of children from England, France, Germany and the United States, showing tousled, hollow-eyed waifs operating machinery with bare feet, or staring vacantly at the camera in coal mines, their faces covered with soot. In the slums of New York City, hundreds of children slept in the streets, curled up in exhausted and wary packs, or on rooftops. Disease carried these children off like flies, and swept through entire families.

The bad effects of industrialization never ceased altogether. On the contrary, the difficulties of dealing with industrial waste which were present at the beginning, seemed to grow more serious with the passage of time: by the late 20th century such waste products as dioxin often became a serious health hazard menacing the population for miles around. Certainly, human experience changed completely with industrialization. Cities grew up, and eventually the vast majority of people became urbanized. This provided numerous advantages in the way of amusement and convenience, but it also meant the end of a calmer, more peaceful, more serene way of life. The bustle of city life created new pressures, spawned ugliness, stirred up tension, and arguably, hardened people to one another's plight.

Of all the good changes effected by the Industrial Revolution the most striking was to the health and well being of the human race. The first generation or two suffered under appalling conditions, but even in the 1820's and 30s benefits were becoming widespread. Sanitation in cities underwent a great change for the better with the development of proper sewers, and the invention of the flush toilet or water closet. New and better crops, such as the potato, improved the diet, and with more plentiful food, more people survived. A peasant could raise enough potatoes on one acre of ground to feed his family for a year. With better nutrition the people were more resistant to disease and lived longer.

Beginning in the 18th century, the population of every country of Europe began to grow. Estimates vary, but the population of Europe as a whole was about 100 to 120 million people in 1700, but 190 million in 1800, and 260 million in 1850. England and Wales grew from 6 million in 1750 to over 10 million in 1800; France reached 26 million in 1789, and Russia numbered 29 million. Cities grew at a striking pace, so that London went from 700,000 in 1700 to one million inhabitants in 1800; Paris reached 500,000; St. Petersburg, a new city in 1703, had 250,000 people by 1800. The increased population came just in time to provide a workforce for the industrial revolution; cheap labor is one of the most crucial components of industrialization.

Presumably the greater quantity of foodstuffs available was the main reason for the dramatic increase in population. But improvements in medicine played a significant role as well. Childbirth, for example, had been a principle cause of death for both mother and baby in all of human history. In the 19th century great strides were taken in overcoming such deaths, including the conquest of puerperal fever, a septic poisoning, which had been the most dangerous single malady. Fortunately, with the new improvements in communications, news of medical progress became available more quickly than before. Louis Pasteur discovered a vaccine for innoculating against rabies, hitherto fatal; and even more important, developed the method of sterilizing milk known afterwards as pasturization, which safeguarded millions of people against disease. Robert Koch, a German microbiologist, discovered the bacilli causing tuberculosis and cholera; Walter Reed, an American, found that yellow fever was transmitted by a virus carried by the anopheles mosquito. Joseph Lister, an Englishman, demonstrated the necessity of sterilizing wounds, thus saving millions of lives in that way. Other medical breakthroughs were the development of laughing gas and ether, which were used in dentistry, childbirth and in surgery.

Part IV

Effects of Industrial Revolution: Intellectual Response

That the Industrial Revolution was changing the texture of English life was no longer in doubt by 1820. Everywhere the effects of industrialization could be seen--in the new cities of Manchester and Liverpool, in the new slums, the new poor, the new factories, the new wealth. Likewise, there was no dearth of intellectual curiosity about the new phenomenon. On the contrary, in the best Enlightenment tradition, 19th century intellectuals were convinced that their society, economy and politics could be scrutinized and analyzed for the purpose of determining the basic underlying laws. Auguste Comte founded the science of sociology at this time. Even more to the point, other observers added to the new science of economics, and still others to political theory. How they responded to the dramatic new changes was also remarkably typical of the Enlightenment, at least in the period immediately after 1815. Leibnitz and Newton in the 17th century had envisioned the world as a clock whose workings had been set in motion by God. The gears and mechanism could be studied, but the device as a whole could not be substantially altered. Adam Smith in the 18th century had followed this philosophy when he expounded laissez-faire economics; governments should not try to interfere in the economic life of their subjects. The free functioning of the market place was the key to prosperity. This had been a direct challenge to the old order of mercantilism, the system whereby governments had systematically attempted to control colonies, markets and trade in order to build up a large supply of bullion in the treasury. Mercantilism was in disfavor, and by 1820 practically everyone interested in economics advocated free trade. If governments were advised to leave merchants freedom in trade, by the same token, governments were also thought inadequate to interfere in the mechanism of industrialization. This hands-off policy had implications which were not particularly cheerful for anyone looking around him at the initial deleterious effects of the industrial revolution.

The first generation of economic observers are known as the classical economists, experts on the lugubrious subject then called the "dismal science". The funereal tone pervading economic writings in those days was due to the inordinate pessimism of the two leading scholars on the subject--David Ricardo (1772-1823) and Thomas Malthus (1766-1834), both of whom agreed that the situation in England was extremely bad, and that nothing could be done to improve it. Thomas Malthus caused widespread dismay when he published his Essay on Population in 1798, a grim statement that the human race was doomed, as the human population is increasing at a geometric ratio, while food production is increasing only at an arithmetic ratio. The misery of the worker was inevitable, he wrote; if one increased his wages and standard of living he would only have more children. Malthus had no idea that there were at least two possibilities in the future to ameliorate the problem--the first being vastly increased food production with the aid of new technology and vigorous new hybrid plants; the second being birth control. At that point in time, and even a hundred years later, birth control was an evil subject never to be mentioned in polite company. Even after 1900 Margaret Sanger was imprisoned on numerous occasions as she tried to convert the American people to its uses in order to avoid the extreme poverty she had seen in New York slums. Changes in attitudes helped, including the sexual revolution begun by Sigmund Freud; so that finally, Malthus' analysis had a plausible solution. However, as of 1983, the population in many countries of the world continues to rise unchecked, with the concommitant miseries documented by the dismal scientists in 1798.

A few years later, in 1817, David Ricardo published the Principles of Political Economy, which drew on Malthus and propounded the Iron Law of Wages. This was a rather fatalistic, cyclical view of economics, whereby increased wages produced more children; more children produced more workers to compete for jobs, so that wages would be lowered; lowered wages meant fewer children; fewer children meant fewer workers in the next generation, who in turn would get high wages again. This pessimistic work justified anyone opposed to labor unions and anyone opposed to higher wages. In France, the government of Louis Phillippe, under his minister Guizot, welcomed this attitude, and essentially encouraged the middle classes to enrich themselves while ignoring the plight of the poor. In England the attitude helped produce the new Poor Law of 1834, which set up workhouses for the poor, which were expressly designed to be as wretched, humiliating and abasing as possible, since poverty was supposedly due to laziness. England also repealed the Corn Laws in 1846, in response to classical economics. The corn laws had created tariffs protecting Bristish grain some years before. But with the potato famine, there was an outcry, promoted by the Anti-Corn Law League, to re-establish free trade in order for the cheaper grain from the continent to come in and lower the price of bread.

The classical economists and their adherents were not the only surveyers of the Bristish scene at this time. A second group whose impact was more humanitarian, was known as the Utilitarians. These were men who advocated the principle of utility, the greatest good for the greatest number, as the basis for government policy. This constituted a radical departure from traditional views of men like Guizot. The utilitarians actually wrote much of the reform legislation passed in England after 1830, the new Poor Law of 1834, the Factory Act of 1833, and the Sanitation Act of 1848. The Poor Law was actually a cruel measure in many ways, for it humiliated the poor, at the same time that it made it extremely difficult for the poor to receive aid; but it did establish that the government was responsible for the care of indigents (instead of the Church, or private charity). The Factory Act of 1833 was one in a series begun in 1819, which forbade child labor below the age of nine, and restricted it to children from ten to eighteen. As with other early legislation against the evils of industrialization, the factory acts provided for very little inspection; but they did constitute a step in the direction of control of abuses and protection of the worker which culminated at last in the National Insurance Act of 1911.

Jeremy Bentham (1748-1832) was the most famous utilitarian, and in point of fact, coined the word. He rejected Enlightenment concern for ethical principals with nature's laws, and dismissed "natural rights" as "nonsense upon stilts"[1]. He believed governments should behave as "passive policemen", while private industry had a free hand. But whenever the pains of the many exceeded the pleasures of the few, the state should interfere on behalf of the general welfare. The most extraordinary man of the day who is sometimes classified as a utilitarian, was John Stuart Mill (1806-1873). Mill went much farther than Bentham. His most famous books were On Liberty and The Subjection of Women, which called for freedom of thought, protection of the individual against the state, and women's rights. He pleaded for education of the masses, and in a sensible realistic way, envisaged improving the standard of living of English workers.

Socialism

The genteel pessimism of Malthus and Ricardo, and the moderate reforms of utilitarians were equally distasteful to certain groups of people in the 19th century Europe, who not only wanted remedies for the evils of industrialization, but radical remedies. Such were the socialists, a small but striking group of free-thinkers who not only wanted to change the distribution of wealth (which they could see was blatantly unequal), but also the production of goods. Socialism is a heady concept which is often misunderstood, and which even a century later was capable of inspiring the fiercest of passions. Underlying all true socialism is the common idea that the community of people (or state) should own the means of production. Ultimately in a socialist state private property would be abolished, and the state would own all railroads, factories and industry and all the land as well. Today, many countries are partly socialistic, such as Britain and Scandinavia, where the nation owns coal mines, railroads, medical services and the like, but private property still exists. The real difference between different schools of socialism is not to be found in the number of industries which are government owned versus the number privately owned, but in the manner in which any of the industrial concerns are to be taken over by the government. The utopian socialists believed this could be accomplished peacefully; the radical socialists asserted that only through violence could it take place.

The uptopian socialists derived their name from Sir Thomas More's Utopia, although Plato had already described what he thought was a perfect society in his Republic, two thousand years before that. In the early 19th century the idea of designing an ideal state was a logical culmination of certain concepts entertained in the Enlightment. If man could discern nature's laws, he could also improve upon them, went one train of thought. Others disagreed (the classical economists, for one); but the impulse behind utopian socialism came from the optimistic conviction that this could be the best of all possible worlds if only certain precepts were followed. It is likely that another factor which accounts for their enthusiasm was that at that moment in time there still existed the distinct opportunity to experiment with new ideas: the American frontier was only half settled; the vast reaches of plain and forest in the United States stretched all the way to the Pacific Ocean, with thousands of miles of land available for experimental communities.

---

[1]Quoted by Brinton, Chrisopher and Wolff, op. cit., p. 574

Many of the utopian socialists were quaint and chimerical in their fanciful blueprints for the perfect state--including in some ways Henri, Count of Saint-Simon (1760-1825), Charles Fourier (1772-1837), and Robert Owen (1772-1858) the three most famous. St. Simon wanted Europe to be a federation of states, with all men acting as brothers. He advocated vague but cheering programs of "organization," "harmony" and "industry" in the case of the social welfare of the poor. He was important because he focused on the needs of all of society rather than the wishes of a select few. Fourier drew up a blueprint for a society organized into units called phalanxes, each self-sufficient, each completely organized from top to bottom, with profits going generously to workers (though stopping short of complete equality). Fourier's most endearing contribution was his "butterfly principle", the imaginative concept that workers suffered from the drudgery of hours of working at the same task, and should therefore routinely (every two hours or so) switch jobs. He was on the track of something which the 20th century psychologists would confirm. But his immediate plans never bore fruit, in part because of the scandalous implications of some of his other proposals, such as complete sexual freedom in the phalanges--hardly a formula which would appeal to strait-laced Victorians. Yet the sexual aspect tended to be a common denominator of early socialists; Robert Owen was just as free-wheeling as Fourier on that subject. Owen was a rich textile industrialist with experimental and very successful factories in New Lanarck, Scotland. He was a pioneer in opposing child labor, setting up special schools in his factory towns, beautifying the environment, and basically, proving that one could earn even more money if one were kind to the workers. However, Owen decided to go farther than that, and set up a community in New Harmony, Indiana, with the aid of his son, Robert Dale Owen. The community caused scandal right and left, partly because of the dubious characters it attracted (including the nortorious Amelia Bloomer in her celebrated trouser--the first woman to insist on wearing pants); partly because of Owen's attacks on religion; but mostly because of his enthusiam for free love.

New Harmony lasted only from 1825 until 1828. It had not been harmonious. But other communes were created in the United States on the same general socialistic principles. Some, like Brooke Farm, the intellectual haven of novelist Nathanial Hawthorne, and Bronson Alcott, the father of Louisa May, failed early on; but Oneida, in upstate New York, was extraordinarily successful under the leadership of John Humphrey Noyes. Founded in 1848, Oneida was an experiment in socialism which lasted until 1881: its members made silverware, shared each others' sexual favors, and raised their children communally. The enthusiastic Noyes fathered many of the children himself; perhaps even as many as he thought he had.

The socialist with the most interesting experiment in Europe was the French revolutionary, Louis Blanc (1811-1882). After the Revolution of 1848 France grew increasingly radical, the provisional government acknowledged the demands of the unemployed workers by authorizing Louis Blanc to create socialistic workshops, which he hoped would eventually replace private property. After only a few weeks, Louis Blanc's political fortunes grew murky: after the June Days his workshops were disbanded, and the reactionary new government was unpleasant to him. They eventually threw him into a dungeon at Mont St. Michel.

More than thirty years of socialist enthusiam found European radicals discouraged with the mild mannered methods of the utopians. Voluntary and peaceful ways of drawing people into communities became popular again over a hundred years later, in the 1960's. But in the short run, serious advocates of socialism came to the conclusion that the only way to establish socialism in a country was through violence.

Marx and Engels

To the modern observer looking back, the utopian socialists look like errant schoolboys compared to the hard and brutal ideology of Karl Marx. Where they had talked of butterfly principles and free love, Karl Marx wrote a systematic denunciation of capitalism and a rather chilling description of its destruction at the hands of a ruthless proletariat. Karl Marx was born in Germany in 1818, of a middle class Jewish family, and attended the University of Berlin, where he was influenced by the great German philosopher, Hegel. Hegel saw history as a series of conflicts, a dialectic, where different civilizations clashed and the result was a new civilization which was a synthesis of the two which had clashed. History was deterministic, and moved forward inexorably, with each new synthesis in turn being challenged, clashing, and giving way to a new order. Marx adapted this theory in a way called dialectical materialism. Hegel was an idealist, and believed that the underlying conflicts inherent in each civilization were based on ideas; Marx was a materialist, and felt that hard economic realities are the basis of the conflicts in the world.

Karl Marx
(The Granger Collection)

Marx believed that capitalism was only a stage in the historical dialectical process, a stage characterized by brutal rivalry between the oppressors, the middle class, and the oppressed, or the workers, whom Marx called the proletariat. The conflict between the two was inevitable, and would finally erupt in a vast economic revolution. The workers would destroy all property. All social class differences would disappear. There would be a preliminary stage which he envisaged as the "dictatorship of the proletariat", but this would be followed by a classless society, where "the state would wither away". Curiously, both Hegel and Marx seemed to believe that their dialectical process would cease once their ideal states were created.

Marx fled from Germany and eventually settled in England, where he lived with his wife and six children in abject poverty. He was greatly aided in his life's work by a man of an altogether different sort, the son of a rich industrialist, who looked more at home on the race track or the boulevards than in the British museum--Freidrich Engels (1820-1895). Though rich, Engels also hated the evils of capitalism, and had already published an angry analysis of the sufferings of the workers in Manchester. Engels helped support Marx in the years that followed, and collaborated with him on his work. The two worked together on The Communist Manifesto, which they published in 1848; and also on Das Kapital, a three-volume analysis of capitalism.

Marx was one of the four greatest seminal thinkers of the past hundred and fifty years (the others being Darwin, Freud and Einstein); he inspired an international movement which bears his name and which changed the course of history for millions of people. Yet ironically, he was wrong in many respects. He predicted that the revolution was inevitable; that it would begin in England, the most wretched example of industrial excesses, but that it would spread immediately around the world; that it would begin with a spontaneous uprising of the proletariat; that it would culminate in a classless society. In reality, none of these things happened. The revolution did not occur in industrial England, where the standard of living was slowly improving (contrary to Marxian analysis of capitalist decay, but in backward agricultural Russia. It did not spread throughout the world, and did not become international; on the contrary, in 1983 one of the striking characteristics of the communist states of Russia and China is their nationalism. The revolution did not begin with the proletariat in any case, but with a small core of hardened intellectual revolutionaries, led by Lenin. The revolution did not produce a classless society, but rather, created new classes and new elites. Furthermore, the revolution did not create an ideal state where all shared power equally, but a dictatorship in every case.

QUESTIONS FOR REFLECTION

1. What was the Protestant Ethic and what did it have to do with the Industrial Revolution? In the 20th century the people of Japan seem to have many of the characteristics typical of early Protestants; how can this be when they are not Protestants or even Christian?

2. List some of the changes produced by the Industrial Revolution: and imagine your own life without them. Have the material benefits outweighed the

pollution and other problems? Would you say mankind is substantially better off today? If so, why do you suppose some countries, like Iran, have religious and other groups who resist industrialization? Is it possible to have an industrial revolution without making a population materialistic?

3. Where did the Industrial Revolution begin? In which countries did it come later? How do you suppose it affected social classes? How did it change political realities? Did it change who held the power in a given society? Did it affect the political powers of countries, or the international balances of power?

4. What were some of the political theories which resulted from the Industrial Revolution? What is the real difference between the socialism of a man like Owen, and the communism of Karl Marx? How do some of the 20th century plans for utopias, such as Walden II of B. F. Skinner, compare with the earliers ones?

SUGGESTED BIBLIOGRAPHY

T. S. Ashton, An Economic History of England: The Eighteenth Century (1955)
T. S. Ashton, The Industrial Revolution, 1760-1830 (1948)
I. Berlin, Karl Marx: His Life and Environment (1963)
W. D. Borrie, The Growth and Control of World Population (1970)
A. Briggs, The Age of Improvement, 1783-1867 (1959)
J. H. Clapham, Economic Development of France and Germany, 1815-1914 (1936)
S. B. Clough, France: A History of Natural Economics (1939)
G. D. H. Cole, The Meaning of Marxism (1948)
G. D. H. Cole, Socialist Thought: The Forerunners, 1789-1850 (1962)
P. Deane, The First Industrial Revolution (1965)
H. J. Habbakuk and M. M. Postan, eds., The Industrial Revolutions and After
   (1965)
E. Halévy, The Growth of Philosophic Radicalism (1955)
J. L. Hammond and B. Hammond, The Town Labourer, 1760-1832 (1917)
W. O. Henderson, The Industrial Revolution on the Continent (1961)
W. O. Henderson, The Rise of German Industrial Power, 1834-1914 (1976)
W. O. Henderson, The Zollverein (1939)
E. E. Lampard, Industrial Revolution: Interpretations and Perspectives (1957)
D. Landes, The Unbound Prometheus: Technological Change and Industrial
   Development in Western Europe from 1750 to the Present (1969)
T. R. Malthus, An Essay on Population
P. Mantoux, The Industrial Revolution in the Eighteenth Century (1929)
F. Manuel, The Prophets of Paris (1962)
K. Marx and F. Engles, The Communist Manifesto (1848)
Karl Marx and Frederick Engles; Selected Works, 2 vols. (1951)
J. S. Mill, Autobiography
J. S. Mill, On Liberty
D. Ricardo, Principles of Political Economy and Taxation
E. Roll, A History of Economic Thought (1942)
W. M. Thomas, The Early Factory Legislation (1948)
E. P. Thompson, The Making of the English Working Class (1963)
A. P. Usher, A History of Mechanical Inventions (1929)

S. Webb and B. Webb, English Local Government: English Poor Law History, 3
    vols. (1927-29)
S. Webb and B. Webb, History of Trade Unionism (1920)
E. Wilson, To the Finland Station (1953)
E. L. Woodward, The Age of Reform, 1815-1870 (1938)

CHAPTER 4 - WAR, EMPIRE AND THE TRIUMPH OF NATIONALISM

1850 - 1870

Part I

The Crimean War

The revolutions of 1848 were mostly failures: Germany and Italy were still not united; and scarcely any countries had become more liberal. Even in France, the one instance where the revolution seemed successful, reaction had set in and within a short space of time the newly elected French President was transformed into Napoleon III, another emperor. To add to the causes for disillusion, cooperation between the big powers broke down and the Crimean War broke out in 1854 between France, England, the Ottoman Empire, and Russia.

The vast steppes of Russia reached all the way to the Pacific Ocean in the East, to central Europe in the West, and stretched from the Arctic Circle in the north to the Black Sea; but with all their great size and potential wealth, the Russians had certain problems which never seemed to go away. The principle one of these was that in the north their Baltic ports were icebound in winter, and in the south what shipping they had in the Black Sea was hindered by Turkish control of Constantinople on the Bosporus Straits, the only passage into the Mediterranean. A constant Russian theme in foreign policy, as one century folded into the next, was the never ending rivalry with the Ottoman Empire on this issue. By the mid 19th century when that decrepit empire was tottering into ruin, the Russians were poised to strike. Two other constants balanced out the game, however; the French had opposed the Russians and befriended the Turks for many years; and the English, while not necessarily friend or foe, stood committed to one overriding principle--defend the balance of power.

The rivalry over the Balkans had been papered over at the Congress of Vienna because of the need for the great powers to keep the peace. Metternich had presided over this attempt until 1848; but he was now ousted from power and there was no statesmen on the scene astute enough to use successful diplomacy on the quarrelsome Turks and Russians. The two began fighting in 1853 in the Crimea ostensibly over religion, but really over Russian hunger for two Turkish provinces, Moldavia and Wallachia. England and France came to Turkey's aid, and Russia was defeated. By the Treaty of Paris of 1856 Russia had to recognize the neutrality of the Black Sea, renounce claims over Christians in the Ottoman Empire, and surrender some territory on the Danube. They had already been forced out of Moldavia and Wallachia. This bloody little war, in which the Charge of Light Brigade and other disasters produced terrible casualties, was the first in a series of Balkan conflicts which led to World War I. The only good part about it was the magnificent nursing done by Florence Nightingale. In the meantime, with the concert of Europe at an end, each power felt free to embark on whatever adventures came to mind. And England, acting alone for the most part, was unable to prevent the two immediate challenges to the balance of power which then occurred; the unification of Italy and Germany. At the end of the next twenty years, where before there had been weak and quarrelsome confederations of states in both those areas, there now appeared two united new nations, each determinedly nationalistic, each eager for empire, and one of them extraordinarily powerful.

Part II

The Unification of Italy

The romantic Italian nationalists who had followed the carbonari and Mazzini had failed to create any permanent liberal governments or to unite the country. They had, however, seen the temporary successes of the king of Piedmont against Austria in 1848. This small northern state now assumed the leadership of the cause, under Count Camillo Cavour (1810-1861), the moderate prime minister under the new Piedmont King, Victor Emmanuel II. Cavour in power represented a new breed of ambitious, rather liberal and progressive leader, who wanted no republic, but did want a strong, united Italy, economically viable, and endowed with a limited constitution. He spent considerable time plotting with Napoleon III, offering France Nice and Savoy in exchange for French help in driving Austria out of Italy, an arrangement formalized at Plombiéres, in 1858. In the modest little war which ensued, Austria was indeed driven out with French help; but Napoleon III was alarmed at the new power of Piedmont and signed a separate treaty with Austria at Villa Franca. His alarm came too late, for Piedmont was well on her way: she received Lombardy from Austria; and also the states of Parma, Moderna, Tuscany and Romagna, which had all revolted and now asked to be annexed.

Southern Italy remained outside the Piedmontese kingdom, but this was soon remedied by a dramatic gesture: an adventurer named Garibaldi landed on Sicily with a colorful ragtag army known as the Redshirts, and proceeded to conquer the Kingdom of Naples, one of the most desperately corrupt regimes in the peninsula. As Garibaldi and his successful band marched in disorderly fashion toward the north, Cavour grew alarmed at the possibility that Garibaldi would overrun the papal States and Rome which would surely alarm Louis Napoleon of France. To avert such an eventuality, he sent a Piedmontese Army to occupy the papal states and to head off Garibaldi in Southern Italy near Naples. Garibaldi acceded to this superior force, and southern Italy joined the north in 1860. In March of 1861 Victor Emmanuel II became king of Italy under a conservative constitution. Unfortunately the canny Cavour died soon after, and left no one on hand shrewd enough to deal with Italy's two overriding problems after unification--the great disparity in wealth and industrialization between north and south; and the hostility of the Vatican. The latter finally ended when the pope joined the rest of the country in 1870. From that moment until the advent of Mussolini, Italy was an uncertain, slightly corrupt, and unstable constitutional monarchy.

Part III

The Unification of Germany

It took a clever prime minister to unite Italy, and a clever prime minister to unite Germany. In both cases, the efforts of two generations of

THE UNIFICATION OF ITALY

THE KINGDOM OF SARDINIA AT THE TIME OF THE CONGRESS OF VIENNA, 1815

TERRITORIES ACQUIRED, 1859-1860

TERRITORIES ACQUIRED, 1860-1870

FRANCE

SWITZERLAND

AUSTRIA

SAVOY
(TO FRANCE IN 1860)

LOMBARDY

VENETIA

KINGDOM OF SARDINIA

MILAN

VENICE

PARMA

MODENA

BOLOGNA

GENOA

LUCCA

FLORENCE

PAPAL STATES

ADRIATIC SEA

TUSCANY

UMBRIA

CORSICA
(TO FRANCE)

ROME

KINGDOM OF THE TWO SICILIES

KINGDOM OF SARDINIA

TYRRHENIAN

SEA

NAPLES

MEDITERRANEAN

PALERMO

MESSINA

SICILY

SEA

revolutionaries had failed to produce tangible results. The king of Prussia had temporarily accepted German unification under Prussian leadership in 1848; but afterwards he changed his mind again, and for ten years there was a lull. During that time, thousands of Germans left the country for America, many of them taking their idealism with them. The advent of a new king of Prussia, William I, and a forceful dipmomatist as his minister, Otto Von Bismarck (1815-1898), changed the picture.

Otto von Bismarck was an aristocratic Prussian Junker of extremely conservative views. Tall, with a spine ramrod straight and bulging eyes like ripe gooseberries, Bismark was an anomaly. He called for a policy of "blood and iron", yet he was often moved to tears at public occasions. Bismark wanted a united Germany under Prussian leadership with a strong industrial base; and although he distrusted parliamentary government he was willing to allow at least a moderate constitution. When he came to power in 1862 he clashed with the liberal Prussian parliament when they refused to increase taxes at his request for the army. Then and in the years that followed he outwitted the parliament at every turn, dissolving them, calling for new elections, dissolving them again. He had already decided to unify Germany in his own way, without Austria, and opposed Austrian efforts at reform, as well as Austria's efforts to enter the Zollverein, the German customs union. One cannot be quite certain to what extent the central steps in German unification were planned in advance by Bismarck, or to what extent he merely seized opportunities which presented themselves. Whatever version is correct, he fought three wars--the first against Denmark, the second against Austria, and the third against France, and when he had quite finished Germany was united.

The war against Denmark was ostensibly fought over the Schleswig-Holstein question, two provinces who neither belonged wholly to Denmark nor wholly to Germany. Bismarck seized his opportunity when Denmark tried to annex Schleswig in 1863. He secured Austria as an ally, and after defeating the Danes, Prussia and Austria shared the administration of the two provinces. Bismarck then quarreled with Austria in 1865 in order to justify a second war. Prussia secured the neutrality of France, and defeated the Austrians in seven weeks. By the end of the second war, northern Germany was united into a rather large and potentially powerful new state, but the south, including Bavaria and the Palatinate, was still outside. In 1870 he fought the third war, against France. This accomplished his objective and unified all of Germany; but the cost was very high. Some authorities were persuaded that Bismark had serious doubts about the wisdom of tangling with France. Certainly the conduct of that war was different. For the third time the Germans defeated the enemy in six weeks, but instead of securing an immediate and satisfactory peace, they occupied France for many months, produced an overthrow of the government and a Paris revolution, and demanded peace terms so humiliating that the French never forgave them. The Franco-Prussian War of 1870 was one of the leading causes of World War I.

The war with France began because of the problems of yet another country, Spain. The Spanish queen Isabel II had been overthrown in 1868 because of rather dubious behavior in the boudoir; and since the paternity of the royal children was in doubt, the Spanish prime minister Prim (aptly named) set out to find a new king of Spain. Candidates threw themselves in his path all over Europe, from Italy to the Baltic Sea, but the young man he settled on was none

THE UNIFICATION OF GERMANY 1866-71

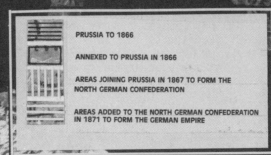

	PRUSSIA TO 1866
	ANNEXED TO PRUSSIA IN 1866
	AREAS JOINING PRUSSIA IN 1867 TO FORM THE NORTH GERMAN CONFEDERATION
	AREAS ADDED TO THE NORTH GERMAN CONFEDERATION IN 1871 TO FORM THE GERMAN EMPIRE

other than the crown prince of Prussia. The most serious disadvantage of this choice was that Napoleon III of France felt that his country would be surrounded on all sides by Germans, and he remembered the aggravation France had suffered the last time such a situation had transpired, in the time of the Holy Roman Emperor Charles V. He demanded that the Prussian prince withdraw his candidacy and when this was done, he further demanded suitable apologies to his person from the Prussian king. King William was at that point bathing in hot sulphuric mud at the watering spa called Ems (a favorite occupation of rotund European monarchs). He sent a dispatch to Bismarck clothed in suitable terms, but Bismarck edited the document, which was later published in newspapers all over Europe as the "Ems Telegram". In Bismarck's shorter version Napoleon found vague and menacing insults, and thus declared war.

Within six weeks the French were defeated and Napoleon himself was captured at the Battle of Sedan. In the ensuing clamor for a new government, the city of Paris fell into the hands of a group of revolutionaries who set up a leftist Commune. The more moderate politicians including Gambetta, escaped the city in a hot air balloon, landing with dignity intact in a nearby field. Thus France had to defuse an internal threat to the peace and stability of the country at the same time that they had to settle with a foreign army and persuade them to leave. They managed to accomplish both of these goals, but not without difficulty. France became officially known as the Third Republic, and the communards were finally routed, although more than 70,000 people were killed. For their part, the Germans seized two French provinces, Alsace and Lorraine, and demanded an indemnity of five billion francs. Their army was to occupy France until the money was paid, which they expected would take quite some time. The French paid the indemnity much more quickly than Germany expected, and thus saw the last of German troops; but the scars from this experience did not heal in the next fifty years. In his short story, Boule de suif the French writer Maupassant sums up all the antipathy and hatred the average French citizen felt for the invading army. From then until World War I a common toast in France was, "Revanche!"--or revenge for the harm that had been done to them.

Part IV

The United States

At the same time that the balance of power of Europe was irrefutably changed by the creation of two ambitious new states, the balance of power of the entire western world was altered by the emergence of the United States into a position of great importance. In 1800 England's former colony was a small and determinedly isolationist outpost across the Atlantic. They had a tiny navy, a small army, and a blueprint for government which hadn't even been completely unfolded. Most of the early presidents believed that power was a dangerous thing and practiced rigorous self-control in denying all opportunities to wield it. Thomas Jefferson, president from 1800-1808, was an aristocrat by background and temperament, but a democrat in philosophy; he opposed special privileges for the wealthy, and championed the rights of the little man, especially the small farmer. Ironically, Jefferson's greatest deed as president was in defiance of his own beliefs; for Napoleon offered him the chance to purchase the magnificent territory of Louisiana for an absurdly small sum. He believed that such an act was unconstitutional for the president, since the Constitution said nothing about it; but he bought Louisiana just the same, more than doubling the size of American territory.

In 1812 another war began with Great Britain. In Europe Napoleon had been conquering a vast empire. The English had been fighting him for a generation, and took to impressing, or kidnapping, American sailors, and otherwise angering Americans, who were always sympathetic to the French. The English burned the White House to the ground, but the Americans trounced them in the satisfying Battle of New Orleans, fought after the war had already ended. After that, the United States was even more determined to steer clear of European entanglements, and in 1823 issued the Monroe Doctrine, a foreign policy statement warning other countries to keep clear of the Americas.

For twenty-five years the young American nation focused inward, steadily expanding their control of the frontier lands, bringing one new state after another into the union. Arts and letters began to flourish, immigrants poured in from Europe, new cities such as Cincinnati and Chicago burst out of the prairies, and nationalism grew at a fever pitch. The popular president Andrew Jackson (the hero of the Battle of New Orleans) presided over the broadening of the franchise in 1828 so that the small farmers and ordinary citizens felt the government belonged to them. They demonstrated this when they swarmed over the capital on Jackson's inauguration day, devouring a gigantic cheese, swilling lemonade, and threatening the president with suffocation in their enthusiastic embrace. "Old Hickory", as he was called, was a simple rough-hewn man, with popular prejudices against the Indians ("the only good Indian is a dead Indian"), who did not necessarily represent all that was good and just in the American people. However he did represent one of the two mainstreams of American political history--the popular man of the people; the other mainstream, the constantly recurring president who stood for the rule of the elite (and eventually, big business) alternated with men such as Jackson.

The fervor for expansion called "Manifest Destiny" led the United States into a war with Mexico in 1846 and 1847, initially over the free republic of Texas. Texas was originally part of Mexico, but had filled up with Americans and their slaves, and defied Mexico by declaring independence in 1836 after the tragic Battle of the Alamo. The war ended with the Treaty of Guadalupe Hidalgo in 1848, giving the Americans vast stretches of territory not only in Texas, but in California and Utah. California was a particular treasure, for gold had been discovered there, and a frantic gold rush ensued, drawing thousands of fortune seekers out west by covered wagon over the Oregon Trail. One of the few congressmen who defied President Polk and challenged the claim that Mexico had wickedly started the war was a lanky backwoodsman named Abraham Lincoln. The people of Illinois were irate with Lincoln, and after only two years in congress gave him to understand that his career was over. But ten years later he emerged from his country law practice again to challenge a national inequity, slavery, and so was elected president of the United States just at the moment that a dreadful Civil War was about to ravage the land.

From the Missouri Compromise of 1820 until the Kansas-Nebraska Debates of 1853, slavery had been determinedly ignored as a blight on the land by a

THE SLAVERY ISSUE 1861

MAINE
VT.
N.H.
MASS.
R.I.
CONN.
NEW YORK
NEW JERSEY
PENN.
DELAWARE
MARYLAND
W. VA.
VIRGINIA
OHIO
INDIANA
KENTUCKY
N. CAROLINA
S. CAROLINA
GEORGIA
FLORIDA
MICHIGAN
WISCONSIN
ILLINOIS
TENNESSEE
ALABAMA
MISS.
MINNESOTA
IOWA
MISSOURI
ARKANSAS
LOUISIANA
NEBRASKA TERRITORY
KANSAS TERRITORY
INDIAN TERRITORY
TEXAS
WASHINGTON TERRITORY
UTAH TERRITORY
NEW MEXICO TERRITORY
OREGON
CALIF.

ATLANTIC OCEAN
GULF OF MEXICO
PACIFIC OCEAN

SLAVE
FREE
BOTH SLAVE AND FREE
CONFEDERATE STATES
POPULAR SOVEREIGNTY

series of government compromises which kept the peace. The southerners were satisfied that each time a new state wanted to enter the union all those north of line 36'30" might be free, but all those south of it were to be slave. This kept the national government evenly balanced between the southern and northern states, although it did little to cheer up the slaves. And trouble was coming in the person of the ambitious little Chicago entrepreneur, Stephen Douglas. In the 1850's Douglas wanted to build a gaint railroad to the Pacific Northwest, with Chicago as its terminus, and as he needed southern votes in Congress to acquire the federal permissions necessary to this end, he was not above throwing out the one right antislavery forces had won--the right to have free states north of 36'30". To win over the South, Douglas proposed a high-sounding principle of popular sovereignity, ostensibly to permit each territory to make the decision for itself. But the hypocrisy of this supposedly democratic proposal was not lost on Abraham Lincoln, and while the determined settlers of Kansas and Nebraska settled the slavery issue by shooting each other with rifles, Lincoln challenged Douglas to a series of debates in 1858. Lincoln argued that slavery was a blight and an evil and must not be allowed to spread. He frightened the south notwithstanding his moderate words, for he never threatened to abolish slavery where it already existed. When he was elected president in 1860, seven southern states seceded, and in April of 1861, the war began. Four more states joined the Confederacy later, and for four years the rest of the world watched the industrial northern free states battle against the agrarian southern slave states, and eventually wear them down.

Lincoln freed the slaves in January of 1863, and won the war by April of 1865, one week before he was shot dead by a southern sympathiser in Ford's Theatre in Washington, D.C. His death unleashed a stream of northern invective and demand for revenge against the prostrate south. During Reconstruction. The south was treated like a conquered territory, and with the abuse and reprisals which ensued, did not recover economically or morally from the war for one hundred years. The north, on the other hand, emerged strong and powerful, and launched a period of frenetic speculation, industrialization and growth. By 1870 a new breed of millionaires were becoming famous, typified by Rockefeller and Carnegie who started the oil and steel industries. In foreign policy the United States remained isolationist, but with their burgeoning energy and wealth they signified a vast new power to be reckoned with.

QUESTIONS FOR REFLECTION

1. What were some of the most important foreign policy concerns of Russia in the 19th century? What changes in the 20th century have altered the picture? Are their traditional goals and fears completely gone do you suppose?

2. Define nationalism. How many nations can you think of which have more than one racial, religious, or linguistic group of people? Make an effort during the remainder of this course to determine if the countries you are studying have more than one religion, or more than one language. Begin a list of conflicts which are still occurring over these issues.

3. Look up the following countries in a political handbook or encyclopedia, to evaluate their degree of success in resolving religious or linguistic (or other) conflicts: Switzerland, Belgium, Canada, the Soviet Union, India, Lebanon.

4. What were some of the alternative ways to unite (1) Italy and (2) Germany. Which way succeeded and why? What implications did this manner of success have upon the future of those two countries?

5. What were some of the mistakes made in the United States after the Civil War? Both the United States and Russia had similar problems with newly liberated people: compare the two countries and the lot of the ex-slaves and the ex-serfs.

6. What were some of the causes and consequences of the Spanish-American War? What is "dollar diplomacy"? Is that policy uniquely American? Is it a good basis for foreign policy?

SUGGESTED BIBLIOGRAPHY

M. S. Anderson, The Eastern Question (1966)
D. Beales, The Risorgimento and the Unification of Italy (1971)
R. C. Brinkley, Realism and Nationalism, 1852-1871 (1935)
T. S. Hamerow, The Social Foundation of German Unification, 1858-1871 (1969)
A. J. May, The Hapsburg Monarch, 1867-1914 (1951)
W. E. Mosse, The European Powers and the German Question, 1848-1871 (1958)
O. Pflanze, Bismark and the Development of Germany: The Period of
    Unification, 1815-1871 (1963)
P. W. Schroeder, Austria, Great Britain, and The Crimean War: The
    Destruction of the European Concert (1973)
D. Mack Smith, Cavour and Garibaldi, 1860: A Study in Political Conflict
    (1954)
D. Mack Smith, Garibaldi (1956)
D. Mack Smith, Victor Emmanuel, Cavour and the Risorgimento (1971)
A. J. P. Taylor, Bismark: The Man and the Statesman (1955)
G. M. Trevelyan, Garibaldi and the Thousand (1911)
G. M. Trevelyan, Garibaldi and the Making of Italy

CHAPTER 5 - THE BIG POWERS - 1870 - 1914

Part I

Russia

In the course of the 19th century as the United States, England and France continued to respond to the higher and higher demands for representative government, Germany, Russia and Austria-Hungary withstood such demands and with only a few concessions to liberalism, were still rigidly autocratic in 1914.

The largest of the three, Russia, lay sprawled across the map like a sleeping brontosaurus. Its peasants were still bound to medieval traditions, and its government was autocratic and absolute. After the repressive and imperious Nicholas I, Alexander II (1855-81) began to rule with indications he would abolish or reform some of the antequated or repressive institutions of the country. At the same time that the United States came to violence over slavery and began to fight their bloody Civil War, Alexander wanted to free the serfs of Russia, whose families had been enslaved for hundred of years. He corresponded with Abraham Lincoln on the subject, and finally freed the serfs in 1861. Lincoln freed the American slaves in 1863, but although he fought a war over the issue and Alexander did not, the two countries had very similar problems: in both cases the newly emancipated people were economically destitute and within a few years were virtually enslaved all over again by the local community. In the United States this was called share-cropping, with ever increasing indebtedness of the former slaves to the country store. In Russia it was institutionalized in that the land for the newly freed serfs was given to a village mir (council) to administer, and was to be paid for over forty-nine years by the village community. Thus in both countries, economic and social problems lasted for years after the purported liberations, with both population groups undergoing intense suffering.

Alexander II was reform-minded in other ways as well. He endowed the universities with greater academic freedom and provided some local self-government through elected assemblies called zemstvos. He was just signing a bill calling for a national assembly, the Duma, when he was killed--for Lincoln and Alexander were both murdered by assassins. In Alexander's case, he was neither as liberal as his admirers like to believe, nor as villainous as his critics said. The latter were growing in number every day, and included two particular groups in the period after the 1860's. One group who followed socialists like Alexander Herzen were called Narodniki (go-to-the-people), for they went out to the villages and tried to stir up Russian peasants to fight a revolution. The second group were the nihilists, who believed in "nothing", were adamant opponents of the regime, and disliked all social conventions. They began to follow Mikail Bakunin, the anarchist, and in the space of about twenty years supported the asssassination of as many people in government as possible. The international commune of anarchists did in fact kill a number of important people--two American presidents (Arthur and McKinley), the Hapsburg empress Elizabeth, ministers, heads-of-states, and one archduke.

In 1881 Alexander II was mortally wounded by an exploding bomb, and was carried into his palace, where he bled to death in the presence of his son, the future Alexander III, and his grandson, the future Nicholas II. Neither of his heirs ever forgot the lesson, that liberal concession led to terrible trouble. They intended to keep the lid on, and did. Alexander III followed a policy of the strictest repression, striking out against nationalist movements and education, and launching virulent pogroms against the Jews. For his part, Nicholas was a small slender youth with a fetching moustache and soulful eyes, who was completely dominated by his large bear-like father. The czar kept Nicholas in ignorance of all affairs of state, and his future looked bleak. His one bright spot was that he was enamoured of a German princess, Alexandra, a granddaughter of Queen Victoria. She arrived at the summer palace to meet the family, when abruptly Alexander III surprised one and all (himself, mostly) by dying. He had been ill, but was only forty-nine. Thus Nicholas and Alexandra, the most famous couple in Russian history, had a hasty marriage and then a tragic coronation. Several hundred of the common people were killed during a mad rush to get at the feast laid out for them. Nicholas and Alexandra handled the tragedy badly, and were unpopular from the beginning.

A decade passed before Nicholas learned how serious his troubles would be. In 1904 he embarked on the Russo-Japanese War and lost to Japan--the first time a European nation had ever been defeated by an oriental one at war. Because of this on January 22, 1905, a group of peaceful protestors tried to march on the Winter Palace in St. Petersberg, and were fired upon by the czar's own troops, an event called Bloody Sunday. The people were shocked and outraged, and over the next few days there were strikes and mutinies in the country. These eventually died down, but Nicholas reluctantly granted some mild concessions, specifically the October Manifesto of 1905, which called for the election of a Duma by almost universal male suffrage. Any euphoria over this soon dissipated, because the czar also ordered thousands of arrests of people who had demonstrated against him, and also systematically interfered in the elections in question. There was one outstanding minister, Peter Stolypin, who was personally quite conservative but astute enough to see the necessity of giving the people certain concessions. He worked with the moderate "Octobrists" in the Duma, and began an ambitious plan of distributing communal land of the mir to the peasants. He actually gave out land to some nine million people during his time as chief minister. At the same moment, Stolyin had dissidents arrested, including Lenin, Trotsky and Stalin, and had them either dispatched to Siberia or sent into exile (many went to Switzerland). Russia fairly crawled with secret police, and there were spies who spied on spies. In 1911 one such informant notified the czar of a plot to assassinate Stolypin while attending a performance of the opera. Every precaution was taken to insure Stolypin's safety, and on the night in question the informant himself leapt up and shot Stolypin dead.

The loss of Stolypin hastened the revolution to come; and three unfortunate events guaranteed it--the birth of a prince with haemophilia, the influence of the Rasputin, and the outbreak of World War I. The prince, Tsarevich Alexis, was born in 1904, and because the slightest mishap might cause him to bleed to death, had bodyguards hovering over him day and night to catch him if he fell. Sadly, at age eight, he had a serious hemmorrhage and almost died, but was most miraculously "saved" by an unkempt, unwashed, hypnotic kind of man, a Siberian peasant who passed himself off as a holy

Czar Alexander III. The future Nicolas II is standing
directly behind his father. (The Granger Collection)

monk, Gregory Rasputin. Despite a sordid reputation, by saving the prince Rasputin gained such control over the czar and czarina that henceforth no minister could hold or lose a post unless he wished it. Scandal about Rasputin spread all over Russia, and although he was eventually assassinated (in 1916), the deed came too late to prevent the revolution. World War I broke out in August in 1914, and the Russians suffered dreadful casualties at the hands of the Germans on the Eastern front. Russian soldiers were sent into battles without boots or guns. Stories were told that at the Battle of Tannenberg there was such a mountain of corpses that the Germans actually had to stop shooting to clear a path for their bullets. By the spring of 1917 the people had had enough.

Part II

Austria-Hungary

After the revolution of 1848 was put down in the Hapsburg Empire, the various nationalities remained both ambitious and frustrated, and their wish for self-fulfillment merely grew stronger during the next half century. The emperor was a dour young man named Francis Joseph (1830-1916) who had no intention of changing the imperial government in any liberal way. He ruled for an exceedingly long time, from 1849 until 1916, and managed to preserve the empire with only one authentic concession to nationalism--the compromise (Ausgleich) of 1867. Austria had suffered during the unification of both Italy and Germany, for each had fought a war against her, the first in 1859 (when she was defeated by France and Piedmont), and the second in 1866 (when she was defeated by Prussia). Now in her weakened condition, Austria was besieged with demands from nationality groups, and was obliged to give way before the most vociferous ones, the Hungarians. In 1867 a dual monarch was created, with the emperor ruling overall, but with two separate governments under him in Austria and Hungary. This brought no joy to the other nationalities, the Serbs, Slovenes, Croatians, Ruthenians, Czechs, Poles or Rumanians, for the Hungarians were if anything more repressive in the Hungarian half of the monarchy than were the Austrians in their half. School children were taught in Hungarian schools, and eventually all railroad employees and other state officials had to speak Hungarian. Feelings ran very high over that state of affairs.

During his reign, the emperor also gave out one eventual concession to liberalism--although not until 1907--when he reluctantly bowed to pressure and granted universal manhood suffrage for elections to the lower house of the Austrian half of the empire. Unfortunately, this concession produced mostly chaos in the assembly. The large number of non-German delegates were so hostile that they disrupted each other's speeches by throwing inkwells, emitting raspberries, and the like, until no business could be transacted. The government had to be run by decree. In the Hungarian half no concessions of this nature ever were given, with the result that the upper class magyars completely controlled parliament.

The Hapsburg family had a series of misfortunes during this period which contributed to the general dissatisfaction and ultimate tragic outcome for the

Archduke Franz Ferdinand and his wife Sophie. (The Granger Collection)

empire. Three of the four episodes were at least partly due to the irascible and compromisingly severe attitude of the emperor, who was so reactionary that one story had it that he liked to shoot a peasant every morning before breakfast. According to this, his advisors thought ill of this pasttime, but found a satisfactory compromise. They hired a peasant to pose on the palace grounds every morning, and fall dramatically into a heap when the emperor fired a blank shot at him, so that the old man never knew about the charade.

The first tragedy occurred in 1889 when the crown prince and heir to the throne, Rudolph, persuaded a 17-yeard old lover, the Baroness Marie Vetsera, to join him in a double suicide at Mayerling, the royal hunting lodge. This ghastly tragedy was at least partly laid at the emperor's door, for he had continually snubbed his son, forced him into a miserable marriage, and refused to give him responsibility and take him into the government. Rudolph was substantially more liberal than his father and might have assisted in solving the problems of the nationalities. The second tragedy was that his wife, the Empress Elizabeth, nicknamed the Reiserin Kaiserin (the traveling empress), was more or less driven out of Vienna by the rigid and gloomy emperor. She was assassinated at Lake Geneva by an anarchist in 1898. The emperor's brother, Maximilian, also came to an unfortunate end, for during the American Civil War he loaned himself to a madcap scheme of French Emperor Napolean III for conquering Mexico, and lasted only a short time in this adventure before he was shot by a firing squad.

The final tragedy involved the emperor's nephew, Francis Ferdinand, a stout, well-intentioned man, now heir to the throne, who had the courage to marry the woman of his choice, and to openly sympathize with the nationalities of the monarchy--both contrary to the wishes of Francis Joseph. However the archduke's sympathy for southern Slavs alienated Serbia, for the Serbs hoped that further hostilities between Slav and Hapsburgs would eventually lead to an enlarged Serbia, with all southern Slavs in their own boundaries. Knowing this, when Francis Ferdinand was invited on a good will mission to Sarajevo in the troubled area of Bosnia-Herzegovina, he still accepted, and even took his wife. When they alighted from the train to embark on a well-publicized tour of the city, a half dozen assassins lay in wait for them, all Serbian nationalists. The first threw a bomb at the car, which failed to detonate. The anguished mayor sped to the town hall with his distinguished visitor, where they hastily revised their plans, and the assassins all repaired to the nearest coffeehouse to drown their sorrows--all except one. The mayor's car returned down the street where Gavrilo Princips stood awkwardly holding his gun, the chaffeur stalled the car directly in front of him, and Princips shot the archduke and his wife dead on the spot. The assassin was seized and taken straight to prison, where he died in less than a year of bad treatment. Today there is a marker at the place, not in honor of the archduke, but of the assassin. This was the deed which led directly to World War I.

Part III

Germany

When Bismarck accomplished his purpose in 1871 of unifying the German states into one centralized monarchy (which they called an empire), and of

NATIONALITIES OF THE HABSBURG EMPIRE

RUSSIA

GERMANY

BOHEMIA SILESIA
MORAVIA GALACIA

AUSTRIA BUKOVINA

SALZBURG
TYROL CARNIOLA H U N G A R Y
CARINTHIA STYRIA

GORZ TRANSYVANIA

ISTRIA CROATIA SLAVONIA

BOSNIA

ITALY DALMATIA RUMANIA

ADRIATIC SEA

SERBIA

TYRRHENIAN

SEA

CROATS

CZECHS

GERMANS

ITALIANS

LITTLE RUSSIANS

MAGYARS

POLES

RUMANIANS

SERBS

SLOVAKS

SLOVENES

defeating France, in one stroke he created one of the most powerful countries in the world. Within twenty-five years the nation had 50 million people (67 million by 1914), one of the most productive coal and steel industries in the world, great munitions makers such as Krupp, vast modern electric and chemical industries, and a merchant marine second only to Great Britain.

One of Bismarck's main critics in Germany was the Social Democratic Party, the largest socialist party in Europe. The SPD was created in 1875 when a Marxian group, led by William Liebknecht, and a non-Marxian group, led by Ferdinand Lasalle, united to form one socialist party, and although they were persecuted by the German government, they became increasingly important as social and political critics. In a clever move, Bismarck's government stole much of their thunder by putting through extensive programs of social and economic reform, including factory inspection acts (1878), an industrial sanitary and safety code (1891), and also measures for health, accidents and old-age insurance--all of which were way ahead of their time and became models for other countries. Despite this, by 1912 the SPD was the largest party in the Reichstag.

While Bismarck was chancellor, Germany was a world leader in diplomacy: one of his greatest accomplishments was keeping the peace from 1871 until 1890, due in large part to his success in keeping his enemy, France, isolated in Europe. In 1872, Bismarck brought Germany, Austria and Russia in an alliance, the Three Emperor's League, although the three emperors (all rivals) had a serious falling out in 1875, when a war broke out between Russia and Turkey over the Balkans. This war ended with the Treaty of San Stefano of 1878, with Austria occupying two Turkish provinces, Bosnia and Herzegovia. Another compromise had to be reached the same year, with Bismark's help, at the Congress of Berlin. At Berlin Russia lost the large state of Bulgaria they had occupied since the war; the area was reduced in size, and Serbia, Montenegro, and Rumania got full independence; however Austria kept Bosnia and Herzegovina. Russia felt cheated by this, but nevertheless succumbed to Bismarck's overtures to make a new Three Emperor's League in 1881. The next year Bismarck managed a Triple Alliance betweeen Germany, Austria and Italy, further rounding out his plans to make agreements on the continent which isolated France. Russia continued to feel threatened by Austia's menacing attitude toward the Balkans, so Bismarck signed a Reinsurance Treaty with Russia alone in 1887, which provided for the benevolent neutrality of each country in case the other got into war, and German recognition of Russia interests in Bulgaria and the entrance to the Black Sea. However Bismarck neutralized this encouragement given to Russia by still another series of moves. With the Mediterranean Agreements signed the same year, he encouraged England, Austria and Italy to maintain the status quo in the Balkans. Bismarck's objective throughout was peace, and as long as he was there to manipulate the intricate threads of his diplomacy, the pattern was peaceful. But Kaiser William II succeeded to power in 1890, and dismissed Bismarck. Bismark wanted a strong compact European empire while Kaiser William II was interested in in an overseas empire. The loss of Bismark tangled up the diplomatic alliance into a monstrous snarl. The first to defect was Russia. After four years of persuasion, Russia allied with France thus ending French isolation which Bismarck had so carefully arranged.

Firing Bismarck was only the first in a series of thoughtless gestures on the part of a ruler who had virtually absolute power in Germany, and very little common sense. William II was the son of the king of Germany and the eldest daughter of Queen Victoria of England. A birth, William had a withered arm and symptoms which indicated neurological damage. As he grew, young "Willy" was given to tantrums and fits of anger which left the entire family exasperated; but as the eldest grandson of Queen Victoria, and the only grandchild ever seen by her Prince Albert, before he died, William kept a place in the old lady's heart which he did not really deserve. He spent his summers in England, but abused his place regularly once he reached his teenage years. For example, as a boy he actually spied on the English fleet, and sent dispatches back to Berlin. As a man William II did not hesitate to challenge England on many occasions. In regard to the Ottoman Empire, where England had been Turkey's main defender, William II proclaimed in 1899 that he was the great friend of the world's Moslems, and wooed the sultan for the Berlin-to-Baghdad railroad. In the Far East he made claims to part of China, and to the Gilbert and Soloman Islands in the Pacific. Worst of all, he meddled in the Boer War. After the first skirmish over the Jameson Raid, William fired off a telegram to Kruger congratulating the Boers in their victory over the English. When the telegram was made public, English rioted in public all over their land in fury at the German.

England had one or two consistent policies in foreign affairs for most of the 19th century, including splendid isolation for herself, and intervention whenever necessary to maintain the balance of power on the continent. Despite her efforts, the balance of power had changed irrevocably when Germany became a great nation, and now with the irascible temperament of William II, her chances of keeping the peace seemed slim. Thus England after many years abandoned her policy of isolation. Aside from Germany, her main concern had been Russia, fear of Russian aggrandizement either in the Far East or in the Balkans. Thus England allied first with Japan in 1902, and then with France in 1904. The Japanese made good use of this new friendship, and promptly defeated Russia in the Russo-Japanese War. That humiliating defeat caused the events of Bloody Sunday inside Russia, and convinced the czar that they also should revise their diplomatic situation. The Russians had already broken with Germany and allied with France in 1894; now in 1907 they courted England. Thus the three most important allied powers of World War I, France, England and Russia, fell into each other's camp, and were allies from that day forward, held together by what was referred to as the "Triple Entente".

For his part, the kaiser continued to disrupt the peace of Europe. All the great powers had been vying for colonies, and sparks flew whenever anyone of them felt challenged. France had an empire second only to Great Britain, and had just formed an agreement with Italy in 1902 to protect Italian interest in Tripoli and Libya, and French interest in Morocco. The French then signed an accord with the English as well. To challenge France, in 1905 the kaiser went to Morocco in a flamboyant gesture, precipitating what is known as the First Moroccan Crisis. The French foreign minister Delcassé resigned and war seemed eminent; but at an international conference at Algeciras the dispute was settled, for all the powers except Austria abandoned Germany. In 1911 the dispute broke out again, when the French sent troops to Morocco to settle some native disturbances, and the Germans protested. The kaiser sent the gunboat, Panther, to the Moroccan port of Agadir, challenged the French again, and demanded that Germany be given compensation elsewhere. This time German intimidation succeeded, for in return for keeping Morocco, the French gave to Germany part of the French Congo--altogether a bad precedent.

The Germans were not the only malefactors in the years before the war: the most central crisis of all was precipitated by Austria when she annexed Bosnia Herzegovina in 1908. The opportunity arose because some patriotic liberals who called themselves "young Turks", revolted in the Ottoman Empire in 1908, and overthrew the sultan. Adul-Hamid II had been a rather nasty ruler, who was remembered more for his murder and mayhem against the Armenians than perhaps any other thing. This revolt caused the empire to crack like a piece of glass, with large bits being chipped off at once by nationalistic minorities. Bulgaria declared independence in 1908; Crete united with Greece in 1912; Albania became independent in 1913. While this was happening, Austria told Russia she would annex Bosnia and Herzegoviana, and Russia could take the Turkish straits. However, the wiley Austrians did not wait for Russia to claim her part of the bargain; without further ado they annexed the two provinces. This act angered every major country in Europe, except her ally Germany. The Russians were outraged, for they had been duped. The English and French wanted an international conference. The residents of Bosnia and Herzegovina were enfuriated. And perhaps angriest of all was Serbia, for they had wanted the area themselves. This was the event which lead to the central tragedy of 1914: it led the Serbian extremists to plot the death of the Hapsburg heir; it angered and frightened the czar so that the next time Austria acted aggressively in the Balkans he felt forced to take a stand. It also showed France and England that a policy of opposition not backed up with force was useless. Meanwhile, the troubled Balkans now provided the stage for two small wars, one in 1912, the second in 1913, where Serbia, Bulgaria, Greece and Turkey came to blows twice over the crumbling Ottoman Empire. Again Austria blocked the ambitions of Serbia, thus exacerbating the hatred already felt there against the Hapsburgs. Another unfortunate result of these squabbles was the conclusion many Europeans drew, that the conflicts were at least localized and tended to always involve the same participants. Thus no one in Europe thought in the summer of 1914 that a minor fracas between Austria and Serbia might turn into the most colossal, bloody war the world had ever seen.

Part IV

The United States

The Civil War was fought from 1861 until 1865, but its effects lasted well into the 20th century. The last shot in the war was fired on April 13, 1865, when a vengeful Southern actor, John Wilkes Booth, assassinated the president of the United States. The cost to the nation of removing the one man with wisdom and ability from the scene was incalculable. Andrew Johnson, Lincoln's ineffective successor, was almost found guilty of impeachment, and during his short time in office failed to implement Lincoln's policy of moderation toward the defeated South. Radical Republicans Charles Sumner and Thaddeus Stevens, who controlled federal policy, treated the South like a conquered province.

In the period known as Reconstruction, northerners called "carpetbaggers" and southerners called "scaliwags" seized control, confiscated property, and did what they could to ruin former Southern white leaders economically and politically. Many of the newly freed slaves were illiterate, but during this time they were elected to offices throughout the South. Some of them were corrupt and incompetent, and the disenfranchised white leaders got their revenge all too soon. Meanwhile, though the Confederacy was reduced to a wasteland, the North began to boom after the war, and soon the yankee fortune-seekers headed back again and left the freed men with no more protection. By 1890 many white southerns had joined the Klu Klux Klan to intimidate the frightened black people and prevent their voting; at the same time the dream of forty acres and a mule, promised to all the former slaves by unscrupulous carpetbaggers, turned out to be a myth, and thousands of black people found themselves in a new form of slavery as share croppers, indebted to the country store. The Supreme Court decision Plessey v. Ferguson of 1896 established the "separate but equal" doctrine for transportation and accepted as legal, thereafter, a double standard of institutions for black and white people, specifically schools, so that segregation became an accepted way of life. Black people were discouraged from voting and office-holding, and were forbidden to enter white hotels, restaurants, theaters, parks or restrooms, not only in the South, but throughout the country. Black people who objected to their unjust treatment were in danger of life and limb; for more than fifty years dozens of black people were lynched every year in the United States.[1]

In the northern and western states, the period from 1870 until 1900 was one of vast industrialization, building of railroads and great prosperity. The new figure on the scene was the industrial tycoon, the millionaire, including John D. Rockefeller, in oil; Andrew Carnegie, in steel; J. P. Morgan, in banking; and later on, Henry Ford. The gap between rich and poor was striking, in that era before income taxes, for the numbers of poor had been streaming in by the millions from the troubled countries of Europe. By 1900 more than one million immigrants arrived every year, and whereas earlier in the century the nationalities had been primarily German and Irish, by 1900 they were preponderantly Italian and Russian. Some of the immigrants made their way out to farmland and began to prosper, but many stayed in the city, particularly New York, where they lived in misery. Great city machines grew up at this time, such as Tammany Hall in New York, which provided a rudimentary form of social assistance to the immigrants in return for their loyal vote. Political corruption grew to proportions never seen before, and even included figures in the government of President Ulysses S. Grant.

This Gilded Age was not one of the more attractive periods in American History. Gay Gould, Jim Fisk and other notorious men of the time made millions through corruption; John Rockefeller and his contemporaries made millions by exploiting the poor. The rich lived like oriental potentates, and even middle class Americans aspired to gingerbread houses and opulent display. The workers struggled for better hours and pay, and the strikes of that era, such as the Pullman Strike, and the Carnegie Steel, Homestead Strike, were violent affairs, put down by the factory owners with hired muscle

---

[1]See Ralph Ginzburg, 100 Years of Lynchings (N.Y.: Lancer Books, 1962); and Arthur F. Raper, The Tragedy of Lynching (N.Y.: Dover Publications, 1970)

or federal troops or both. Some few laws were passed on minimum wage, child labor, women's labor, and workmen's compensation, but they tended to be passed at the state level, so that conditions varied greatly; and in any case, in social and economic legislation the United States lagged behind Great Britain and even Germany.

For most of the 19th century in foreign policy the United States was determinedly isolationist. While European countries were carving out empires in Africa and Asia, the United States had an empire already on hand to conquer, the frontier, which for most of the century still consisted of thousands of square miles of wilderness land. With the Monroe Doctrine of 1823, the United States announced that no European intervention in the Americas would be tolerated. Since Great Britain concurred with this policy, there was remarkably little European intervention. But in the 1890's, the American attitude in foreign policy underwent a significant change. According to Frederick Jackson Turner, because the frontier land had been exhausted, Americans had to seek any future adventures overseas, like everyone else. Turner argued that the frontier had been a safety value, acting on the poor, the ambitious and the lawless with equal effect, drawing an unceasing stream of people to leave their settled homes and strike out for the unknown. Now that frontierland was no longer available, men at every level in society who wanted a challenge of some kind, were obliged to look elsewhere. Furthermore, the generation of the 1890's was the generation reared on stories of the Civil War. Antietam, Gettysberg and the other battles had been glorified in the telling almost beyond recognition, and most American men in their twenties and thirties longed for a chance to win military glory themselves. In still another way they were only sharing the attitude common to all Western nations at that time, an attitude exemplified by Rudyard Kipling, Winston Churchill and Teddy Roosevelt alike, that war was a necessary and worthwhile pursuit. These attitudes were written up for all to see in a new kind of popular press, called "Yellow Journalism", particularly in the Hearst and Pulitzer newspaper chains, which in the 1890's went to unprecedented lengths in sensational stories in order to sell newspapers.

All these factors and others besides, including a widespread American sentiment that Americans were nobler than other folk and liked to come to the aid of people in need, caused the United States to embark on a new imperialistic adventure, the Spanish-American War of 1898. Teddy Roosevelt, the Vice President, said, "It wasn't much of a war, but it was the best war we had;" and of President McKinley who tried half-heartedly to prevent it, he said McKinley "had no more backbone than a chocolate eclair." The war began when the American battleship, Maine, was sunk by an explosion in the Havana harbor. Although to this day the malefactors were never found out, the American public was led to believe that they were Spanish. The war ended quickly: The Americans defeated the Spanish and gave Cuba her independence. Also, Spain ceded the Philipine Islands, Puerto Rico and Guam to the U.S. in return for a payment of $20,000,000. Through the Platt Amendment the United States established a protectorate over the Cuban island to ensure a democratic government.

This war was not openly imperialistic in the European model, for the United States did not openly seize the island. However, it did establish a new model for the future of American political interference, for the Platt

THE WORLD'S CONSTABLE.

Theodore Roosevelt: "The World's Constable", a cartoon by Dalrymple
(The Granger Collection)

Amendment gave Washington the right to intervene in cases of Cuban political
corruption--surely a most ironic clause at a time when American government was
symbolized by Tammany Hall. It also began a kind of economic imperialism
which was an American eccentricity, nicknamed "Dollar Diplomacy". In the
free-wheeling American way, with no government support or participation,
American businessmen invested heavily in Cuban sugar and tobacco, and
afterwards if any trouble arose, expected the American government to
intervene. Teddy Roosevelt, who became president upon the death of McKinley,
incorporated this point of view in a new statement of American foreign policy,
the Roosevelt Corollary to the Monroe Doctrine. This said that no other
countries were to intervene in Latin America, but the United States would
intervene if any trouble arose, including the nonpayment of debts by Latin
governments. In the 20th century the United States acted on this premise on
numerous occasions, sending ships, occasionally landing marines, and always
taking the position that it was their prerogative to supervise Latin American
affairs. The policy was very offensive to the countries in question. It
temporarily abated with the Good Neighbor Policy of Franklin Delano Roosevelt
in the 1930's. Nevertheless, in the 1950's when Fidel Castro seized power in
Cuba, President Eisenhower followed the dictates of Americans who controlled
Cuban sugar and tobacco, and did not recognize him. When Salvador Allende was
the Communist president of Chile, the United States followed American copper
interests and provided CIA assistance to the dictator Pinochet, who overthrew

81

Allende and murdered him. To this day the amount of American money invested in a Latin American country, not the degree of democracy, or respect for human rights to be found in the country, is more likely to determine the degree of sympathy of the American government.

Teddy Roosevelt was one of the most colorful of all American presidents. Popular and charismatic, he embarked on a vigorous foreign policy ("Speak softly but carry a big stick"), and an equally ambitious domestic program. During his administration the federal government began the policy of establishing millions of acres in national parks; he began to "bust trusts", establishing the principle that the giant corporations of the day would have to be guided more by the public interest. Following the lead of Upton Sinclair and other writers called "muckrakers", who attacked the abuses of the food industry and other examples of corruption, the government also began to enforce pure food and drug laws.

Teddy Roosevelt played an important role in international affairs. After the Russo-Japanese War he presided over the peace conference in New Hampshire. Yet despite this and despite the vast industrial complex the United States had built up by 1914, when World War I began Americans took it for granted that it was none of their business.

Part V

France

When the German army occupied France in 1871 the empire of Napoleon III came to an abrupt and embarassing end. There was an enemy army occupying France; Paris was seized by the radical communards, and no one could agree on what should constitute the new government. There were monarchists aplenty, but they quarreled among themselves, for some followed the Bourbons, some the House of Orleans, and some still wanted a Bonaparte. By the same token, the republicans were also divided, partly on the issue of just how soon and just how thoroughly France should take revenge on Germany. Thus the Third Republic which fell into place was a sort of step-child, a government which was everyone's second choice, based on no constitution, but rather on a series of laws which eventually called for a president with no power, and a two-house legislature with the lower house elected by universal manhood suffrage. The overriding characteristic of the new government was its instability: for it fell more than fifty times in the first forty years. Even so, it survived longer than any other French government since 1789, lasting from 1871 unitl the Nazi conquest of 1940.

Three serious crises threatened the republic before World War I, each of which could have spelled the end. The first was the threat presented by General Georges Boulanger, a "man-on-horseback" who wanted to seize power through a military coup. His moment came in 1889, but his nerve failed and he fled from Paris at the last moment, eventually trailed into Belgium, and committed suicide on the grave of his mistress. The second scandal had to do with the Panama Canal. A number of radical deputies had accepted large bribes from the Panama Canal Company, which had wanted government support for the construction. The scandal destroyed the company but not the republic, and the canal was eventually built by the United States.

The third crisis was the most serious of all, a charge of treason leveled against the first Jewish officer in the French army, Captain Alfred Dreyfus. Dreyfus was accused of leaking French military secrets to Germany, and for this he was condemned to life imprisonment at the most ignominious hell-hole known to man, Devil's Island (later publicized in the popular book, Papillon). However, in point of fact Dreyfus was innocent, for the documents had been forged by an antisemitic Hungarian named Esterhazy (who later committed suicide); and the real issue quickly became whether one supported the reactionary antisemitic political right, which supported monarchy, church, and army; or whether one supported the republic. Emile Zola, the celebrated novelist, led the forces defending Dreyfus, in a cause which only after five years of interminable haggling and scandal procured his release (a broken man) from prison. The first result of the republic's victory was that the radical republicans brought about a separation of church and state in France. A second result was that at a time when antisemitism was on the rise in Russia, Austria-Hungary and Germany, in France it was defeated.

Part VI

Great Britain

Of the countries which dominated Europe from 1870 to 1914, the most democratic was England. Because of their practice of steady evolution in political freedom, they were also the only country that escaped serious revolutions in the 19th century. The British political system was one of accomodation. Beginning with the Reform Bill of 1832, the British slowly modified the qualifications for voting, so that after deliberate and measured changes in 1867 and again in 1880 they were on the verge of universal manhood suffrage. Two important pressure groups in the early part of the century were the Anti-Corn Law League and the Chartists. The former was created from economic necessity, when the tariffs on import of European grain kept the cost of English bread at a high price during the depression after the Napoleonic Wars. The league eventually got its way, and the corn laws were repealed. The chartists were more consciously political. They were created out of the need of working class Englishmen to gain seats in Parliament in order to pass legislation to improve their lot in the factories. The steps to accomplish this were straightforward: a People's Charter called for universal manhood suffrage, secret ballot, abolition of propery requirement for members of Parliament, salaries for members, equal electoral districts, and annual elections. In 1839 more than a hundred thousand people signed petitions calling Parliament to adopt this charter, and they unsuccessfully renewed the assault in 1842 and in 1848. The chartists disbanded after three defeats, but by World War I every one of their demands had been met except that calling for annual elections. By the turn of the century members of Parliament were receiving a salary, which meant that ordinary middle class people could finally serve in the government. And a final very important measure was passed in 1911 when Parliament abolished the absolute veto of the House of Lords.

Economic and social reforms were passed as well. The Education Act of 1870 was due to the embarrassing circumstance that the Reform Bill of 1867 had enfranchised men who were illiterate. Now belatedly, the government sought to provide at least of modicum of public education, and with some success. In ten years, attendance in elementary schools rose from one to four million. There were reforms in public housing, food and drug legislation, and union rights. The British worker won the right to strike, old age pension, accident compensation, and unemployment insurance. These extraordinary measures were passed because of the efforts of both Conservative and Liberal leaders in Parliament. William Gladstone (1809-1898), Liberal, and Benjamin Disraeli (1804-1881), Conservative, were acerbic political rivals, but both saw the need for reform, and in the years when they alternated in power, both sponsored important new legislation.

The one important British failure during this time was their inability to resolve the problem of Ireland. The Irish had been chafing under British rule for two centuries. They had lost much of their land to absentee British landlords, and they had been underrepresented or not represented at all in Parliament until the 1820's. Laws had restricted the Catholic vote. By the 1870's the leading Irish statesman, Charles Stuart Parnell, actively sought home rule for Ireland. Gladstone twice tried to establish Home Rule for the Irish, but each time was defeated, although other measures were passed to help the Irish tenants purchase land. In 1912 the Liberals introduced a third Home Rule Bill, but by the time it became law in 1914 World War I had broken out, and the whole process had to be postponed. Only after the war did part of Ireland obtain its independence.

The period from 1870 until 1914 was otherwise a time of great power and prestige for the British Empire, when their fleet controlled the seas, and their colonies stretched around the globe. The fortunate ruler who presided over this glorious situation was a plump little person who looked like a pouter pigeon, who almost unanimously received credit for the events of her long and glorious reign, but who in fact had little power at all. Queen Victoria ascended to the throne as a girl of eighteen (in 1837), and reigned until 1901. With her German husband, Prince Albert, she lived in happiness, and gave birth to nine children; but upon his death in 1861 she retired from view for three years and never completely recovered from his death. Personally she was puritanical (and gave the entire era the nickname "Victorian" for straitlaced behavior) and imperialistic, highly opinionated, and not very bright. Gladstone deferred to her but was never very successfully in her graces; but Disraeli handled her with charm and tact, and guided her in many important decisions. In 1876 against many objections, he obtained the title for her of Empress of India, which pleased her enormously; and in truth, in the later year of her life she was the most popular monarch in the world. Her real successes were that after numerous licentious kings, she embodied middle class morality and honesty. However, her own son, the Prince of Wales (Edward VII), who ruled 1901-1910 was notoriously dissolute in his private life.

On the eve of World War I, Great Britain was the most powerful country in the world--prosperous, extremely democratic, and understandably proud. Few would have predicted that her days of glory were almost over. During the war four empires fell: the Ottoman, Russian, Austria, Hungarian, and German. And the remaining great empire, the British, suffered a mortal blow.

QUESTIONS FOR REFLECTION

1. Which of the major democratic nations was the most "democratic" by 1914? In addition to being "democratic" does the government you have in mind also qualify for being "liberal" in economic matters? What specific acts or laws can you cite to justify your arguments on political behavior, and on economic legislation?

2. Which of the democratic countries was the most "stable", and which was the most "volatile" in the period before World War II. Do you equate stability with national well-being?

3. Which of the three governments under consideration would you say was the most autocratic in the time before World War I? Evaluate life under the three different regimes; were they equally prosperous? Was there a strong middle class? Was there any freedom at all? Were there any efforts at reform?

4. If you had been a ruled with sympathy for the nationality groups under the Hapsburg, how would you have handled the problem?

5. If you had been in charge of foreign policy in Britain (or France, or the United States), how would you have handled the kaiser? Do you think the great democracies could have prevented the first World War if they had been forewarned?

SUGGESTED BIBLIOGRAPHY

O. Aubry, The Second Empire (1940)
R. A. Billington, Westward Expansion (1967)
J. Bowle, Politics and Opinion in the Nineteenth Century (1954)
A. Briggs, The Age of Improvement, 1783-1867 (1959)
D. W. Brogran, The French Nation from Napoleon to Pétain (Colophon)
G. Dangerfield, The Awakening of American Nationalism (1965)
G. Dangerfield, The Era of Good Feelings (1952)
G. Dangerfield, The Strange Death of Liberal England (1961)
B. D. Gooch, ed., Napolean III: Man of Destiny--Enlightened Statesman or
    Proto-Fascist? (1963)
A. Guérard, Napoleon III (1943)
A. Guérard, Reflections on the Napoleonic Legend (1924)
M. T. Florinsky, Russia: A History and an Interpretation, Vol. II (1953)
E. Halévy, History of the English People in the Nineteenth Century, Vols V and
    VI (1936)
E. J. Hobsbawn, The Age of Capitalism, 1848-1875 (1976)
H. S. Hughes, Consciousness and Society: The Reorientation of Social Thought
    1850-1930 (1958)
O. Jaszi, The Dissolution of the Habsburg Monarchy (1929)
D. Johnson, France and the Dreyfus Affair (1967)
G. Kitson-Clark, The Making of Victorian England (1962)

W. L. Langer, European Alliances and Alignments, 2nd ed. (1950)

E. Longford, Queen Victoria (Pyramid)

H. W. Morgan, America's Road to Empire: The War with Spain and Overseas Expansion (1965)

S. E. Morison, History of the United States (1965)

F. C. Palm, England and Napoleon III: A Study in the Rise of a Utopian Dictator (1948)

B. Pares, The Fall of the Russian Monarchy (1939)

J. W. Pratt, Expansionists of 1898 (1936)

J. G. Randall and D. Donald, The Civil War and Reconstruction (1961)

J. C. G. Rohl, Germany Without Bismark: The Crisis of Government in the Second Reich, 1890-1900 (1967)

A. Rosenberg, Democracy and Socialism (1939)

H. Seton-Watson, The Russian Empire, 1801-1917 (1967)

F. A. Simpson, Louis Napoleon and the Recovery of France, 1848-1856, 3rd. ed. (1951)

F. A. Simpson, The Rise of Louis Napoleon (1950)

K. M. Stampp, The Era of Reconstruction (1965)

K. M. Stampp, The Peculiar Institution (1956)

A. J. P. Taylor, The Struggle for Mastery in Europe, 1848-1918 (1954)

J. M. Thompson, Louis Napoleon and the Second Empire (1955)

D. Thomson, Democracy in France Since 1870, 4th ed. (1964)

A. K. Weinberg, Manifest Destiny (1935)

R. W. Williams, Gaslight and Shadow: The World of Napoleon III (1957)

C. V. Woodward, Origins of the New South, 1877-1913 (1951)

E. L. Woodward, The Age of Reform, new ed., (Caredon, 1962)

Gordon Wright, France in Modern Times (Rand McNally, 1960)

G. M. Young, Victorian England: Portrait of an Age (1936)

CHAPTER 6 - CULTURAL CHANGES 1850-1914

Part I

Darwin

The Theory of Evolution of Charles Darwin (1809-1882) was a milestone which dramatically changed the way man thought about himself. Darwin was a modest genial man, the son of a successful doctor, who considered himself fortunate to be hired as a naturalist on board the H.M.S. Beagle in 1831 as it embarked on a round-the-world research voyage for the royal navy. For five years he collected specimens of plants and animals in South America and in the Pacific, and as he observed the fascinating geological differences in the land, Darwin attempted to accommodate his findings with a theory of natural changes. When he returned to England he lived a life of scholarly seclusion, devoting the rest of his days to the project, spending entire years on certain specific problems, such as the anatomy of the barnacle. In 1859 he published his book, On the Origin of Species by Means of Natural Selection, or the Preservation of Favored Races in the Struggle for Life.

Darwin believed that species were not immutable, constant entities, but were always changing and evolving even as the entire world had evolved over the course of time. By a process of natural selection taking millions of years, the evolution occurred as follows: first there would be minute variations of offspring from parents; second (from an idea inspired by Malthus), it took large numbers of offspring to ensure the continuation of the species; thirdly, the competition of the millions of these offspring for survival ensured that those which did survive would be the most fit, endowed with tiny differences which constituted an advantage over their fellow creatures; lastly, the accumulation and passing on of these advantageous variations over many generations made up such numbers of changes that the eventual result was a new species. Sometimes advantageous mutations occurred spontaneously which speeded up the process, but usually it was exceedingly slow. There was no place in his scientific world for a deity or a divine purpose, and in contrast to the fanciful story of creation in the Book of Genesis, Darwin believed that man shared the experience of all other living creatures of having evolved in the course of time from a more primitive form of existence, one stage of which was the "Old World" monkey. The furor created by the book took Darwin by surprise, and he soon found himself to be the most vilified man in England. Clergymen attacked him from the pulpit, and delicate ladies fainted in the streets. But his impact was as long-lasting as it was immediate. In the scientific world new evidence came forth every day on natural selection, adaption of creatures to the environment, survival of the fittest, and other key points.

A group of writers known as the Social Darwinists caused an impact of their own by applying Darwin's biological ideas to social issues. The most famous of these interpreters was Herbert Spencer. Among the ideas which became popular in the latter half of the century, were the following: the concept that life for people was the same as for plants and animals, so that the fittest, or those best adapted to their environment, would survive. Life for people was seen as a jungle, where struggle was a natural phenomenon, and where the strongest would win out, rightfully, over the weakest. There was also a distinct implication that men did not bear the responsibility of their deeds; they were only higher versions of animals, doing what nature would have them do; the consequences were neither good nor evil but inevitable. Translated into application for human behavior, for national policy, empire building and industrialization, some of the notions of the Social Darwinists tended to justify every kind of dubious behavior.

The poor, in particular were viewed differently by this generation. The poor had been pitied, ridiculed, hated or ignored in differing fashion since the beginning of time, depending on the prevailing philosophy of the culture in question. Early Christianity had been sympathetic to the indigent, and had harshly criticized the rich. But by the time of the Puritan community of John Calvin, attitudes had changed. The puritans believed in predestination. They affirmed that a small select group of individuals was saved out of each generation, and all the rest of mankind was doomed to burn eternally in Hell. When searching for clues as to the identity of the small group of saved they fell more or less naturally upon the proposition that those who were saved were undoubtedly those who were thriving. Their stony theology held no pity for those unfortunates who had been doomed. Thus in Puritan New England the poor were despised as evil, and other characteristics came to mind, such as lazy and good-for-nothing. This attitude did not change much from 1650 to 1850 and was still present in Protestant England, borne out by the new Poor Law of 1834. With the advent of the Social Darwinists this attitude shifted--but not to the benefit of the poor people in question. Rather, there was a new scientific reason to dispise them. Hitherto, they had been considered evil, bad, immoral. After the 1870s and 1880s the poor came to be regarded as unfit biological specimens. Life was a jungle; prominent successful men deserved their success and power because they were stronger; and the wretched widows and orphans being driven to the wall were an inferior species which nothing could help. This attitude justified the industrialists newly arrived on the scene, and at the same time erased any thought of public assistance or social legislation to help the unfortunates. If social legislation was passed in one or two countries, including England and Germany, it was not due to sympathy for the poor, but to political pressure from the growing force of labor.

Friedrich Nietzche (1844-1900) was a German philosopher who contributed a number of ideas to the pot. Nietzsche was intensely antidemocratic, and felt that democracy meant only the triumph of mediocrity. Actually, Social Darwinism in all its forms was antidemocratic, for it favored the strongest or fittest over ordinary creatures. Nietzsche contributed the idea of the Superman, as embodied in his most famous work, Thus Spake Zarathustra. Here he criticized Christianity, as the cult of the weak, and called for the triumph of the natural aristocracy of the strong and fit, leading to a superman who would be above good and evil.

Social Darwinism was used to justify not only the triumph of one individual superman, but also of races and of nations. Arthur Gobineau wrote racist tracts at this time, arguing that some races were inherently superior to others and therefore had the natural right to rule. Racism was already distinctly popular: the British and Americans believed in the superiority of the "Anglosaxon race"; the Spanish believed just as strongly in the superiority of the Latins; the Germans were just beginning to promote the mythical concept of the Ayran race. One of the few corners of the earth where there was racial homogeneity was Japan; yet the great powers of the west despised the Japanese (and all other orientals), and talked of the "yellow peril". When Russia embarked on a war with Japan in 1904 no one dreamed that the great imperial throne of the czars was threatened by a conflict with an oriental race, and their defeat sent them reeling. In the United States this unsavory attitude came out in riots against the Chinese. Other aspects of racism were the claims that Anglo-American had the duty to help their "little brown brothers", meaning the "racially inferior" peoples of Asia (such as the Filipinos). And in general, "Social Darwinism" was grasped by white Europeans as further justification for imperialistic domination, subjugation of non-white areas throughout the world during the last half of the 19th Century.

Part II

Literature

As romanticism warned, it was replaced by realism in the 19th century as more and more political power gravitated to the middle class, writers began to write of middle class characters. Also, rather than avoiding the horrors of industrialization and urbanization, beginning with Charles Dickens (1812-70), writers began to portray poverty and economic misery. The leading characters continued to be genteel in Dickens: in David Copperfield the hero is a likely young lad who has many misfortunes but is strictly middle class at heart and ultimately succeeds in winning his rightful place in society. In Oliver Twist the hero is ostensibly a poor orphan who lives a life of abject poverty and falls into the hands of thieves and villains. But Oliver is also really a middle class boy, and luckily finds his prosperous family, who recognize his sterling qualities instantly. In Dickens his keen young boys and girls are all endearing; but it is the panoply of other characters who make his works the great novels which they are. An entire canvas of humanity is portrayed in a novel like David Copperfield or Nicholas Nickleby--villainous aristocrats, swarmy petit bourgeoisie, disreputable thieves--actors, clerks, stage coach drivers, fishermen, nursemaids.

Other fine realistic novelists appeared in the years that followed. In the United States a good example was Mark Twain (Samuel Langhorne Clemens, 1835-1910) who created a whole new world of characters based on folk who lived in small-town-America after the Civil War. In Huckleberry Finn he portrayed the first realistic black character in literature. Twain was humorous; other writers in describing the humdrum lives and petty mediocrity of the middle class were merciless. In France, Guy de Maupassant (1850-1893) and Gustave Flaubert (1821-80) were outstanding. Flaubert's Madame Bovary is a great masterpiece, an account in relentless and exact detail of a bored wife of a French country doctor, who persuades herself of her need for romantic love affairs. Her unremittingly boring and tedious husband is laid out for all to see; one sympathizes with her life even as one grows more restless with her self-serving quest for gratification. She finds no great love affair, but only sex with a series of disinterested partners. She undergoes no change of

89

heart, no growth, only disillusion and ruin, and her suicide at the end is described with the horrific detachment only a practicing medical doctor could provide.

Throughout the western world realism became the dominant genre in the late 19th century, from the Norwegian Henrik Ibsen (1828-1906) to the Russians Ivan Turgenev (1818-83) (Fathers and Sons) and Leo Tolstoy (1828-1910). Tolstoy was one of the great writers of all time. In Anna Karenina and War and Peace he wrote of a rather upper-class Russia.

Realism was an often moving, sometimes charming, genre mostly concerned with the middle class. The next generation of writers developed a new approach, already heralded by realists like Flaubert and Maupassant, a basically pitiless account of life as a dreadful experience, life of the lower classes, life in the slums, life of pathetic mortals in the depths of a human jungle. This was Naturalism: writers who were influenced by the ideas of Darwin as interpreted in social terms by men like Herbert Spencer. Man was the victim of forces beyond his control. Man lived in a jungle. Life was a struggle, just as in the animal world, where only the fittest survive. There was a grim fatalism to these works, a pessimism, a scatological realism, and a depressing philosophy that human character and free will had no bearing on success or life. In the United States, Jack London (1876-1916) came the closest to showing man in genuine conflict with nature and grappling with natural forces beyond his control (Call of the Wild), but in other writers, the jungle was loosely defined as the city. Chicago came in for more than its share of criticism in such books as Sister Carrie by Theodore Dreiser (who also wrote the unrelievably depressing An American Tragedy) and The Jungle by Upton Sinclair, a merciless account of the Chicago meat-packing industry. In Europe the leading naturalist writer was Emile Zola (1840-1902), who wrote such novels as Nana. Zola's characters were helpless and not necessarily endearing victims of social problems such as poverty and alcoholism. With clarity and precision he wrote of social ills, portraying human failures in the most pessimistic terms. In real life Zola was an activist who fought in justice in the Dreyfus case, when he championed the cause of a falsely accused Jew.

By the turn of the century there were a number of writers who expressed a growing interest in psychology, a field just then being explored by Sigmund Freud, and destined to provide some of the most original new literary writing. Writers such as Thomas Hardy (1840-1928) depicted life (in his case, rural England) which was realistic enough, but were bordering on naturalism in the searing exposure of the human personality. One of the most memorable psychological works of this period was Remembrance of Things Past by the Frenchman, Marcel Proust (1871-1922). Proust not only portrayed his class with great psychological accuracy, but also began the exploration of the unconscious, the importance of dreams and fantasies, the inner life of the subject. These concerns also influenced James Joyce (1882-1941), an Irishman, who created scandal by the sexual explicitness of his stream-of-consciousness book, Ulysses. Ulysses was banned in the United States for many years, and the complicated use of language, literary references, symbolism and stream-of-consciousness made it one of the most difficult books in all of literature. His impact, however, was incalculable.

Part III

Painting

    Generally speaking, trends in music, literature and painting tend to
resemble each other; romanticism could be observed in all three, as a movement
toward freedom, emotionalism, breaking with conventions, highly colored
passions sometimes verging on sentamentality. The realism which became
popular in fiction was not apparent in painting, however--for an obvious
research. This was the century when the camera was invented; and after that
technological marvel painting could never be the same again. Henceforth if
anyone wanted a realistic portrayal of someone, the camera was infinitely more
reliable than the paintbrush. The generation of artists at the turn of the
century turned to nature for inspiration; found a whole new world to explore
in variations of light and color. In the first wave of this movement,
Impressionism, the artists tried to convey the essense of a scene as in a
first impression. The nickname came from a painting by Claude Monet
(1840-1926), "Impression of the Rising Sun", which was ridiculed by the more
established painters of the day (1875). For Monet and his contemporaries, the
play of light and shadow on the world around them created a realm of
constantly changing images. He did several series of paintings, one of a
haystack, one of a cathedral, another on water lilies, each showing the
exquisite differences created by the shifting light in the course of a day, or
in different seasons. Impressionists conveyed their scenes with a few quick
strokes of color, with no fine edges and little detail. Close inspection
showed only blurs of red and blue and green, reminiscent of the style of the
great Spanish artist of the 17th century, René Velasquez. Some of the famous
impressionists were Pierre Renoir (1841-1919), Edgar Degas (1834-1917), and
Georges Seurat (1859-91), the first noted for his blushing rosy maidens and
little girls with golden hair; the second for his ballerinas; and the third
for his "pointilism", a technique Seurat invented of painting with little dots
of color, which blended together when one moved to a distant perspective.

    Even as the impressionists were still trying to capture the fleeting light
of a setting sun, their detractors were already challenging them, demanding
that art show more than a moment of light, but a concept that was eternal.
Paul Cezanne felt that an artist must organize a scene into his own
conception, reduce it to its geometrical verities. He painted bowls of fruit,
landscapes, groups of people, in a flat foreshortened way emphasizing cones,
squares and triangles. From Cezanne it was only a step to the work of Pablo
Picasso, then a young man about Paris, who conceived of cubism, which was
paintings of objects broken down into geometric segments. To some artists,
Cubism represented a 20th century concept where the subject matter is taken
apart by the unconscious mind. Other artists went in different directions,
each searching for some other way of conveying an eternal meaning. For Paul
Gauguin it was the lost innocence of the world as seen in the people of
Tahiti. For Henri Rousseau it was the childlike beauty of the primitive.
For Vincent Van Gogh, the tormented Dutchman who was psychotic and eventually
committed suicide in Southern France, it was the way in which colors
themselves could express emotions. Van Gogh's paintings of himself, of his
room, a sun, and the stars in the sky, were all passionate evocations of

91

mood. They were still representative, but the school of painting most influenced by Van Gogh, Expressionist, left behind any attempt to represent a real object, and used color alone to convey feeling, in their most often a feeling of despair.

Part IV

Music

Late 19th century music was dominated by one man, Richard Wagner (1813-1883), who in turn was dominated by romanticism, long after if had run its course. Wagner was a German who was infused with the spirit of German folk stories and legends from the distant past; he was every bit the romantic in his own life, for he had taken part in the 1849 revolution in Dresden; he believed in emotional music, and above all in the redeeming power of a love that ignored all conventions. Such themes could be seen in his operas Lohengrin and especially Tristan and Isolde, although his most famous work was a four-opera cycle called the Ring of the Nibelungen, a murky, overwhelming effort of dark gods and greedy humans lusting for gold, pulsating with themes of incest and murder. Wagner tried to create a new art form in this latter work, combining music, drama and poetry. In Germany he became a cult figure, with his operas performed yearly at Bayreuth, to the mesmerized adulation of thousands of German listeners--and at least one Austrian. As a young man in Vienna, and later in Germany, Adolph Hitler conceived such a passion for Wagner that he heard his operas some two thousand times. The overblown emotionalism, the implied theme of anarchy for love, and especially the exaggerated nationalism did not carry well beyond the borders of Wagner's native land, and lent themselves to political causes which were contrary to most democratic principles.

Franz Liszt was Wagner's father-in-law, but even so was less than enthusiastic about the post-romantic quality of Wagner's music. Liszt felt that German music had run its course, caught in the inertia of a symphonic tradition where the same basic rythmns repeated themselves endlessly. In this old age, Liszt was very excited in meeting the Russian composer Alexander Borodin who was like a breath of fresh air. Borodin had marvelous new sources of inspiration--peasant music, folkdances, strange haunting songs of the serfs, and wonderful sounds from the balalaika. Mikhail Glinka had incorporated peasant music into his work in the 1830's and had caused a scandal by it among the Russian aristocracy. This coachman's music, as it was called, became the most important new musical development by the end of the century, and influenced the group of Russian musicians known as "The Mightly Five". Along with Borodin, the five included also Nikolai Rimsky-Korsakov, and the talented Modeste Moussorgsky, whose most famous work was the opera Boris Godunov. Moussorgsky had not only pursued peasant music farther than anyone, he also incorporated qualities into his music which seem particularly Russian, qualities of dissonance and coarseness which alienated compatriots such as Peter Tshaikovsky, but which inspired other musicians with his originality and genius.

Tchaikovsky stood halfway between the new Russian genre and the traditional German music. He imitated classical German models most of the time, and used European sources of inspiration, such as Italian street music, but Tchaikovsky was above all a Slavic composer. Other nationalistic composers began to write at the same time, using their own folksongs for inspiration, such as the Norwegian Edvard Grieg, the Czech Antonin Dvorak, and the Finn, Jan Sibelius. At the same time that composers began to consciously incorporate their own national heritage into their music (music which was "lower class", "peasant" music, and never before considered worthy of serious attention), many of them were also strikingly influenced by the Orient. This was true of the Russian Rimsky-Korsakov (although the Orient had a great influence upon Russians at all times), and the Frechmen Claude Debussy and Maurice Ravel.

By the turn of the century in literature and painting one of the greatest new influences was Freud's preoccupation with the subconscious mind. This influence had an impact on music as well, above all on the German composer Gustav Mahler (who had actually had a session of psychoanalysis with Freud in 1910). On the one hand Mahler wrote intensely on the beauties of faith and nature; but his lasting contribution was his sarcastic treatment of parade music, parodies of traditional harmonies. A desperately unhappy man, a Jew, from a poor family where nine of his siblings had died, and who felt alienated from the world, Mahler wrote brilliantly in the new surrealistic way (which few people then understood), on the unconscious self.

Part V

Origins of Psychology

The origin of much of the cultural brilliance in painting, writing and music by 1900 was Sigmund Freud (1856-1939), whose genius affected the lives in one way or the other of most people in the 20th century. Freud was a Viennese doctor who specialized in nervous disorders. He formulated a theory which other people had only guessed at, that the mind has two parts, the conscious and the unconscious. He believed that much of what we do in our lives is because we are impelled by drives or motives or fears which we are not aware of. Illness in particular has two origins--the organic illnesses caused by actual disease; and the psychosomatic, which are caused by disorders of the mind. The latter could sometimes be cured by hypnosis, sometimes by a treatment of psychoanalysis, where Freud persuaded his patients to recount their childhood experiences, and also their dreams. He found that by suggesting that the patients "forget" traumatic experiences of their childhood, many of their grownup afflictions disappeared. Eventually Freud concluded that most mental ills could be traced to sexual problems of one kind or another, especially to sexual repression. He defined the Oedipus Complex as an experience shared by all people, where as children they feel sexual love for the opposite parent, an experience which causes guilt and anxiety unless properly handled.

Like Darwin, Freud's influence was incalculable, although his ideas were often distorted by a simple-minded public. For example, one of his overriding

93

concerns, as expounded in his book, Civilization and its Discontents, is that children are born as little bundles of uncontrollable animal drives, two in particular, sex and aggression. The parents raise the child by "civilizing" him, teaching him to bring his drives under control in an acceptable way. He does this in part by sublimation, by taking out his sexual or aggressive fantasies in an acceptable way, such as by painting pictures, playing sports, or reading books. Unfortunately, some parents overdo their training (much was made of severe toilet training, for example, which supposedly leads to compulsive adults who are perfectionists), so that many people of his generation were anxious, repressed in some way or other, and unable to enjoy life. Freud believed that sex was not to be feared, but enjoyed; it was not evil or unnatural; man could be civilized and still enjoy sexual fulfillment.

He helped create a sexual revolution in the 20th century which began to manifest itself after World War I, aided in large part by the Henry Ford car, and later in the century, by the pill. But Freud loosely interpreted came to mean that one could have sex anytime with anyone, that inhibitions and self control were bad. As a result of such distortions, many acts have been committed in his name by people who had only the vaguest notion of his teaching.

Another important implication of his theories was that man was a victim of his inner self, of his unconscious drives. Darwin, loosely interpreted, had given rise to the view that man was the victim of his environment, that he was shaped by outer forces beyond his control; Freud emphasized inner forces, such as the hidden memory traumas suffered when one was young and vulnerable. Both

The young Sigmund Freud, with his fiancée, Marta Bernays.
(The Granger Collection)

94

points of view had the result that the individual was thought to be not responsible for his behavior. In the field of criminology this conclusion was enormously important. It shifted the blame for criminal behavior from the criminal himself to society, in the case of Darwin. In the case of Freud it shifted blame from the criminal to his unconscious self. The two theories converged in a way, because the traumas a criminal might have suffered which might have led him to crime, could also have come from outside the child, from his environment. Western civilization eventually reformed law codes and trial procedures to accommodate these views, and one of the most visible results has been the murderer or rapist of the 20th century who is considered mentally ill, not criminal. The focus for them is cure instead of punishment, rehabilitation instead of revenge.

A contemporary of Freud who was also a pathfinder in psychology was the Russian scientist Ivan Pavlov. Pavlov's most famous contribution was his experiment with dogs to modify their behavior. He found that by giving them food whenever he rang a bell, he could "condition" them to expect food, so that even when he rang the bell without giving them food at all, they would still salivate with expectation. This was behaviorlist psychology, a field which held that human beings also could change their behavior if they were properly conditioned. For example, a favorable environment and favorable conditioning could produce well educated, well balanced children. This tended to negate the importance of heredity in a child, and led to a running battle between different schools of psychologists and educators on the role schools could have in minimizing the impact of a low I.Q. It appeared that a child's I.Q. could be manipulated at will, and was not inborn. Not all of the findings of Pavlov were happy ones: at the hands of evildoers behaviorist psychology led the way to brainwashing and modern forms of torture in order to condition people for political purposes.

Anthropology

Another science was born at this same time which explored these same ideas, the field of cultural anthropology. Some of the earliest scholars in the field were Americans U. G. Sumner and especially Franz Boas, who in turn trained Margaret Mead and Ruth Benedict with innovative new methods of inquiry. Anthropologists began to compare such different cultures as the American Indians and the natives of Samoa. One of their original premises was that there were no superior or inferior races, merely races which were different due to the impact of different environments. Mead, one of the great innovators in the field, found that even behavior always associated with males and females in western society was sometimes reversed on primitive islands, with the females acting aggressive and the males passive. She also found an absence of puritanical constraints, and a naive enjoyment of sexual freedom among the young. Her book Coming of Age in Samoa became a runaway best seller, and helped produce the 20th century attitude of cultural relativism. No one had the courage to challenge Mead's findings in her lifetime, but soon after her death, a man named Derek Freeman caused a controversy in scholarly circles by trying to undermine all her work.

QUESTIONS FOR REFLECTION

1. What were the most important aspects to the Theory of Evolution? How did Darwin's ideas affect man's thinking about man? Social Darwinism was a way of justifying racism and exploitation of the poor. It changed man's ideas. But did it also change man's behavior?

2. The period from 1870 to 1914 was generally speaking a period of prosperity and stability in Europe and the United States. The period from 1789 to 1848 had been a period of constant turmoil and revolutions. Is it just a coincidence that the earlier period produced a literature and art which was escapist? Is it probably true that only during periods of prosperity and well-being that a people want to face reality in their literature?

3. How many of your own concepts can you identify which go back to Freud? Do you agree with his assessment of human experience? Do you like his approach to mental illness?

4. How many changes and developments in the 20th century can be traced back to Pavlov? Do you think it's true that people can be conditioned in the same way animals can?

SUGGESTED BIBLIOGRAPHY

L. Barnett, The Universe and Dr. Einstein (1952)
J. Barzun, Darwin, Marx, Wagner (1958)
G. Brandes, Main Currents in Nineteenth-Century Literature, 6 vols. (1923)
C. Brinton, Ideas and Men (1950)
O. Chadwick, The Secularization of the European Mind in the Nineteenth Century
    (1976)
G. Costigan, Sigmund Freud: A Short Biography (1965)
E. Fromm, Escape from Freedom (1941)
C. Gray, History of Music (1947)
R. Hofstadter, Social Darwinism in American Thought (1955)
E. Jones, The Life and World of Sigmund Freud, 3 vols. (1953-57)
J. H. Randall, The Making of the Modern Mind (1926, 1940)
R. Raydal, The Nineteenth Century: New Sources of Emotion from Goya to Gauguin
    (1951)
P. Reiff, Freud: The Mind of the Moralist (1959)
P. B. Sears, Charles Darwin: The Naturalist as a Cultural Force (1950)
E. Wilson, Axel's Castle: A Study in the Imaginative Literature of 1870-1930
    (1958)

CHAPTER 7 - THE WORLD: 19th CENTURY

Part I

Imperialism

In the 19th century one of the important characteristics of advanced industrial nations was the rise of a new form of nationalism. For the first time the masses had become aware of a new identity larger than their village or province, and of the necessity for some of these people to rouse up enough fervor to cause a revolution in order to unite. All nationality groups began to think more or less at the same time that each separate one of them was better than all the others. Once they succeeded in creating the nation they wanted, their arrogance and pride which had been so necessary in the first step, now led them to the next: the conclusion that if they were so superior, they should rule other people. All the great powers of Europe acquired colonies in the 19th century, first Great Britain, then France, who obtained Algeria, Morocco and Indochina. Belgium had the Congo; the Netherlands had Indonesia. The Italians and Germans were too late on the scene to plunder the best areas, a circumstance which created a great deal of tension in the world. Italy was defeated in her attempt to acquire Abyssinia in the 1860's (later Ethopia) - the only European nation defeated by a backward African country. They did get Libya and Somaliland, but their defeat at Adowa smarted for the next 40 years. The Germans acquired some desert areas of Africa, and some islands in the Pacific - but mostly they also failed in their quest for empire - and were as a result twice as aggressive and twice as bellicose as the nations who had been more successful.

The competition for colonies in the first place, and then the slow and steady dissolution of the empires as the natives struggled for independence are a major chapter of world history since 1770.

Part II

Latin America

The Latin American revolutions against Spain had run their course by the 1820's: one country after another declared itself an independent nation, beginning with Argentina in 1816, and leaving only Cuba still within the empire. Expectations ran high as the liberators presided over the drawing up of constitutions and the establishment of new governments on the model of the United States. But disillusionment was not long in coming. The North American colonies had over a hundred and fifty years of experience with varying degrees of self-government. But things had been quite different in the Spanish Empire. Latin America had been settled by the crown, not joint stock companies, and it had not been colonized by families. It had been conquered by armies (the <u>conquistadores</u>) and then converted by priests, and

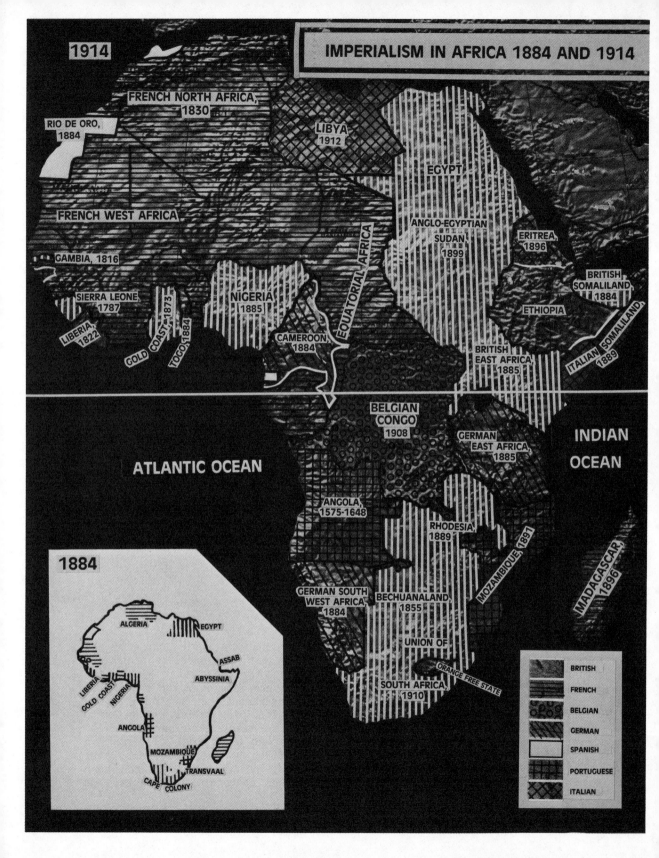

IMPERIALISM IN AFRICA 1884 AND 1914

1914

FRENCH NORTH AFRICA, 1830

RIO DE ORO, 1884

LIBYA 1912

EGYPT

FRENCH WEST AFRICA

ANGLO-EGYPTIAN SUDAN 1899

ERITREA, 1896

GAMBIA, 1816

BRITISH SOMALILAND 1884

SIERRA LEONE 1787

NIGERIA 1885

EQUATORIAL AFRICA

ETHIOPIA

LIBERIA, 1822

GOLD COAST, 1873

TOGO, 1884

CAMEROON 1884

BRITISH EAST AFRICA, 1885

ITALIAN SOMALILAND, 1889

BELGIAN CONGO 1908

GERMAN EAST AFRICA, 1885

INDIAN OCEAN

ATLANTIC OCEAN

ANGOLA, 1575-1648

RHODESIA 1889

MOZAMBIQUE, 1891

MADAGASCAR, 1896

1884

ALGERIA

EGYPT

ASSAB

ABYSSINIA

LIBERIA

GOLD COAST

NIGERIA

ANGOLA

MOZAMBIQUE

TRANSVAAL

CAPE COLONY

GERMAN SOUTH WEST AFRICA, 1884

BECHUANALAND 1855

UNION OF

ORANGE FREE STATE

SOUTH AFRICA, 1910

	BRITISH
	FRENCH
	BELGIAN
	GERMAN
	SPANISH
	PORTUGUESE
	ITALIAN

rather than fostering individual initiative and hard work, the wondrous wealth encountered there had done quite the opposite. The Spanish had found treasures of gold and silver of dazzling splendour, and had transported gold and silver back to Spain in silver fleets sailing twice a year from the new world. The wealth had caused a disastrous inflation in Spain, and rather than contributing to the national well-being had probably been a great evil. Among other things, it had created a new class of aristocrats who bought titles and then forever ceased to work. In Latin America, therefore, there were few entrepreneurs or hard-working middle class colonists, but mostly treasure hunters who were understandably dazzled by the money. The economic difference was compounded by the religious difference. The Protestant emphasis on hardwork and individualism was never fostered. Instead, the Catholic emphasis on obedience and hierarchy dominated the region. The population of Latin America had the political concept of an all-powerful king and his representatives, the viceroys; and the religious concept of an all-powerful Pope and a hierachy of obedient faithful.

Within a decade of independence virtually every new country in Latin America had discovered that democracy did not work overnight, especially among populations who had never had any experience in self-government. Dictators sprang up in all directions. Even Simon Bolivar (1783-1830) who had tried to be the George Washington of Latin America, found the temptation too great to resist and was on his way to becoming dictator of Colombia when he suddenly died. In Argentina a series of dictators began to rule early on, the most famous of whom was Juan Manuel de Rosas (1793-1877), who organized the gauchos to help establish his power, and then subjected the new country to a regime of unspeakable cruelty. He was eventually overthrown in a revolution in 1852, but the pattern was never completely broken. In Mexico the first dictator was Antonio Lopez de Santa Anna (1794-1876), a charismatic but capricious man who contributed greatly to the instability of life in Mexico during the first thirty years of independence. Santa Anna was impulsive and capricious. He would seize power for himself then turn it over to another, only to overthrow him again, as the whim came up. He was the dictator of Mexico at the time when Texas attempted to break away and join the United States, and Santa Anna earned a black spot in the hearts of all American schoolchildren by killing Davy Crockett and Jim Bowie at the Alamo in 1836. Later in the century there was more stability when Mexico was ruled by Benito Juarez (1855-72), but until the Mexican Revolution of 1911 there was virtually no experience in self-government or rights for the Indians.

Economically, Latin America remained underdeveloped until after World War II, despite the great copper mines of Chile or the rubber industry of Brazil, or all the coffee, nitrates or sugar.

Part III

The British Empire

During the 19th century the British Empire grew to majestic proportions, and became known as the "empire upon which the sun never set", the largest empire in the history of the world. Before the 19th century, only North

America had been settled to any large degree by Englishmen, but by the end of the century, Englishmen had transported themselves to Africa, Australia and the Far East.

Canada. The British had gained full control of Canada from the French in 1763, only a few years before they lost control of the United States. But defeating the French had created problems for them which have persisted ever since: the French and English have lived in Canada from that time forth in a state of continuous tension. In 1837 there was a small uprising against British rule, and to prevent further trouble the Canadian governor, Lord Durham, wrote a Report suggesting the reunion of Upper Canada (Ontario) and Lower Canada (Quebec). This was done in the Union Act of 1840. Although the people had self-government, the French/English antipathy persisted, and led to a new effort at solution in the British North America Act of 1867. Ontario and Quebec again were separated, and with New Brunswick and Nova Scotia became the Dominion of Canada. This remarkable event amounted to the friendly liberation of a colony, for Canada henceforth had complete control over its domestic affairs, and virtual control over policy, thus constituting the first step in the establishment of the British Commonwealth.

Australia. Australia gained self-government in 1850 and dominion status in 1901. New Zealand began self-government in 1876 and became a dominion in 1907. South Africa folowed in 1910, but only after a much more complicated series of events.

South Africa. South Africa had attracted the notice of Europeans several hundred years earlier. The Portuguese were the first to pass that way, first with Bartolomeu Diaz in 1488, whose sailors mutinued under him at the Cape of Good Hope; then with Vasco da Gama, who successfully rounded the Cape on his way to India in 1497. The Portuguese settled Angola in Africa, but left no permanent mark on the areas farther south. The first to really settle there were the Dutch, who became a great naval power when Spain and Portugal went into decline. In the 1600's the Dutch sent settlers as far afield as New Amsterdam (which became New York) and South Africa, where they became known as Boers. They tended to be stern Calvinists of the Dutch Reformed Church, with unremittingly strict puritanical behavior, and a general intolerance for other people (this was typical of Puritans everywhere). England acquired the Dutch Cape Colony in 1806, and the first English arrivals clashed with the Boers from the start. The British by the 1820's were among the most liberal group of people in the world; the Boers were dour conservatives from the first, and in addition, had been cut off from liberal ideas for a hundred and fifty years. The Boers began the Great Trek away from the English in the 1830's, eventually founding two new Dutch colonies to the north, the Transvaal and the Orange Free State. England recognized the independence of these states in 1852, but their generosity was as sawdust in their mouths when the Dutch found diamonds and gold on their land.

British feeling at this time was probably exemplified by emperor-builder Cecil Rhodes, who owned interests in the diamond and gold fields, and who became the outspoken prime minister of the Cape Colony in 1890. Quarrels between the British and the Dutch president of the Transvaal, Paul Kruger, led to the ill-fated Jameson raid upon the Dutch in 1896. Kruger defeated the British raiders. Unfortunately, the German Kaiser, William II, chose this

Queen Victoria and her children, beside a bust of Prince Albert.
(The Granger Collection)

moment to express his hostility to the English by sending Kruger a telegram congratulating him. This incident was headline-news all over Europe and aroused feelings of great hatred in the British public against the Kaiser. The Boer War finally broke out in 1899. The British were spoiling for a fight, and the popular mood of the day was exceedingly bellicose. Young Winston Churchill was on an English troop train in South Africa ambushed by the Boers, and persuaded the engineer to fight them off while the troops escaped; he was himself captured and held in a concentration camp. Then he escaped, and with a reward on his head, made his way back to the British lines. Back in England, after that promising adventure he ran successfully for Parliament, thus beginning his long and brilliant political career.

The British won the Boer war in 1902. A lenient peace led to the creation of the Union of South Africa in 1910, which had a former Boer general as its first prime minister. By establishing a democratic form of government, the liberal British citizens of the new state were soon outvoted by the conservative Boers. In the seventy years since that time, South Africa has become increasingly inflexible toward its black inhabitants, citizens who in 1910 had the vote. Today the black population is only one or two steps higher than slavery.

India. The Seven Years' War ending in 1763 gave England complete control of Canada and also of India. But as with other areas of the British empire in those days, the responsibility lay in the hands not of the British government, but a joint stock company -- in the case of India, the East India Company. Beginning in 1773 the crown began to appoint the governor general, and ten years later established a way to supervise the company's political activities. The company began to take over more and more Indian states, allowing the residents a large measure of autonomy, but in 1814 Parliament took away its monopoly on Indian trade, and after the 1830's the company began to focus less on India and more on China. Meanwhile, hostilities cropped up between the British and the Indians, in part due to their widely divergent views on religion and tradition.

The dominant religion in India was Hinduism, an ancient faith which affirmed the truth of reincarnation. One's condition in this life was due to one's state of sinfulness in the previous life, a belief which strongly discouraged efforts to change the social or religious order. Indian society was organized in a caste system of the Brahmins or priest/scholar caste; the soldiers; the farmers and merchants; and the laborers. At the lowest level were the pariahs or untouchables, whose very shadow could contaminate one of the others, and who were given the most vile and evil jobs to perform in Indian society. No one thought of complaining about his station in life, as it was inexorably linked to a previous existence. Animals were also part of the reincarnation cycle, and killing even an insect could thus have serious consequences. Cows were worshipped.

The English objected to a number of specific practices resulting from the Hindu faith, such as infanticide, slavery, and sati (the custom of burning widows on the funeral pyres of their husbands), and made them illegal. In 1833 the English went contrary to the caste system by stating in the Charter Act that no Indian native could be prevented from holding an office because of religion, color or descent (roughly the same language as the Civil Rights Act

102

not passed in the United States for another 150 years). The Indians feared that the British would soon decree forced conversion to Christianity. In 1857 these misunderstandings led the Indians to a widespread revolt against the British forces, with numerous atrocities against British prisoners. The British reacted by ending the tenure of the East India Company. In the Government of India Act of 1858, the British government took over full control of India, reformed the British army, and undertook a series of economic improvements. They irrigated the land, they built 25,000 miles of railroads and 170,000 miles of roadways. They also brought in health services, which had such a beneficial result that Indian population jumped from 150 million in 1850 to 250 million in 1881. There were also political reforms: in 1886, they allowed the National Congress to have its first meeting; that was the first important native political party, and the forebear of the Indian Congress Party of today. By 1907 some factions were already asking for independence, but most Indians were content with the increasing provision the British gave them for representative government. One exception was a brilliant young lawyer, Mohandas Gandhi, who became involved in the inequities based on color in South Africa before World War I. He returned to his native land with the decision to work for the liberation of India from the British.

Part IV

The Far East: Japan and China

Japan

After Vasco da Gama opened the sea route to India in the 1490's, the Portuguese eventually made their way to Japan, and by the 1540's were sending numbers of Jesuit priests to that distant land in hopes of converting it to Catholicism. Francis Xavier and his intrepid colleagues were mightily impressed with Japanese accomplishments--their vast cities, advanced technology, cleanliness and personal habits. They learned the Japanese language, adopted Japanese dress, and made important religious inroads until the Japanese people finally turned against them and in 1616 ordered the Europeans out, shutting themselves off from contact with the outside world except for a few Dutch traders. Japan had been in advance of Europe in many important ways in the 1500's; but in the two-hundred year period of their isolation, Europe began the Industrial Revolution which brought changes undreamed of. One change was that a new country was created which was rapidly becoming enormously powerful--the United States. In 1853, the American navy under Commander Matthew Perry plowed the Japanese seas with a new kind of ship powered by steam, and brandishing guns never seen in those islands. They forced Japan out of their seclusion and opened trade with them by force; but unlike her neighbor, China, Japan did not fall victim to the advanced military might of the west. On the contrary, with a speed and efficiency seldom seen in other countries, they undertook to copy the advanced forms of government, law, banking, and industrialization of the western powers. They imitated the army of the Germans, the navy of the British; and the banks of the Belgians.

The shogun and the emperor disagreed on the appropriate policy to take toward the west; the shogun advised collaboration, but the emperor favored opposition. In 1867 this struggle came to a head when the Meiji emperor forced the last shogun to resign, and taking direct control of the nation himself, moved his capital from Kyoto to Tokyo. This brought in the Meiji period, which lasted until 1912, which was a time of great industrialization and modernization for the country. The traditional warrior class, the samurai, were decisively crushed in the Satsuma Rebellion of 1877, which meant the true end of feudalism in Japan. In 1889 a constitution was put into effect which established an Imperial Diet of two houses, the lower house based on limited voting. There was no ministerial responsibility, and the emperor, who would issue decrees with the force of law, was the real executive, but it gave a forum to the rising middle class and was a beginning of political participation.

Japan began a vigorous foreign policy in the 1890's, in particular by opposing the interests of China and Russia in Korea. One conflict occurred with China in 1895, with the Japanese successful. A second conflict was the Russo-Japanese War, which broke out in 1904. The two nations were a startling contrast at that moment in time, with the Japanese well on their way to becoming a modern industrial state, while the Russians were still lumbering in the Middle Ages. However, the Russians were not short on pride, and along with most other Europeans at the turn of the century, were convinced that the Japanese were an inferior race and could never pose a genuine threat to them. This opinion changed when the Japanese sank the Russian fleet in a brief little skirmish at sea. The peace treaty was signed at Portsmouth, New Hampshire, in 1905, under the auspices of Teddy Roosevelt. It recognized Japanese interest in Korea, Japanese control of the Liaotung Peninsula and the southern half of the island of Sakhalin, as well as railroad concessions in southern Manchuria.

China

The Chinese had a great and ancient civilization, and at many points in time had been far in advance of Europe technologically. They invented gunpowder, for example, and for hundreds of years did not use if for weapons but for religious festivals in fireworks. In ironic contrast, within one generation of establishing contact with China in the 1500's, Europeans were melting down church bells to make canons. Like the Japanese, the Chinese were dubious of any benefits they might gain from contact with the Europeans, and severely restricted European visitors to their land. In 1757 they closed all their ports except Canton to European traders. As might be expected, the nation most annoyed at this was the nation with the greatest amount of trade in the world, Great Britain. The British quarreled not only over the number of ports open to them, but also about the one commodity they had found which the Chinese wanted to import--opium. The Chinese government took a strong stand against the opium traffic in 1839. Despite British opposition, it destroyed vast amounts of it, and the British retaliated by beginning the Opium War. The different attitudes about gunpowder now became rather relevant, for with superior weapons the British made short work of the Chinese. The war ended with the Treaty of Nanking (1842) by which the British gained the right to trade at four ports besides Canton, and also acquired the island of Hong Kong.

The Nanking treaty marked the beginning of western exploitation of China, an empire which by then was technologically far inferior, and which had many troubles politically. The invading powers established the principle of extraterritoriality, which placed all foreigners under the control of their own consuls, rather than under Chinese law or government. Westerners flocked in, either to build up trading empires in the vast populous land, or as missionaries, who scattered in all directions in an effort to convert the heathens to Christianity. The Manchu dynasty, which was then in power, was in general conflict with the foreigners, and also with certain dissadents in their own population. Another conflict erupted, the Taiping Rebellion, which ended in 1858 with the Europeans victorious over both the Manchu dynasty and against the Chinese rebels. They gained even more ports, the Yangtze River was opened to foreign navigation, and the opium trade was legalized. But Chinese opposition, especially to the opium, led to renewed hostilities. The foreigners invaded Peking and burned a royal palace, so that some of them (particularly the Russians) gained even more trading concessions. For about twenty years, there was an uneasy peace, marked by numerous incidents of hostility between Chinese and western individuals. However, not all threats to China emanated from Europe or the United States. In 1895 the newly powerful country of Japan fought China over the independence of Korea, and won. That war encouraged the European powers to demand new concessions from China for themselves, and by 1898 virtually every major Western power had acquired mining rights, railway concessions, and varieties of other trading benefits in China. Russia got Port Arthur; Germany got special rights on the Shantung Peninsula; and France and England also acquired new privileges. One of the few industrial nations which had not participated in this feast was the United States, as the United States had been occupied through the century in settling her own frontier. In China, she insisted on an "Open Door" policy, where all countries would have equal trading opportunities. Her wish for equality was based in part on the unfortunate fact that all the best morsals had already been gobbled up.

Foreign encroachment had repercussions in China, and in 1898 again there was an internal attempt to challenge the Manchu Dynasty, this time with the approval of the emperor himself. The dowager empress Tz'u Hsi opposed the efforts at reform, and had the emperor enprisoned. She ruled with an iron hand until her death in 1908. Meanwhile, there was a serious rebellion against the foreigners, an armed uprising called the Boxer rebellion. The foreign interests in China put together an expeditionary force which crushed the rebellion and again sacked Peking. But once the dowager empress died, opposition to the Manchus and to the foreigners erupted one final time, in the Revolution of 1911. The leader of the Revolution was Sun Yat-sen, who headed up the Kuomintang, or Nationalist People's Party, which intended to reform China and free it from foreign exploitation. Unfortunately, their success in finally ousting the Manchus was not equaled by any success in establishing a unified, successful government. On the contrary, anarchy and civil war broke out, and were not to be dispelled for many years.

QUESTIONS FOR REFLECTION

1. When did most of Latin America gain independence? What kind of political and economic experience did they tend to have in the 19th century? What was the main concern of the United States?

2. Familiarize yourself with the colonies held by European countries in Africa by World War I. Were all the mother countries the same? Were any of them "enlightened" in the way they administered their empire?

3. Which power controlled the Middle East during this period? What were some of the problems in the area by 1914?

4. How did India take steps in opposition to England in the 19th century? What progress had they made by 1914?

5. Compare the fate of China and Japan historically, and in this time of western imperialism. Why were the two so different? What kinds of relations did each have with Europe and the United States?

SUGGESTED BIBLIOGRAPHY

G. M. Beckmann, The Modernization of China and Japan (1962)
S. L. Easton, The Rise and Fall of Western Colonialism (1964)
C. C. Eldridge, England's Mission: The Imperial Idea in the Age of Gladstone and Disraeli, 1868-1880 (1974)
J. K. Fairbank, The United States and China (1963)
D. K. Fieldhouse, The Colonial Empires (1966)
J. A. Hobson, Imperialism: A Study (1902)
W. L. Langer, The Diplomacy of Imperialism, 1890-1902, 2nd ed., 2 vols. (1951)
K. S. Latourette, The Chinese: Their History and Culture, rev. ed. (1964)
W. W. Lockwood, The Economic Development of Japan (1954)
C. J. Lowe, The Reluctant Imperialists: British Foreign Policy, 1878-1902 (1967)
P. T. Moon, Imperialism and World Politics (1926)
B. Porter, The Lion's Share: A Short History of British Imperialism, 1850-1970 (1976)
E. O. Reischauer and A. M. Craig, A History of East Asian Civilization, Vol. II.: East Asia: The Modern Transformation (1965)
E. O. Reischauer, Japan: Past and Present (1956)
J. A. Schumpeter, Imperialism and Social Classes (1955)
Ssu-yu Teng and J. K. Fairbank, China's Response to the West: A Documentary Survey, 1839-1923 (1954)
A. Tiedemann, Modern Japan: A Brief History (1955)

CHAPTER 8 - WORLD WAR I

Part I

The War

It was particularly ironic that the assassination of Archduke Francis Ferdinand caused the outbreak of World War I, for his death, although shocking to all the great powers, was not a source of particular grief to the old emperor. Francis Joseph had disapproved of him in the first place. The crown princes of Europe was told not to come to the funeral, and the funeral was almost insulting in its simplicity and modest guest list. The coffin was spirited away by dead of night and transported, amid a violent thunder storm, to a rural burying place.

But despite his insensitive behavior about his nephew, Francis Joseph decided to use the assassination as a pretext for punishing Serbia. On July 23 Austria gave Serbia an impossibly difficult ultimatum. Serbia complied to almost all of it, and made every effort to avoid hostilities, but Austria declared war on July 28. Germany, in the meantime, had promised to stand by her ally come what may; although the German government did everything possible to keep Russia from getting involved on Serbia's side. Russia was not to be persuaded, however. Ever since Austria's treachery in 1908 over the annexation of Bosnia-Herzegovina, the Russians had been wary, and now that Austria seemed about to wolf down Serbia, they had no intentions of standing by. Russia began to mobilize, first in only a limited way, as a gesture to Austria. But they were worried about the difficulties of getting their war machine operating if general hostilities were to break out; and soon switched back to general mobilization. Meanwhile, the czar and the kaiser, who were cousins, exchanged letters, telegrams and telephone conversations throughout the crisis, even as they had for years, signing the messages "Willy" and "your loving Nicky". But to no avail. One tragic error that summer was the kaiser's assumption that England would stay out of any continental war (based partly on idle remarks made by George V of England). In fact, the British Foreign Secretary, Sir Edward Grey, tall, tight-lipped and taciturn, gave warning that the British would not stay out. Someone high up in the German government, perhaps the kaiser, edited this warning out of a message Grey was sending to Vienna. Thus Austria did not believe England would come into a Balkan war.

Throughout the crucial hours preceding the war, the heads of state were unable or unwilling to stop the machinery from turning. Austria declared war on Serbia July 28; Germany declared war on Russia August 1. The same day the French ordered general mobilization. As the kaiser signed his own order for mobilization in Germany, he suddenly seemed to see into the future. Turning to his naval and military chiefs he said in a tragic voice, "You will live to regret this." Lord Grey in London had a similar premonition. He said, "The lamps are going out all over Europe. We shall not see them lit again in our life time."[1]

─────────────────

[1]Edmond Taylor, The Fall of The Dynasties, (N.Y.: Doubleday & Co., 1963), pp. 228-9.

Gavrilo Princip immediately after his assassination of
Archduke Ferdinand at Sarajevo. (The Granger Collection)

Germany immediately proceeded to put into effect an invasion plan named
after Count Schleiffen, who had been on Germany's general staff at the turn of
the century. Schleiffen called for an attack on France at her most vulnerable
point, the northern boundary with Belgium, followed by a rapid scythe-like
movement to separate Paris from the sea and knock France out of the war.
After that was accomplished they could move in a more leisurely fashion
against Russia. However, this meant moving the German army through neutral
Belgium. William asked King Albert for a free passage through Belgium, but
Albert not only refused, he and his people held off the Germany army for two
weeks, giving the British time to move their troops across the Channel to help
the French. The Belgians resorted to sabotage, and the Germans responded
angrily, setting fire to the medieval library at Louvain and killing thousands
of innocent civilians. These acts turned the British public instantly against
Germany, and rallied public opinion everywhere against German "atrocities".
Soon stories were circulating that Germans made lamp shades out of little
Belgian children; and posters were painted of wrathful Huns impaling Belgian
babies on their dripping sabres.

The Schlieffen Plan failed, and while still engaged with France the
Germans also had to battle the Russians on the Eastern front. There they
scored decisive victories, most notably at Tannenberg, where Russia lost
250,000 men. But in the West, the French held firm at the Battle of the
Marne, after which the western front was laid out in a line extending from

Switzerland to the North Sea--a line which scarcely wavered for the next four years, but which kept two entire armies facing each other, ready to fight to the death over a single inch. At Verdun, one of the eastern points on the line, over one million men were killed. Everyone's expectation that this would be just another localized Balkan War was quickly scotched; the months and months of slaughter and the enormous casulties caused a despair and disillusionment that lasted long after the war ended. Numerous books were written about it: Erich Maria Remarque, "All Quiet on the Western Front; Vicente Blasco-Ibanez, The Four Horsemen of the Apocalypse; Ernest Hemingway, Farewell to Arms. Renoirs' great film, The Grand Illusion, was only one of a series of masterpieces which had as its theme the end of an era, the death of a world.

Meanwhile, the war spread in many directions. One of the more tragic campaigns was the British attack against the Gallipoli Peninusula and the Turkish Straits, the brain child of Winston Churchill, who was then First Lord of the Admiralty. For a number of reasons the attack failed (partly because Lord Kitchener disliked Churchill, and refused to cooperate). The British suffered such terrible casualities that Churchill was forced to resign from his post. On the seas the Germans also began to gain decisive victories with their submarine warfare directed at all allied shipping, including the American merchant marine. It was the submarine campaign which was their downfall, for it brought the United States into the war.

Public opinion in the United States in 1914 was quite different from a generation later, since the foreign power most distrusted by Americans was still their traditional enemy, Great Britain. Germany was widely admired, partly because millions of immigrants had come from German shores, still spoke German, and even published American newspapers in German. The first event which changed this feeling was the sinking of the Lusitania, in May 1915, a British passenger ship with 114 Americans on board. The German government had placed an ad in The New York Times before the ship sailed, warning neutral travelers not to sail on board the Lusitania; but hardly anyone took the notice seriously. The Lusitania was an unarmed luxery liner, but the Germans sank it without warning off the coast of Ireland, claiming it was carrying armaments to England. The cold-blooded slaughter of 1,195 innocent civilians caused a sensation, and turned the American public against Germany. The latter temporarily suspended their submarine warfare on neutral shipping, but on February 1, 1917, they resumed it. Two days later the United State broke relations. The Zimmerman telegram was made public at this point, a message sent by the German foreign secretary urging Mexico to declare war on the United States. These two factors were the decisive ones in leading President Woodrow Wilson to declare war on Germany on April 6, 1917. This was a fortuitous turn of events from the allied point of view, for their cause was just then being seriously undermined: the czar had been overthrown.

Part II

The Russian Revolution

For more than fifty years there had been intellectuals and political activists dissenting with the autocratic government of the czars. Programs of

109

the narodniki and the anarchists had called for the overthrow of the government for years, but for most of that time they had been in a distinct minority. However, the number of dissenters was growing. In 1861 several million serfs had been freed, but were not given land or any satisfactory way to acquire it (except for a brief moment under Stolypin). By 1914 many of these people had become uprooted and even more miserable by becoming industrial workers, who then constituted more than 20% of the population. Those who remained in the countryside were bitter; and those who had moved away were also bitter. Added to this were numerous other problems: the personality of the last czar, and his unpopular, misguided and rather fanatical wife; the scandal about Rasputin and his control over the royal family; the legacy of Bloody Sunday of 1905, when the czar had handled a peaceful demonstration with cruel stupidity; the disillusionment of the Russo-Japanese War; and to a large degree, the considerably greater disillusionment with World War I: in the first year of the war alone Russia lost one million men. They were to lose nine million before the war was over, or 76.3 percent of the men mobilized. In addition to these factors, there were three very able men--Lenin, Stalin and Trotsky--who had been plotting for years to produce a Marxist Revolution. Curiously in the spring of 1917 all three were in exile, and had absolutely nothing to do with overthrowing the czar: that event took place because of spontaneous demonstrations all over Russia. More than a million men had deserted from the army, there were food riots in the cities, there were riots in the countryside for land. In March (February, by the Russian calendar) there were demonstrations in Petrograd (formerly St. Petersberg), and the police refused to shoot. The government

Rasputin. (The Granger Collection)

110

fell, the czar abdicated. An unknown political leader named Alexander Kerensky became the most visible man in the new government. The allies persuaded him to keep Russia in the war, a serious mistake from which the fragile new government could not recover. Lenin had been in Lausanne, Switzerland, at the moment the czar was overthrown, and in April he returned with the help of the German General-Staff in a sealed train to Russia. There with his cohorts Stalin and Trotsky he produced a second revolution in October, overthrowing Kerensky and establishing a Communist government.

Lenin was born Vladimir Ilyich Ulianov in 1870, in Simbirsk, Russia, in a family of minor gentry. When his brother Aleksandr was executed in 1887 for plotting to kill Czar Alexander III, Lenin became an avowed revolutionary, with a particular admiration for Karl Marx. But whereas Marx had predicted revolution would break out in an industrialized country, specifically in Great Britain, and as a spontaneous uprising of the proletariat which would then spread worldwide, Lenin disagreed: he aimed to have it in Russia. Russia was not advanced and industrialized, but was one of the most backward countries in Europe, still primarily agricultural, with peasants only newly freed from serfdom. Lenin also disregarded the admonition that the revolution would come from a spontaneous uprising of the workers and then lead to a dictatorship of the proletariat. Rather, he envisaged a small group of elite workers (including himself) who would lead the people.

In 1864, three years before the publication of Das Kapital, Karl Marx had joined in the formation of the First International Workingmen's Association, which was an effort to unite workers from every country and every variety of belief. It was too amorphous to be effective, and was opposed by governments all over Europe, and also by some of its own quarrelsome members. The Second International was organized in 1889, which lasted until the Russian Revolution. More cohesive than the first organization, and more political, it represented one specific point of view--the Marxian Socialist or Social Democratic parties, which were becoming an important voice in Europe (the German Social Democratic Party was the largest in the Reichstag in 1912). One major division continued to plague their members--those who adhered to a solidly Marxist line, and those who were willing to compromise with the middle classes and with democratic government--"revisionists", who favored avertising the horrors of a class war.

By 1903 at the Party Congress of Brussels and London, the split became formal, with the more moderate faction henceforth following Plekhanov, and called Mensheviks; and the upcompromising radicals following Lenin, henceforth called Bolsheviks. It was this latter group which Lenin brought to power in the fall of 1917; however, Lenin was really a dictator who adapted Marx as he thought best. His first act was to call for the dissolution of the provisional government and for a republic of soviets. He demanded confiscation of land, abolition of the army, nationalization of property, dissolution of the civil service and the police, and above all, peace. The latter point he obtained by the Treaty of Brest-Litovsk, signed with Germany on March 3, 1918. In this astonishing treaty Russia lost the entire Ukraine, the Baltic provinces, Finland, and some of the Caucasus; one third of her population, eighty per cent of her iron and ninety percent of her coal. But Lenin's motives were clear: even then a civil war in Russia was breaking out between the supporters of the Communist state (the reds), and the defenders of the old Regime (the whites), and he had quite enough to do merely keeping his government intact. Even without the civil war, the World War had been so devastating for Russia, with nine million men killed, that there was no hope for a government supported by the people unless the war were ended. However, Lenin also believed that communism would soon be spreading worldwide, and with the advent of their international triumph, national borders would disappear, rendering it purely academic whether Germany or Russia temporarily held the Ukraine. With Russia out of the war in early 1918, the situation would have looked rather grim for the allies; but the defection of Russia was assuaged by the entrance of the United States, coming in with vigorous fresh young troops, and an arsenal of weapons and supplies. The Americans decided the outcome, and won more than their fair share of credit; for in fact, the American troops saw relatively little combat, compared to the European soldiers who fought for four years.

Part III

The End of the War

By 1917, the war had become worldwide. The Central Powers included Germany, Austria, Turkey and Bulgaria. Italy, which had been their ally until the hostilities began, joined the Allies, including France, England, Russia, Serbia, later Japan, the United States and Romania. As the war turned into a stalemate in the west, the battles overseas became increasingly important. Through submarines the Germans attempted to destroy British shipping and to isolate the British Isles. By the end of 1917 they had sunk eight million tons of shipping, and at one point that year, the Germans had reduced the English to only enough supplies to last them a month. The German superiority at sea was also brought home by the Battle of Jutland, fought in the North Sea on May 31 and June 1, 1916, in which the British lost twice as many tons as the Germans. However, there was no follow-up, and the British remained in control of the seas. The Germans not only failed to push home their advantage, but at the same time made the serious error of launching unrestricted submarine warfare on the United States. Toward the end of the war the Germans decided once again to launch a sea battle, but the navy refused to take the ships out. This was the mutiny at Kiel which brought down the imperial government and ended the war. The distant territories of Germany overseas were also the site of many struggles, and although the German colonials fought effectively in every case, by the war's end they had been defeated in Africa and the Far East, and German territories were taken over by other western nations.

In the Ottoman Empire yet another struggle was going on, which brought to the public eye one of the most original characters and genuine romantics of the era--T. E. Lawrence, who became known through his exploits as Lawrence of Arabia. In The Seven Pillars of Wisdom, Lawrence recounts how he led the Arabs in a revolt against the Turks, with many acts of sabotage on the trains of the Berlin-to-Baghdad Railroad. He spoke fluent Arabic and liked to wear Arabic dress, certainly the only time in history when an unpreposseing Englishman became an Arabic hero. He failed in his ambitious goal of creating a united Arabic republic, due largely to quarrels among the Arab factions; but

112

he did see the day when the British took Jersualem. By 1918 they had driven Turkey out of the war.

The future Arabic states of Lebanon, Jordon, Syria, and Saudia Arabia thus won their independence from Turkey; but they did not become free self-governing nations for many years to come; rather, they were included in the mandate system after the war, with Palestine and Jordon going to the British to administer, and Syria and Lebanon to France. In a sense they had exchanged one ruler for another. Worse, from their point of view, their belief that the English were their unequivocal friends was badly tarnished when the British issued the Balfour Declaration in November, 1917. Beginning in the 1890's, at the instigation of men like Theodore Herzl, many European Jews reacted to the growing antisemitism in the Austro-Hungarian Empire and Russia by going back to what they considered their Holy Land, Palestine. By 1917, several thousand Jews had moved there. The British in the Balfour Declaration recognized the establishment in Palestine of a national home for the Jewish people, although they added, rather vaguely, that nothing should be done to prejudice the civil and religious rights of the non-Jewish communities there. Most Arabs, and particularly Palestinian Arabs, were incensed at this British stand--certainly an important step leading to the conflict which would rend the Middle East after World War II.

Part IV

The Treaty of Versailles

World War I marked the end of an era, the end of a way of life. Four empires fell before it was over--the Austro-Hungarian, Ottoman, Russian and German; and the British Empire was beginning to show cracks. A social class was destroyed as well--the aristocratic class, an international elite which met regularly at Biarritz, London and Paris, where they spoke French together. Their sybaritic way of life, with their elegant country estates and stable of impeccable servants was gone forever; for the war had a democratic effect on the class structure of Western societies. In the war for the first time many ordinary men had become officers; after this war many aristocratic men began to work for a living. Servants entered other occupations. The landed estates became too expensive to keep up. In England the end of power of the House of Lords in 1911 was merely the first step in a society in which birth was no longer the only way or even the main way to succeed.

Another result was that communism had been established for the first time, but only through a bloody revolution which destroyed the Russian monarchy and the entire upper class. The image of the czar, his wife, and five children being shot in the head and thrown into a pit, struck terror in the hearts of ordinary people, and left fears which periodically were fanned into mania in the years which followed. A symptom of these fears was the extraordinary myth which persisted for three or four decades that the youngest daughter of the czar, Anastasia, had escaped from death, and had made her way to Paris, where, for the rest of her life, she tried to claim her inheritance. The notion that a slip of a girl could elude four or five determined Soviet assassins captured the fancy of the world and eventually was the subject of books and films, not

113

TERRITORIAL CHANGES IN EUROPE AND THE NEAR EAST RESULTING FROM WORLD WAR I

Legend:
- TO GREAT BRITAIN
- TO FRANCE
- TO DENMARK
- TO YUGOSLAVIA
- TO GREECE
- TO ITALY
- TO BELGIUM
- TO RUMANIA
- BECAME INDEPENDENT
- 1914 BOUNDARIES
- NEW BOUNDARIES AS A RESULT OF POSTWAR TREATIES

ATLANTIC OCEAN

GREAT BRITAIN

NORTH SEA

NORWAY
SWEDEN
FINLAND
ESTONIA
LATVIA
LITHUANIA
GULF OF BOTHNIA
BALTIC SEA

SOVIET RUSSIA

DENMARK
NETHERLANDS
BELG.
GERMANY
POLAND

CZECHOSLOVAKIA
AUSTRIA
HUNGARY
RUMANIA

FRANCE

SPAIN
PORTUGAL

ITALY
YUGOSLAVIA
ADRIATIC SEA
GREECE

BLACK SEA

TURKEY

CASPIAN SEA

PERSIA
IRAQ
SYRIA
TRANS-JORDAN
ARABIA

MEDITERRANEAN SEA

MOROCCO
ALGERIA
TUNISIA

only because of the purely romantic quality of the story, but because it eased the terror inspired by communism: if a mere girl could escape from this new threat to humanity, then there was hope for the human race. The same ingredients were found in the story of Anne Frank, in World War II. Both girls, in fact, were killed.

These fears of communism were exacerbated by additional revolutions which broke out in southern Germany in 1918, and in Romania under Bela Kun. Both were put down, but western publics for years were subject to waves of hysteria, "red scares", and became used to the idea of enduring practically any political ill, provided only that communism were kept away. Hitler capitalized on this when he came to power in 1933.

Where the great empires had once ruled, new nations were now created. In October, 1918, Czechoslavakia declared its independence from Austro-Hungary; in November, Yugoslavia did the same. Both Hungary and Austria also became independent republics. Finland, Latvia, Lithuania and Estonia were recognized as independent. In Germany, the Weimar Republic was created in November of 1918.

The peace conference opened on January 18, 1919. As at Vienna a hundred years before, the victorious powers sent their delegates which one overriding idea--to prevent the enemy from ever posing another threat. The delegates were the "Big Four", Georges Clemenceau, David Lloyd George, Vittorio Orlando, and the hero of the hour, Woodrow Wilson. The Americans had entered the war late in the day, suffered by far the fewest casualties, and in point of fact, had profited enormously. The Americans as a people, and also their President, Wilson, interpreted the cause of the war in their own way, embuing what had been a European power struggle with tinges of idealism typical of the rather naive American republic. The most famous expression of these ideals came when Wilson announced that the war was being fought to "Save the World for Democracy"--which actually was not the case at all, particularly on the part of the czarist Russians, who were accustomed to imprisoning people who demanded democracy. One reason for the idealistic pronouncements was that the Russian Bolsheviks, once they acceded to power, published details of the secret alliances signed by the big powers revealing their war aims. This caused a mad scramble on the part of the allies to dissassociate themselves from such crass behavior--and particularly by the United States, which had not been a party to it in the first place.

In January 1918 Woodrow Wilson announced his Fourteen Points as the American conception of a just peace. They were: 1) Open convenants of peace, openly arrived at; 2) freedom of the seas; 3) removal of all economic trade barriers; 4) reduction of arms to the lowest point consistent with safety; 5) impartial adjustment of colonial claims; 6) evacuation of all Russian territory, and an intelligent and symapthetic attitude toward Russia; 7) evacuation and restoration of Belgium; 8) the restoration of Alsace-Lorraine to France; 9) the readjustment of the frontier of Italy along nationality lines; 10) freest opportunity for autonomous development for the people of Austro-Hungary; 11) the evacuation and restoration of Romania, Serbia and Montenegro; 12) the autonomy of the non-Turkish people of the Ottoman Empire, and the opening of the Dardanelles to all nations; 13) the creation of a free and independent Poland, with access to the sea; 14) the formation of an association of nations, with its goal being the guarantee of political independence and territorial integrity to all states.

Both the Allies and the Central Powers agreed to accept the Fourteen Points as their basis for peace, but that notwithstanding, the participants at Versailles faced insurmountable obstacles. The scope of their task was gigantic: unlike the Congress of Vienna which had reordered Europe after the defeat of Napoleon, the men at Versailles had to make decisions concerning the whole world. They had to deal with the dismemberment of the Ottoman Empire, and they also had to reallocate Germany's former colonies. When it came to pratical decisions, the principles enunciated in the Fourteen Points did not carry as much weight as prior secret treaties, or the wishes of France, England and Japan, who wanted not to create new independent states but simply to annex Germany's possessions. They compromised on the "Mandate System", which provided for turning over portions of both Turkish and German empires to foreign control, subject to the League of Nations. The similarity between mandates and genuine colonies was not lost on many observers, including the Germans.

Other disagreements centered over the demand of France that the Left Bank of the Rhine be made into a buffer state as future protection against Germany. Such an idea ran counter to Wilson's principles. Eventually, after long hours of debate the powers agreed to create a permanent demilitarized zone out of the Rhineland, to be occupied by Allied forces for thirteen years. The Saar was to be administered by the League of Nations for fifteen years, while France gained control of its coal mines. These provisions were not so extraordinary when compared to German seizure of Alsace Lorraine after the previous war; and there was also a precedent for reparations: in 1871 the Germans had insisted on occupying France until the French paid them 5 billion francs. It is relevant to observe, furthermore, that the reparations of 1871 had nothing to do with the blame for causing that war. In 1919, however, the reparations leveled on Germany were out of reason--5 billion dollars a year until the Germans had ultimately paid for the total damage done to civilian property during the war. The sum was astronomical even though it was never precisely defined, for the Big Four could not agree on exactly how much damage had been done. To justify this bill, they added the famous "War Guilt" clause, stating that Germany was to blame for the war.

The war guilt clause was the provision that caused the treaty to be condemned more than any other treaty in history for the damage it caused by its harsh provisions--for arguably, Versailles was one of the leading causes of World War II. In the first place, Germany was not to blame for the war; Austria had been the aggressive party in issuing her intolerable ultimatum to Serbia. Secondly, Russia had compunded the crisis by going into general mobilization, an act widely interpreted as aggressive and portending actual hostilities. True, the Germans had behaved very badly in Belgium, but those acts, however cruel, had not actually started war; the war had already begun. Secondly, the idea that Europe and especially France needed protection against a powerful and aggressive German state was the reason behind the creation of the buffer state; but if on the one hand they wanted an emasculated, defenseless Germany, stripped of its iron and coal, then they were illogical in the extreme to demand the kind of reparations that only a powerful Germany could have paid. The treaty also reduced the Germany army to 100,000 men, and

The Big Four: Woodrow Wilson, Georges Clemenceau, David Lloyd George, and Vittorio Orlando at Versailles. (The Granger Collection)

their navy to six battleships of ten thousand tons, and some smaller ships. Their "war criminals", including the kaiser, were to be prosecuted. Germany lost in all, 13 percent of their territory, fifteen percent of their coal, 50 percent of their iron, and 19 percent of their iron and steel industry. Quite apart from the reparations, 7 billion dollars in German foreign assets was seized; some of its rivers were internationalized, and provisions were made to prohibit Germany from imposing high tariffs, or in other ways from becoming strong again economically or militarily. The Germans were given only 15 days to comment on the treaty, still another unfortunate detail; for afterwards they would claim that it had been dictated to them.

Another conflict broke out when Italy insisted on having the Adriatic port of Fiume, which had been incorporated into the new state of Yugoslavia. A genuine crisis erupted over this issue, and the Italians finally left Paris in protest. But if the Italians were offended and were denied their "just" claim, the Japanese were rewarded with the Shantung Peninula, which had formerly been the property of Germany, even though this violated the rights of China. Throughout the war the Japanese had behaved in an aggressive way toward the Chinese, to the point of issuing "Twenty-One Demands", which were an intolerable infringement on Chinese sovereignty. At this point Wilson felt obliged to give in to the Japanese for fear they would also leave the conference and refuse to join the League of Nations.

Other treaties were signed with Germany's allies in 1919 and 1920. The Treaty of St. Germain with Austria formalized Austria's loss of Czechoslovaia, Poland, Italy, Yugoslavia and Hungary. Austria also had to pay reparations and promise never to unite with Germany. Hungary, Bulgaria and Turkey signed separate treaties. In the case of Turkey, the final treaty was signed at Lausanne in 1923, after the sultan had been overthrown and a republic created under Mustapha Kemal "Ataturk". This treaty was actually more moderate than an earlier one of 1920; it permitted Turkey to keep Asia Minor and a small portion of Europe; they paid no reparations; the Straits were demilitarized and opened to all ships in time of peace, but could be closed in time of war.

There may have been some satisfactory provisions made by the Treaty of Versailles, but they were lost in the plethora of unfortunate aspects of the treaty and its aftermath. One extremely unfortunate circumstance had to do with the United States. Woodrow Wilson was the only American President ever to have a Ph.D. in political science, yet he made one of the most disastrous moves politically that any president has ever made: ignoring the bipartisan nature of the war effort and any Republican votes he might later need, he took only Democrats with him to the Versailles Peace Conference. The leading Republican Senator of the day, Henry Cabot Lodge, took umbrage at this slight. He was born into not one, but the two most distinguished families of New England, the Cabots and the Lodges. It was said that, "Boston is the land of the bean and the cod, where the Cabots speak only to the Lodges, and the Lodges speak only to God." Henry Cabot Lodge may or may not have thought he had a message from God, when he defeated the treaty in the U.S. Senate. As a result of this deed, the United States was never a party to the Treaty of Versailles, and also never joined the League of Nations. Since Germany was not allowed to join until 1926, and Russia was not included until 1934, that organization struggled into existence with three of the five great powers of the world absent.

Part V

Peace Conferences

The world emerged from World War I in an uneasy mood, their worries in no way assuaged by the League of Nations. Foremost in the minds of many Europeans were fears that communists would take over their country; or if not that, the fear that Germany would threaten world peace again. Since this latter is exactly what did happen, one may wonder at the futility of international peace conferences as a genuine deterrant to aggression. As it was, the major powers met on numerous occasions to try to disarm themselves and to try to work out a formula for peace which would be effective. Two disarmanent conferences were held in Washington in 1921 and 1922, the first attempt to control the size of the navies of the great powers. By this time one of the main causes for alarm was the rising influence of Japan. The United States was not so worried about disarming land forces as they were about sea power; thus at the two Washington conferences, the powers agreed on a ten-year naval "holiday", and the scrapping of a number of ships. A formula was provided that capital ships of the United States, Britain and Japan should be in a fixed ratio of 5:5:3. The powers also reaffirmed the Open Door policy toward China. Later attempts to work out further naval agreements failed, largely because of the dissatisfaction of Japan, France and Italy, who quite naturally resented the preferred status of England and the United States.

A different conference was held at Rapallo in April of 1922, although it also was for the purpose of furthering peace. There a treaty was signed between Russia and Germany, two countries which had been mutually suspicious ever since the war, when the memory of the Treaty of Brest-Litovsk soured their relations. This treaty of friendship did not lead to any mutual alliance or economic rapprochement, at least openly. However other powers looked on with distrust, for many feared that it was actually a military alliance. They were right to be concerned, for toward the end of the 1920's, when Gustav Stresemann was chancellor, Germany got around the 100,000-man limit on its army by having the Russians train German troops. Stresemann passed himself off as a strong ally of England and France, and his true colors were not known for forty years, when the secret documents of his government finally revealed the Russian arrangement.

The Treaty of Versailles stated that in 1925 the Allies would begin phasing out their occupation of the Rhineland. However, the Allies refused to take the step because of military violations Germany had made. Stresemann astutely saw a way to dispel their fears by proposing the Locarno treaty, through which France (who was the most fearful), England, Italy, and Belgium, along with Germany, would guarantee the status quo in Europe. With this wily maneuver, Stresemann succeeded in persuading those countries that they were ushering in a new era of good will and peace. To the hopeful admirers of the spirit of Locarno was soon added the misleading platitudes of the Kellogg-Briand Pact.

In September 1928 the American Secretary of State Frank Kellogg, then a wizened little old man, made the trip to Paris to preside over an international renunciation of war, with his elderly co-host Aristide Briand.

Stresemann was there, also old and ill, the first German foreign minister to come to Paris since the Franco-Prussian war, and he had even a shorter time to live than Kellogg. In many ways the pact, signed utimately by sixty-two countries, was as ineffectual as the old men who dreamed it up. Jubilantly, all sixty-two nations denounced war as a means of foreign policy--an act which in its practical application was about as successful, as one observer pointed out, as a declaration against sin.[1]

By that fall of 1928 peace did look promising in Europe, but not because of the wielding of gold-plated fountain pens at signing treaties. Rather, a couple of circumstances had contributed to a German economic recovery, which had benefical results on every aspect of German life.

QUESTIONS FOR REFLECTION

1. Why did the assassination of the archduke start a world war? What was doubly and triply ironic about the fact? Name at least three things which could have stopped the war from breaking out. Name three others which caused it inexorably to happen. Why did German's Schlieffen plan fail?

2. How did the war spread worldwide? How did the United States get involved?

3. Why were there two Russian revolutions? How did the first one bear out the predictions of Karl Marx? What role did Lenin, Stalin and Trotsky play in each? Why did the revolution affect the course of World War I?

4. Compare the goals of the men at Versailles with those of the men at Vienna a hundred years before. What were the mistakes of the men at Versailles? If Germany had been left strong with a powerful army, would World War II have been prevented?

SUGGESTED BIBLIOGRAPHY

L. Albertini, The Origins of the War of 1914, 3 vols. (1952-57)
T. A. Bailey, Wilson and the Peacemakers (1947)
E. H. Carr, A History of Soviet Russia: The Bolshevik Revolution, 1917-1923, 3 vols. (1950-53)
G. P. Hayes, World War I: A Compact History (1972)
J. M. Keynes, The Economic Consequences of the Peace (1920)
D. E. Lee, Europe's Crucial Years: The Diplomatic Background of World War I, 1902-1914 (1974)
B. H. Liddell Hart, The War in Outline (1936)
A. J. May, The Passing of the Hapsburg Monarchy, 2 vols. (1966)
J. Reed, Ten Days That Shook the World (1919)
B. Schmitt, The Coming of the War, 1914, 2 vols. (Scribner's, 1930)
Z. A. B. Seman, The Gentlemen Negotiators: A Diplomatic History of the First World War (1971)

---

[1] Emerey Kelen, Peace in Their Time (New York: Alfred Knopf, 1963), pp. 168-9

A. J. P. Taylor, The Struggle for the Mastery of Europe, 1848-1914 (Claredon, 1954)

D. Thomson, ed., The Era of Violence, 1898-1945 (1960)

Barbara Tuchman, The Proud Tower (Macmillan)

Barbara Tuchman, The Guns of August (Dell)

B. D. Wolfe, Three Who Made A Revolution (1955)

E. L. Woodward, Great Britain and the War of 1914-1918 (1967)

A. Yarmolinsky, Road to Revolution (1957)

CHAPTER 9 - BETWEEN THE WARS: TOTALITARIANISM

Part I

Communism Versus Fascism

One of the difficulties in understanding political ideology in the 20th century is that the far left and the far right had so much in common that it was sometimes hard to distinguish between them. If one were to imagine political regimes of the world lined up from left to right, we would have on the far left, communism, and on the far right, fascism. Democracy, or, more accurately, representative government, would be in the middle. If we then imagined the line to be a piece of string, and then, taking each end, bring the ends around until they touch, forming a circle, we would have a better understanding of the fact that communism and fascism are so similar in some ways, they are practically cheek by jowl; whereas both of them are far away from democracy.

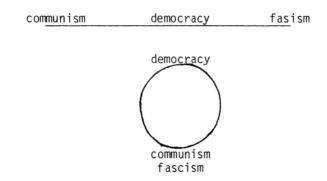

Communism and fascism, both theoretically and in practice, have important differences; but they are alike in that both hate democracy, both oppose freedom and liberty, both are police states.

Differences. Communists are (1) opposed to capitalism or free enterprise; they have state ownership of the means of production; (2) communists theoretically call for an egalitarian society where everyone is equal; the old elite (the landed aristocracy, army officers) is abolished; (3) communism is atheistic; (4) communism tends not to have a cult of personality; although both Lenin and Mao have been idolized, the government isn't tied up with the fate of one man, which is often the case with fascism. When Hitler, Mussolini and Franco died, all three of their countries (Germany, Italy and Spain) became democratic; when communists leaders have died, such as Lenin, Stalin or Mao, the communist regimes have continued; (5) communists are theoretically international, and claim the revolution will spread worldwide, that all workers are brothers.

Fascists are (1) strongly in favor of capitalism, but subservient to the State, and depend on giant industrialists to finance them (such as Krupp in Germany); (2) fascists have an elite society, based on landed aristrocrats, a conservative (usually Catholic) church, and an old style army, with officers who are upper class; (3) fascists are religious (usually Catholics); (4) fascists have often had governments tied to one man, as was the case with Hitler, Mussolini, Franco, and Peron of Argentina; (5) fascists have symbols, such as swastikas and other devices (such as salutes or goose steps) to stir up the people. Governments are usually military, with the dictator and his top men in uniform; they depend on speeches from balconies, constant parades, military music and other devices to keep the people fired up. Some communist leaders such as Fidel Castro have appeared in uniform, but if so, it is not as an aristocratic, heavily decorated officer, but as a common soldier in army fatigues; (6) fascists are nationalistic: Germans were told the Third Reich would last a thousand years; they were told they were racially and culturally superior to all other people.

Similarities: Both Communists and fascists are (1) anti-democratic; they have no freedom of press, speech or religion; they have censorship of the media; (2) in practice both have an elite, for communist regimes may have killed the old aristocrats, but they now have scientists, ballerinas, Olympic atheletes, and Community Party members all living far better than the average person; (3) both have secret police; (4) both are totalitarian, which means they try to maintain total control of the populace; (5) both use extensive government propaganda, often based on lies, with no free press to challenge it (as with Goebbels); (6) in fact, both are nationalistic. In spite of their claims, communist states have important differences and are very competitive at nationalistic events, such as the Olympic Games.

Both communist and fascist regimes have been committed to war against the democracies, and it's a toss-up as to which is potentially more dangerous. At different moments in time, the democracies have feared one more than the other. The Russian Revolution frightened the German people so much that in the 1920's every effort was made to put down communist groups in Germany, while tolerating equally violent and threatening groups which were fascists. By 1933, the democracies began to fear Hitler, and from then until the end of World War II they combined every effort to defeat him, even when it meant coming to the aid of Stalinist Russia. On the other hand, since World War II and the defeat of Hitler, they have swung back in the other direction, and have recognized and supported numerous fascist governments in Latin America and elsewhere, while going to great lengths to fight communist ones.

Part II

Italy

Although Italy had been an ally of Germany and Austria in 1914, she had fought in World War I on the allied side. She thus was at least theoretically one of the victorious nations, and Orlando was one of the leading actors at Versailles. However, Versailles did not bring to Italians what they felt they deserved, the territory of Dalmatia, which was granted instead to the newly created Yugoslavia. Orlando walked out of the peace conference over this issue, and the Italian people felt that they had been badly treated. Gabriele d'Annunzio, a romantic poet and novelist, often called the first fascist, provided his countrymen with a little genuine romanticism at this point when he formed a group of audacious volunteers, and with winning bravado, seized the city of Fiume. There he popularized a uniform of black shirts, a straight-armed salute, and harangues to the people from his balcony, all of which later became integral parts of fascist technique. D'Annunzio was ousted in 1920, but the Italian people were ready for another adventurer to rescue them from their desolation; he emerged in 1923 as the first fascist dictator.

Benito Mussolini shared with other authoritarian rulers of that era a streak of opportunism and a talent for machiavellian politics. In his youth and during World War I he was a socialist and even editor of the most important socialist newspaper, Avanti (which meant he was supposed to be a pacifist); however, he changed expeditiously from the far left to the far right. At the end of the war he began to attack communism, to defend the Catholic Church, to espouse military conquest, and to attack democracy. He began his rise to power in 1919 when he founded the fasci di combattimento, an ultraconservative group of fighters. He urged revolutionary violence, expropriation of land, and attacks on shopkeepers, and when d'Annunzio was defeated in Fiume, Mussolini became the natural leader of all the right-wing dissidents who were angry about the war, out of work, and frightened of Bolshevism. By 1921 there were 100,000 followers, and by 1922, three times that number. As they gained in popularity, so also did they gain in violence. Between 1920 and 1922, hundreds of people were murdered.

Benito Musolini after being appointed prime minister by the kind of Italy.
(The Granger Collection)

In May of 1921 Mussolini was elected to Parliament, along with thirty-four other fascists, by now drawing much popularity by attacking labor, and buttering up big landowners and industrialists. The other legislators were alarmed, but both the army and the king were won over. In 1922 Mussolini had his followers make a famous "March on Rome", cooly arriving himself by train, and the king made him prime minister. He became a dictator within a month, with his own private army to support him. There were still elections to come in 1924, but Mussolini maneuvered cleverly against the opposition. His biggest crisis came over an attack against him by the socialist Giacomo Matteotti, in a book describing fascist outrages. Matteotti was murdered, apparently at Mussolini's own command. The scandal led the opposition deputies in Parliament to pack up and leave, declaring theey would not return until the crime was solved. This was a mistake: it gave Mussolini his big opportunity, for he governed without them. Mussolini took even more control, establishing press censorship and arresting opponents. Eventually all opposition parties were abolished, and Mussolini gained the right to rule by decree. He made much of a concept called the "Corporate State"--blending of government control of the economy (business and labor), but the forms of "private property" remained. He also claimed to follow syndicalism, drawn from the ideas of Georges Sorel, that class warfare would be eliminated if government were based on representatives from economic syndicates--workers, producers, agriculture, sea and air transport--thirteen in all. But in fact Mussolini (who once held eight cabinet posts simultaneously) and his party controlled every aspect of government.

Mussolini received mixed reviews as a dictator. In some ways his government seemed efficient and beneficial: it encouraged Italians to grow their own grain so that Italy became almost able to feed itself; it encouraged tourism, drained swamps, built public works and vastly improved hydroelectric power. It even made the trains run on time. Mussolini also made peace with the Pope in 1929 by the Lateran Treaty, recognizing Catholicism as the state religion. On the other hand, some of the state activities were all fanfare and little lasting improvement. Political freedom, was nonexistent, and a menacing secret police (OVRA) silenced all opposition. Some problems, such as the need for steel or oil, were insurmountable; others were exacerbated: Italy had been overpopulated for years, which is why several million Italians had immigrated to America. But dazzled with prospects of larger armies and military success, Mussolini made emigration a crime, causing unnecessary hardship. And the military glory was not forthcoming. Although Mussolini seized Ethiopia in 1936 and managed to hold onto it despite worldwide outrage, the Italian armies suffered ignominious defeats in the Spanish Civil War (where they helped Franco) and in World War II.

Part III

Germany

The history of Germany between wars is the history of a democracy which did not succeed. The Weimar Republic had an inauspicious birth, coming at the end of a disastrous war. In many ways its creation had been hypocritical, an act to impress the allies with Germany's good intentions, and to win them favorable terms at Versailles. This did not materialize, with the result that the new republic had to bear the onus of losing the war and also losing the peace. The extremists who soon began to attack it from both the far left and the far right made this their first and most devastating criticism. On the far right, of all the malcontents who lounged around the beerhalls of Munich after the war, the most dangerous was a seedy, unprepossesing little man in a worn trenchcoat with pale hypnotic eyes. This was Adolph Hitler, who had been an unremarkable corporal in the war (he got the Iron Cross, but he was never promoted), and had no visible means of support, or any family who cared much about him one way or another.

Adolph Hitler was born in Austria in 1889. His stern humorless father was a customs official, and had provided a middle class homelife, but little or no affection. After his father died, Adolph set out for Vienna to become a painter. Twice he failed the entrance examinations to art school, and then eked out a rude existence in that most anti-semitic of cities, eventually ending up destitute in a home for penniless men. He moved on to Munich to try his luck there, and was rewarded by getting placed in the German army as World War I broke out. His job in the war was delivering messages to the front, a task he filled with reckless abandon rather than courage. In due course he was wounded, and was recuperating in a military hospital when the war ended with Germany's defeat: at this point Hitler went blind, in a case of pure male hysteria. He could not bear to "see" Germany defeated. He was cured by hypnosis, and turned out in the streets like so many thousands of other ex-soldiers with no job, bitter and disillusioned. A popular myth already begun was that the German army had never really been defeated.

When the war ended, Weimar had to deal not only with a sullen and resentful population, but with an economic crisis uprecedented in modern history. There was damage caused by the war, bad unemployment, and outrageous inflation. Because of the unfair and exaggerated reparations bill, the government did not feel pressed to fight the inflation, for the less German money was worth, the easier it would be to pay the bill. They began to print money to spur the inflation on just a bit, but the money became so inflated as to be almost worthless. Bills for ten thousand Deutschmarks had been considered large sums in 1912; in 1922 bills for two billion Deutschmarks were printed on cheap paper and tossed around with contempt, as there was almost nothing they could buy. In desperation some cities printed their own currency, called "Stadtgelt", sometimes on only one side of the paper, purely for local use. The middle classes saw their life savings destroyed, their homes lost; the poorer classes were driven into the streets, to roast potatoes over bonfires, huddling against the cold.

In such a desperate time, political extremists sprang up on all sides. On the far left the Independent Socialists and communist "Spartacists" called for a proletarian revolution. They held several coups, in Munich, and actually set up a Soviet Republic before it was defeated. This created a "Red scare" which haunted Munich for years to come, and encouraged the far right to pose as protectors of the middle classes. The Free Corps, newly formed volunteer units of soldiers, helped put down the Spartacists, and in March 1920 helped the far right hold the "Kapp Putsch", an attempt to overthrow the government in Berlin. Next, a communist revolt took place in the Ruhr valley. After this, the Far Right began a campaign of terrorism against moderates and traitors, and assassinated two prominent Wiemar officials, Matthias Erzberger of the Catholic Center Party, and Walter Rathenau, a Jew. It was at this point, in 1922, when Adolph Hitler emerged as the most vehement spokesman of the radical right, through a small but growing political party. Hitler had stumbled upon the National Socialist German Workers Party, later called Nazis, in Munich in 1919. He joined their tiny force, and urged them forward in a campaign to unite all Germans into a great new nation, to eliminate all Jews from political and economic life, guarantee full employment, nationalize trusts, and encourage small business.

Hitler of the strangely staring blue eyes (which had alarmed the mother of his boyhood friend, Kubizek), Hitler who had tried to sell painted postcards in Vienna, Hitler who had never held a single responsible job other than that of corporal in the war (even though he was thirty-two years old), discovered by 1921 that he had a great and rather unexpected talent: he was a political genuis. His hatred of the Jews, his devotion to Germany, his penchant for violence, and his half-digested socialism coincided with views which were popular all over the country. Furthermore, his way of advancing these views was irresistible: his style of public speaking mesmerized hundreds and later thousands of people in a moment. Witnesses tried to explain how his speaking voice grew more and more insistent, his manner more exciting, until finally whole audiences would rise to their feet cheering him on. By 1921 he was the leader of the party, and had created the SA (Sturmabteilung or storm troops), also called the Brown Shirts, led by Captain Roehm, composed largely of former Free Corps members. These tough and ruthless thugs wore swastikas, patrolled all party meetings, and were soon beating up Jews and leftists in the streets. A menacing outfit, they embodied the concept of violence which Hitler advocated from the start; and it must be said that thousands of middle class and working class Germans were gratified to see "enemies" of the true Germany beaten up in the streets and even murdered out of hand. In 1923 his giddy success inspired Hitler to make his Beerhall Putsch, which was an attempt to take over Munich, preparatory to seizing all of Germany. He was assisted by the right wing Ludendorff, and both were arrested and put on trial--but like so many instances in Weimar, as right wing fanatics they were barely punished. Hitler was sent to prison but served only eight months of a five-year sentence. During that time he was coddled and admired, visited by Nazi leaders, feted with flowers from all over Germany, home-baked cakes, mash notes, and even pleas from confused German women for samples of his used bath water. He used his time well: he wrote Mein Kempf, which became the bible of the movement.

In 1923-24 events took a turn which might still have saved Germany from the tragic years which lay ahead: Weimar recovered from the inflation and economic depression. First, all printing of inflationary currency was stopped, and a new bank was opened to issue new marks, assigned to the prewar value. At the same time, Charles G. Dawes, an American financier, formulated the Dawes Plan which called for the evuacation of the Ruhr by the French, the establishment of a special bank to receive reparations payments, and an international loan to assist German payment the first year. The Nationalists and other Germans vigorously attacked these anti-inflationary policies, but to no avail. As Weimar recovered economically, they also began to "recover" diplomatically--they signed the Locarno Treaties, the Kellogg-Briand Pact, and they entered the League of Nations. They were becoming respected again in the

European Community. In 1929 the Young Plan was formulated, a new reparations plan, also at the behest of the Americans, which reduced the total payment, and assisted Germany to pay at the same time. Later it was established that the United State loaned Germany some six billion dollars to pay their reparations.

At this point the American stock market crash plunged the United States into the Great Depression, and the other advanced inudstrial nations followed. Germany's new depression was all the more dangerous, coming as it did ten years after the postwar crisis which had ruined so many people. The German people now seemed more fearful than before, and blamed the government for all their troubles. The Nazis helped to fan the fears of disaster, and also to blame all the nation's misfortunes on both the Republic and on the Communists.

The economic crisis brought down the German government in 1930, and a call for new elections. President Hindenburg, the stout and sagging old war hero, fancied himself ruling the country by decree, but the Reichstag protested. He dissolved them, and once again they had new elections. Both the Nazis and the Communists gained seats. Over the next several months there was a steadily worsening series of crises, with a constant turnover of chancellors, and a growing number of Nazi seats in the Reichstag, until on July 31, 1932, the Nazis were the biggest single party, with 230 seats. Hindenburg at first refused to name Hitler as chancellor. He appointed Franz von Papen and then General Kurt von Schleicher, but after six more months of crisis he made Hitler chancellor on January 30, 1933.

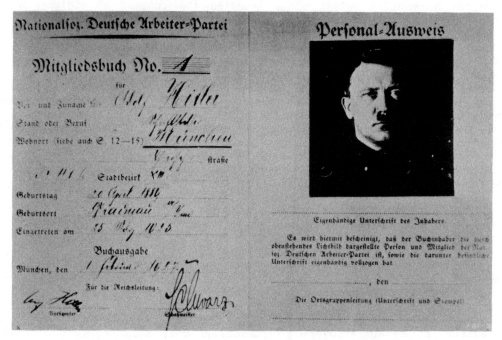

Hitler's membership card of the Nazi Party, Number One.
(The Granger Collection)

Once Hitler became chancellor, he moved decisively in the direction of assuming total power. On February 27, 1933, the Reichstag caught on fire and burned down. At the time, Hitler blamed the Communist party, an excuse which permitted the Nazis to send out their storm troops to use terror against political enemies. However, many caustic observers even at the time regarded the event as all too opportune for Hitler, and blamed the Nazis themselves for the fire. Meanwhile, a demented Dutchman with a great fondness for matches was found wandering near the spot on the fateful night, and may have been the real perpetrator of the deed. Certainly the democratic republic of Weimar was going up in smoke. In March of 1933 Hitler intimidated the Reichstag into passing the Enabling Act, which gave him dictatorial powers. He was above the law from that point onward, and centralized the state, abolished all opposing political parties, assumed the title of president (when Hindenburg died in 1934), and created a ministry of propaganda under Joseph Goebbels. Goebbels, one of the most familiar figures of that era, had been a slavish admirer of Hitler for years. Short and cadaverous, club-footed and dark-haired, Goebbels became the foremost propogator of the creed of Aryanism, the belief that only strong, blond blue-eyed Germans would really inherit the earth. The contradiction was tactfully ignored, as were the un-Aryan features of most of the other leading Nazis, the enormously obese Goering, the buck-toothed Hess, and the dark-haired Himmler and Hitler. Goebbels kept the press under tight control, feeding it constant streams of material on the thousand-year future of the Third Reich, the brilliance of Der Fuhrer, the perfidy of democracies, and the innate evil of the Jews. Most of the familiar rhetoric became canon law at the political rally at Nuremberg in 1934, when more than one hundred thousand Nazis marched smartly past a sea of scarlet flags by day; and by night, past all the shimmering torches needed to set the entire world on fire.

On June 30, 1934, Hitler ordered the murder of several hundred top officials of the SA in an event known as the Night of the Long Knives. Roehm, the homosexual leader of the army, was supposedly planning to turn his one million men against Hitler and seize power for himself. The SS under the direction of Heinrich Himmler, a much more disciplined and elitist outfit, altough perhaps twice as terrifying, replaced the SA; and also formed the basis of the notorious Gestapo, the secret police who would chill the blood for years afterwards.

In 1935 the Nuremberg laws were issued, which defined as Jewish anyone with one Jewish grandparent, obliging such people to wear yellow stars of David, and depriving them of property, livelihood, dignity, freedom, and even their lives. On "Crystal Night" the Nazis began to smash Jewish windows and stores, and soon began to round up Jewish citizens and send them to concentration camps. Jews were said to be racially impure, and biologically and mentally inferior. They were also accused of single-handedly causing not only World War I, but every other ill which had ever beset the German nation. Utimately six million Jews were killed by the nazi regime. To many foreign observers, one appalling aspect of the story was that the German Jews did not protest or revolt against their murderers as they were being led to the slaughter. Such criticisms ignore the teachings of Freudian psychology and German historical tradition, among other things. And they are directly related to the other all-encompassing question, why did the German nation, one of the most technologically, philosophically, and culturally superior nations in the world, cooperate with the demonic leaders of the Nazi era?

Why?

Germans were very advanced in such matters as industrialization, technology, higher education, science, and the arts; but in political matters their experience was limited to obedience to political authority. During the period from the 17th century until World War I, England and France both underwent civil wars which left them with a democratic beginning, so that by 1914 both were comparatively responsive to the wishes of their people. During the same time frame, Germans had evolved only physically, from tiny Brandenberg Prussia to the German Empire. Prussia had been a military state par excellence, and the rigid standards of the German army and the absolute king, both demanding unquestioning obedience, were reflected even in the patriarchal German family. The German people had no experience with democracy when the Weimar Republic was thrust upon them in 1918. Erich Fromm explains in his provocative analysis, Escape from Freedom, that for people raised after centuries of authoritarian obedience, the decisions demanded by a democratic state are a hardship. Freedom is a responsibility, and people who are unused to it often long for the security of authoritarianism.

The Weimar Republic was never popular, and on the contrary, was blamed for the defeat of World War I and for the disastrous peace treaty. It never functioned without serious opposition from both the far left and far right, which included political assassinations, private armies, and a number of attempted coups. However, the men of Weimar cannot escape censure for many foolish decisions they made, which worsened an already bad situation: they purposely inflated German money in the early twenties; they systematically exonerated dangerous enemies of the republic if they were from the far right, even as they systematically punished enemies of the far left; and they secretly trained German troops in Russia in violation of the Treaty of Versailles, which tells us that Weimar diplomats were nationalistic and potentially dangerous to the peace of Europe. They also included in their midst such far-right authoritarian types as Hindenberg and von Papen, who were dangerous in their own right and even more dangerous in their naive evaluation of Hitler.

A good question to ask is this: had there been no Hitler, would some other man have risen to the top in Germany and caused another war? Or was Hitler unique in his abilities for bringing out the very worst ambitions of the German people? It is hard to imagine another man with Hitler's same political genius, for seldom in history has anyone led so many people on such a rabid quest for glory. Part of his genius lay in his extraordinary gifts as an orator, his sense of timing, his intuitive grasp of exactly how far he could go, working the German people up into a frenzy of adulation even when when he was advocating violence and death (one is tempted to say, especially when he was advocating violence and death). Hitler improved the German economy, constructed the famous autobahns, inspired the people to endure any hardships in return for greatness, and through Albert Speer, his architect, even strove for genuine beauty. Had he chosen to limit his goals to such commendable ones as these, the world would regard him as a great man.

Ironically, one reason why the German people succumbed to Hitler's will is the same reason why the Jews did not revolt against him: both groups were raised in the same tradition of obedience to authority. The Jews had been the scapegoats of the Western world for two thousand years. They had learned tactics for survival which had usually served them well: they minded their own business, studied hard and worked. They also obeyed the law in every country where they lived (their crime rate tends to be nonexistent, even in such violent societies as the United States). In Hitler's Germany, these were (ironically) the wrong techniques for survival: obedience cut no ice with the ruthless and hardened Nazi executioners.

Part IV

Russia

The early years of the Soviet regime were difficult. Lenin had to take Russia out of World War I, win the civil war between the reds and the whites, and restore order to a country devastated by anarchy. He accomplished the first two objectives, only to find a new revolt on his hands in 1921, a widespread uprising by Russian peasants against the Communist regime. They objected to losing their entire crop to the state, and also to numerous other communist policies Lenin's new government had announced. Frightened by that development, Lenin temporarily abandoned much of the communism in a program called the New Economic Policy, or NEP. To a considerable extent he realized that the goal of worldwide communism would be long in coming, and Russia needed her economic resources (a departure from his previous sanguine attitude at the Brest-Litovsk Treaty). The state stopped seizing the entire crop of the peasants, permitting them to sell a certain amount; and it permitted some private enterprise to return to light industry and trade, or, as Lenin put it, a partial return to capitalism.

Lenin lived barely long enough to see the NEP effect an economic recovery: he died of a stroke in January 1924. Before his death he had worried about a power struggle between Stalin and Trotsky to succeed him, and did what he could to prevent it by naming Trotsky as his heir. Stalin's high-handed behavior and acquisition of power on a number of crucial committees alarmed Lenin, and his last gesture was an attempt to discredit him--to no avail. The struggle was waged for four years, but Stalin's triumph was probably inevitable. He had become commisar of nationalities, commisar of the Workers' and Peasants' Inspectorate, a member of the Politbureau and general secretary of the Central Committee of the Communist Party. He had helped create the new Union of Socialist Soviet Republics, and had power over some 65 million people. He controlled party patronage, trade unions, managers of industry, and the commission in charge of party "purity", which meant purges. Lastly, he was machiavellian in the extreme, capable of following any party line, supporting any man as long as it served his purpose. He began the cult of Lenin even as he discarded the NEP. He fought Trotsky on every issue, but especially opposed Trotsky's insistence on the internationalism of communism, calling instead for "socialism in one country", and used two important figures, Zinoviev and Kamenev, to help him in his struggle. Trotsky fled the country in 1927, and spent the next decade trying to find a place for himself elsewhere: he was murdered by Stalin's orders in Mexico in 1939. Stalin also turned against both Zinoviev and Kamenev, and consolidated all power unto himself.

The young Stalin.
(The Granger Collection)

In the period from 1928 until his death, Stalin performed remarkable deeds, almost equalling Hitler in his barbarity, and yet succeeding far more than Hitler in his ultimate conquest. He came to power in a country still scarred by civil war and famine, an agricultural country handicapped by medieval attitudes and antequated institutions, and in one generation transformed it into one of the two leading nations of the world, with an arsenal of nuclear weapons. But the toll in human lives may have been eleven to thirteen million. Reversing the NEP, Stalin called for collectivization of agriculture, a policy vigorously opposed by the successful class of peasants called kulaks. The better to confiscate their crops and land, he enlisted the smaller unsuccessful peasants against them, and in 1929 called for liquidating the kulaks as a class. No one knows exactly how many people were killed, perhaps ten million; but hundreds of thousands were machine-gunned or axed to death, or forced into slave labor camps, during the vicious conflict over the land. Crops were burned and more than half the livestock in all of Russia were killed (50% of the horses, 45% of the cattle, 60% of all sheep and goats), which led to a nationwide famine. Within one year 50% of all farmland had been collectivized, and within ten years, 96%, mostly in the form of kolkholzes. In kolkholzes peasants tended to own their own homes and some livestock, and worked the land like factory laborers, turning over a fixed amount of produce to the state. Industry also was collectivized, and also urged on to greater production through five-year plans, which began in 1928. Stalin drove Russians to impossible heights, demanded impossible amounts of pig-iron, electricity, and tractors, and launched two more five-year plans even as the country failed to achieve the goals of the preceding one. The teriffic pace was part of a calculated plan, and it worked extremely well. Workers tended to feel as important as soldiers on the front, and some people said the casualties were almost as high. But by 1941 Russia had almost caught up with Germany in national output. Their standard of living was not as high, and has never been, then or since; but then the standard of living was never the issue.

Like Hitler, Stalin had a bizarre personality with a distinct flair for paranoia; and he indulged his fears as did Hitler, with purges. Hitler had the SA decimated in one night, the Night of the Long Knives. Stalin purged his political enemies more slowly, through a series of sensational public trials in the late thirties. Between 1936 and 1938 some of the most important party leaders in Russia confessed to various crimes, such as plotting Stalin's death. Zinoviev and Kamenev admitted these charges in the first trial, as did several dozen others during those two years, and all were executed. The Western world watched the proceedings, dumbfounded, unable to explain the robot-like way the confessions were presented, and concluded that the participants had been brainwashed. But aside from the comparative handful of public proceedings, thousands of other party figures committed suicide, were executed, or disappeared without a trace during this time, including all the members of Lenin's Politbureau except Stalin; fifty out of seventy-one members of the Central Committee; the top commanders of the Red army--or virtually anyone in the entire state who could ever constitute a threat to Stalin's rule. By World War II, Russia had become an authoritarian state almost as effectively controlled as Germany.

Those old enough to remember life under the czar would have been hard pressed to prove that the country had changed for the better politically: they still had an authoritarian rule, a secret police, and a total absence of human rights or freedom. The former aristocrats had been killed or had fled into exile, their belongings and property seized by the state; but the new Russia threw up an elite of its own, consisting of party members, scientists, and figures of reknown such as ballet dancers and olympic athletes. These people acquired dachas, or country estates, fast cars, and large apartments, vacationed on the Black Sea, and lived as much above the law as the old counts and dukes ever had. For a worker it was hard to see a real difference. The police aspect of Russia became particularly frightening to the West in 1948 when George Orwell, an English writer, published 1984, one of two books (the other was Animal Farm) in which he did a masterly job depicting the evils of communism. Orwell himself had been a communist, and had lived the life of the poorest wretch in the world when he was a starving kitchen worker in Paris (see Down and Out in Paris and London); but when he went to fight in the Spanish Civil War on the Communist side, he suffered a sharp shock to his ideals. His book became one of the most important political statements of the 20th century.

Part V

Spain

Spain was a country with historical differences which set it apart from the rest of Europe. For eight hundred years it had been Arabic, and even

133

after the Moors were finally defeated at Granada, the legacy of the Middle East lingered on. Over-reacting against Islam, the Spanish became the most fervent Catholics of Europe, and turned the Reconquista against the Moors into a religious crusade. After 1492 the Inquisition was created to hound out other internal enemies, the Jews and later the Protestants, and hundreds of religious dissenters were burned in rituals called <u>autos-da-fe</u>.

In the 19th century the Catholic Church of Spain concluded that Liberalism was as dangerous to the faith as Islam, Judaism and Protestantism, and began a new crusade. The church came down on the side of the large landowners, an absolute monarchy and a strong army. This time the Spanish poor, who vastly outnumbered the wealthy (and there was no middle class to speak of), felt that their best interests were being attacked, and they deserted the Church in droves. Many Spanish peasants became anarchists, following the Russian Bakunin. They had no plan for a new state, they had had no real experience with democracy, and only one long ago flirtation with a constitution: all they wanted now was to destroy authority. Anarchists sprouted up like mushrooms in Europe in the 1880's and 90's, but in Spain they were more like thistles--the only thing to grow in the barren soil, tenacious, ubiquitous, and painful to anyone who touched them. One bomb was thrown at King Alfonso XIII on his wedding day: it did not kill the king or his bride, but it killed other people, and cast up a ghastly debris of bloody and broken limbs into the royal carriage.

In the 1920's Alphonso XIII was king, but Spain was actually ruled by a dictator, General Primo de Rivera, until his death in 1930. In 1931 there were elections. When the liberals won, the king abdicated, and a Republic was created. A constitution was drawn up, and any casual observer might have been deceived into predicting a viable new government. But in point of fact, the right and the left in Spain were divided by a chasm which had no possible bridges or common ground whatsoever: the right was rigidly Catholic, monarchist, aristocratic and militaristic; the left was fanatically atheistic, and not really republican at all, but mostly anarchist. Too many people in Spain thought that the best or only means of opposition was violence. There was no tradition of compromise or political debate or democratic exchange of opinions. Both sides began to kill each other, so that Madrid became a sort of battleground long before the Spanish Civil War broke out. After it broke out, over one million people were killed.

In July of 1936 General Francisco Franco launched a military uprising, whereby the army barracks in every important Spanish city were supposed to overthrow the local government. Half of the barracks duly revolted, and Franco flew from the Canary Islands to the mainland to take charge. But the other half, including major urban centers such as Madrid and Barcelona, remained loyal to the Republic. The war lasted three years, and brought out a frenzy of emotion not only in Spaniards, but in conscientious people all over the Western world. The war became the testing ground for fascism versus democracy; and many idealistic young poets and novelists flocked to the scene to immortalize the conflict--including Ernest Hemingway and George Orwell. However, in Spain even more than in most wars, the true nature of good and evil was difficult to distinguish. The fascists included the Falange, the fascist political party founded by the great hero of the right, José Antonio Primo de Rivera (the son of the dictator), and the Carlists, both groups unalterably opposed to democracy, free speech, or any of the basic human rights generally accepted by that time in Western countries. It was easy to oppose such views, and all democratically inclined people did. However, defending the republic became complicated when Russia entered the war on their behalf: after that the conflict changed from fascism versus democracy, to fascism versus communism and anarchism, at least on many battlegrounds. That was really the issue in Madrid, where the tough and desperate citizens held out for three years before finally falling to Franco; it was true in Barcelona, too, where George Orwell found himself surrounded by anarchists and Trotskyites and in more trouble from them than from the haphazard shots of the fascists on the next hill. Atrocities abounded: the leftists murdered priests and nuns, tortured them, and even dug up corpses of the religious dead and desecrated their bodies. The fascists shouted "Long live death!" and performed atrocities themselves: in Badajoz they lined up hundreds of people in the bull ring and symbolically shot them down in the sand.

Italy and Germany entered the war on Franco's behalf, so that in the most serious confrontation between the forces of democracy and totalitarianism before World War II, all the democratic countries stayed out: instead, the totalitarian countries themselves were opposed, Russia on the left; the other two on the right. The United States considered it a crime to fight in the war, but many men did just the same, forming the Abraham Lincoln Brigade and the George Washington Brigade. Frenchmen, Englishmen, and passionate foreigners from all over flocked to join the Republic, creating the International Brigade, an extraordinary outfit which took part in the defense of Madrid, especially in the fighting around the university. The soldiers considered themselves comrades, and every "request" for attack had to be translated into thirty or so different languages. The most important act of foreign intervention was the attack on Guernica, a tiny Basque village, by German pilots, on market day. The massacre of women and children that day was an outrage. Pablo Picasso, Spain's most famous artist, immortalized the tragedy in a striking black and white Cubist painting. The spectacle of Germans trying out their new weapons and bombing civilians gave the war its most famous nickname, the "Dress Rehearsal for World War II". In the summer of 1939 the fascists forces took both Madrid and Barcelona, and their victory was a defeat for freedom everywhere (although it is arguable that a victory by Russia on the other side would also have been a defeat). Only a few weeks later Stalin and Hitler joined forces in an alliance, in a cold-blooded scheme to divide Poland between them. Germany invaded on September 1, and World War II began.

Part VI

Japan

Japan was the only country outside the West to be modern, advanced, industrialized and imperialistic before World War I. For awhile in the early twenties the Japanese were on the brink of democratic government. They attained universal manhood suffrage in 1925, they had political parties and fairly powerful trade unions. However, these democratic strivings were quashed in the 1930's when the naval and army officers, many of them descendants of feudal samurai, manipulated the emperor and Japanese respect for military power into a military dictatorship. Elections to the Diet continued, but the real power gravitated to the military and stayed there. The Japanese tradition of authoritarianism, respect for the past, obedience, and self-control all redounded to the benefit of the dictatorship. The regime continued worship of the emperor, but like the fascists of Europe, they coupled this with a demand for land, using their growing population as an excuse for imperialism. Like the Germans and Italians, they had disdain for equal rights and freedom, and they ruled by secret police. In 1931 they invaded Manchuria, and within ten years were well on their way to carving out an empire.

QUESTIONS FOR REFLECTION

1. Was the rise of Hitler inevitable, do you think? If so, what was it about Germany after World War I which made them so vulnerable? What was more important, the psychological effect of defeat, or the economic chaos?

2. What was particularly ironic about Hitler taking over in Germany? What characteristics did Germany have which made it seem most unlikely, or even impossible? What was there about Hitler's own background which made his success also seem unlikely?

3. How did Hitler come to power? Once chancellor, how did he consolidate his rule? What steps did he take which showed early on his attitude about foreign policy?

4. Could the other countries have stopped him if they had acted forcefully in 1935, 36, or 37?

SUGGESTED BIBLIOGRAPHY

A. Bullock, Hitler: A Study in Tyranny (1964)
E. H. Carr, A History of Soviet Russia (1950-69)
E. Eych, A History of the Weimar Republic, 2 vols. (1962)
J. C. Fest, Hitler (1974)
A. Hitler, Mein Kampf (1939)
G. L. Mosse, The Crisis of German Ideology: Intellectual Origins of the Third Reich (1964)
F. B. Randall, Stalin's Russia: An Historial Reconsideration (1965)
A. Rossi, The Rise of Italian Fascism, 1918-1922 (1938)
D. Schoenbaum, Hitler's Social Revolution, 1933-1939 (1967)
W. L. Shirer, The Rise and Fall of the Third Reich (1960)
B. F. Smith, Adolph Hitler: His Family, Childhood and Youth (1967)
D. Mack Smith, Mussolini's Roman Empire (1976)
H. Thomas, The Spanish Civil War (1961)
D. W. Treadgold, Twentieth Century Russia (1959)
H. R. Trevor-Roper, The Last Days of Hitler (1947)
E. Wiskemann, Fascism in Italy: Its Development and Influence (1969)

Part I

The United States

The United States emerged from World War War I as the greatest power in the world, something no one, least of all the Americans, was ready to admit or incorporate into public policy. On the contrary, despite the very minor losses in the war (115,000 killed, compared to more than one million each in the European countries), Americans reacted strongly against any permanent involvement on the world scene. Their attitude for the next twenty years was determinedly isolationist, summed up by President Harding's malapropism, that the United States wanted to return to "normalcy". For Americans, the normal was a life cut off from European affairs, and the first and most striking evidence of this was the American refusal to sign the Treaty of Versailles or to enter the League of Nations, even though the United States helped create both.

Despite all the talk about normalcy, the United States after World War I was quite a different country from what it had been before, and certainly the era of the "Roaring Twenties", marked as it was with Prohibition, Model T cars, gangsters, the Charleston, and giddy prosperity, was a new experience. One note was set by the marked ambivalence in the nation's moral behavior. The 18th Amendment, on the one hand, was a manifestation of the holier-than-thou puritanical, Bible-belt attitude, that drinking, gambling and other such vices were almost as bad as murder. Several generations of women had smashed up bars along with Carry Nation to win the fight against demon rum. However, the other side of the story is that during the same period when the federal government was trying to legislate private morality, the first salvos were fired in the sexual revolution. After the war, American women shortened their hair (they "bobbed" it), and their skirts. They threw away the whalebone underpinnings of their mothers, and scandalized the older generation with their freely exhibited bodies, their smoking ("Take a Lucky instead of a sweet"), their wild dancing, and their drinking--for some people took the prohibition of drinking as the very act which persuaded them to drink in the first place. Americans have traditionally been defiant of authority (in contrast to the Germans): one of the best ways to persuade an American to do something is to prohibit it. People drank bathtub gin, home-brew beer, "bootleg", and even vanilla extract, before Prohibition was finally repealed in 1933. Two other invitations to immorality were provided by Sigmund Freud, whose teachings began to assume genuine importance among the mass population at this time, specifically the concept that sex was not a dirty word; and by the Model T car, which provided the setting to test out Freud's concept. Birth control was still by no means a polite subject; Margaret Sanger, its foremost advocate, had been repeatedly jailed and abused over the years, but that concept also began to take hold in the twenties. Thus began the sexual revolution which continued unabated on through the 1960's.

Many Americans were disillusioned with World War I, despite their limited contact with it, and a spate of talented novelists, including F. Scott

Fitzgerald and Ernest Hemingway, described the period as the "lost generation". But for most people, Americans were more prosperous than at practically any time in their history, and probably more confident of their own financial prospects than at any time before or since. The stock market boomed and even relatively ordinary folk invested in it. The presidents who presided over this last great era of prosperity and naiveté were all Republican, all in accord with the basic Republican philosophy of government, which was that the least government the better. The country could run itself.

Warren Gamiliel Harding was a good looking but rather vapid man, the only president, so far as is known, who ever fathered a child in the Senate cloak room. He may also be the only president murdered by his irate wife: he died in office from the effects of a poisonous crab. Harding's other claims to fame are also tainted: his administration was involved in a serious piece of corruption known as the Teapot Dome scandal. Calvin Coolidge, his successor, was an individual from Vermont, whose taciturnity was his one distinction. One story told about him was that at a dinner party a gushing middle-aged matron begged him to talk to her, as she had a five-dollar wager that she could persuade him to say three words. Coolidge looked at the woman, and said: "You lose." Another story attributed to numerous wits, including Dorothy Parker, was that someone rushed up with the news that Coolidge was dead. "How could they tell?" asked the wit. Coolidge's other presidential quirk was to take a daily nap and turn off the bell cord--for those were the days of another age when even the president of the United States could lie down on the sofa with a newspaper over his face, knowing nothing important was apt to happen. However, under the term of Herbert Hoover, the third of these Republican presidents, something did happen which affected history inside the country and out, the Great Depression.

Americans of all classes had been borrowing money freely, spending freely, and investing on the Stock Market, at a time when stock watering and borrowing money on margin was widely practiced, with almost no insurance and few controls. The market fell on Black Friday in October of 1929, and plunged steadily downward for the next four years. At its worst, sixteen million Americans were unemployed, or one-third of the national labor force. Millions of people lost all their savings when banks failed; others lost their homes; a mass migration ensued in the direction of dreamland, California. The wretched poor chugged down dusty highways in sputtering rusted vehicles, only to end up in a shantytown of cardboard boxes with newspapers on the walls. These "Oakies", as they were called, were immortalized in The Grapes of Wrath, by John Steinbeck; and their haunted faces still look out of the magnificent photographs of the Library of Congress. Herbert Hoover, as is the way of the American people, was personally blamed for the disaster, and the Democratic Party gathered eagerly for their convention of 1932, knowing the next election was almost certainly theirs. Some people speculate that in times of trouble the country invariably throws up a winner, and it would seem that Washington, Lincoln and Wilson had presided over earlier crises with skill. This time the country threw up the man most historians acknowledge to be the greatest president of them all, Franklin Delano Roosevelt.

Roosevelt was an extraordinarily handsome and rich young man, related to that other president, Theodore, and also related to the the woman he married, Eleanor (generally accepted as the greatest first lady). He earned a

Franklin D. Roosevelt, photographed at sea during World War II.
(The Granger Collection)

gentleman's "C" at Harvard, dabbled in local New York politics, and mostly because of his illustrious connections, became Assistant Secretary of the Navy during World War I. He was nominated for vice-president in 1920, in a race which the Democrats lost; and a short time afterwards suffered a catastrophic bout with polio, becoming paralyzed from the waist down. It is tempting to attribute to polio the character which eventually formed in the sleek young man. For months he lay in a suicidal depression, unable to move. With the encouragement of his wife and treatment at Warm Springs, Georgia, he began to recover his will to live. By 1928 he was a new man. Roosevelt won the race for governor of New York that year, despite his paralysis; and by 1932 was the frontrunner of the Democratic Party. He had emerged as a national leader of sensitivity and great charisma. At all times an innovative man, Roosevelt was the first ever to accept the nomination in person at the Democratic Convention (and also the first to fly there); he was the first president to use the radio effectively (the "fireside chats"); the first since Lincoln to use humor as an effective weapon. During the first hundred days of his administration, Roosevelt persuaded Congress to pass more legislation than any president in U.S. History (a record finally broken by Lyndon Johnson), and began to restore confidence in the country's future with a series of memorable speeches. Some of his words--"The only thing we have to fear is fear itself"--contributed substantially to the economic recovery, and endeared him to millions (although conservative Republicans loathed him, then and later). Roosevelt created the New Deal, wich was an impressive arsenal of weapons against the worst ravages of the Depression, a series of acts which created agencies to help specific groups in American society. These included the National Recovery Act (NRA), the Agricultural Adjustment Act (AAA); the Civilian Conservation Corps (CCC); the Works Progress Administration (WPA); and Social Security.

In 1932, the United States lagged substantially behind the English and the Germans in terms of providing unemployment insurance, old-age pensions, and accident insurance; and in a matter of a few months the New Deal tried to provide all of it. Some of the legislation was intended to help employ people at government expense for the duration of the depression. The WPA, for example, provided any number of useful and interesting jobs for such people as out-of-work artists (commissioned to paint murals) or historians (sent to record the experiences of former slaves, while they still lived to tell the story). The WPA also built sidewalks all over the country, large numbers of them still emblazoned with their acronym; or bridges, or roads. Critics were numerous, and they included the Supreme Court, which in fairly short order declared several of the very first measures (the NRA and the AAA) unconstitutional. Roosevelt was outraged, and in 1937 proposed legislation which would enable him to increase the number of justices on the court (there were then nine). This act was reminiscent of the efforts of King George V to increase the number of lords in England if necessary in order to persuade the House of Lords to give up their right of veto. The existing lords gave into the king, and the existing justices gave in to Roosevelt, so that no new positions were created in either case. In the United States, both sides claimed victory: but it is a fact that the Supreme Court desisted from declaring the New Deal unconstitutional after that moment.

The New Deal constituted a revolution in American history, and vastly expanded the role of the federal government in looking after the population, for better or for worse. Did it work? Certainly there was an initial recovery by 1935; and by 1937 there was another slump; so again, both critics and admirers of Roosevelt claim the victory. In reality, the events producing World War II decisively effaced any traces of real proof one way or other: the fact is that the war created an economic boom for Americans, just as had World War I.

Part II

Great Britain

England lost 750,000 men killed in World War I, and 1,500,000 wounded. They also suffered incalculable economic losses in wasted productivity, in disruption of world trade, and in the encouragement given to other nations, including the United States and Canada, to produce goods which after the war seriously competed with British industry. Unlike the United States, which had come out of World War I substantially richer and more powerful, Britain more closely resembled Germany and France in their straitened economic circumstances. More than a fifth of English laborers were unemployed after the war, and their numbers never went below a million before the next war began--an obvious sign of industrial stagnation. Moreover, one of the most important British industries--coal--was in serious trouble due to international competition. The miners wanted higher wages and better benefits, but in the depressed state of the economy the owners were not sympathetic. In 1926 there was a general strike on behalf of the miners. The strike failed, and although tempers ran high, once again the class conflict bitterly predicted by Karl Marx in England was conspicuous by its absence. Neither communism nor fascism took hold in England.

After World War I England took their suffrage one step further and enfranchised women over thirty (later reduced to twenty-one), a victory at last for dozens of female demonstrators, the suffragettes, who had marched and gone to jail for women's rights. They also got the vote in the United States, but in many countries (including France and Italy) they had to wait another generation.

The political battle in the period was fought between the Labour Party and the Conservative Party, as the old Liberal Party had wasted away to a shadow. The Conservatives won heavily in 1918, and dominated the government between the wars. One of the main conflicts between the parties was the economic crisis posed by the new industrial competition from the United States. The aging plants, featherbedding and other problem of industry made it difficult for the British to compete on the world market. The Conservative Party wanted to encourage industry through high tariffs against foreign competition, relying on the Commonwealth to provide raw materials and markets. The Labour Party had a much more radical plan, to nationalize key industries including transportation, utilities, mines, and later perhaps textiles, with compensation to the owners. They believed that sharing ownership would encourage British workers to produce more efficiently. However they never had the strength in Commons to put through their program.

The British never made a strong economic recovery, and on the contrary, suffered badly during the Depression; but by 1935 several issues other than economics drew the country's attention. The first of these was that the King, Edward VIII, decided to abdicate his throne in order to marry a twice-divorced American, Wallis Simpson. The Duke of Windsor, as the king was subsequently called, had an extraordinary lack of perception about the dangers of fascism and took his new bride to meet Hitler. His behavior undoubtedly embarrassed Winston Churchill, who was keenly sensitive to Hitler's true danger.

A second important issue was the Irish question. After World War I (1919) the Irish were given the Home Rule promised them in 1914, but now power had shifted into the hands of radicals who were no longer satisfied with that solution. The Sinn Fein split in two, with the extremist wing, led by Eamon de Valera, calling for complete independence of the entire island. The other wing was moderate, and negotiated with London in 1921 to win dominion status for 26 counties of southern Catholic Ireland as the Irish Free State, while the six counties of Protestant Ulster would remain as part of Great Britain, sending delegates to Parliament. Bitter feelings over this disagreement fed more violence, but with the murder of moderate leader Michael Collins, public opinion turned against the extremists. The moderate compromise prevailed; in World War II the Irish Free State remained neutral in the war. In 1949 England recognized it as the completely independent Republic of Eire.

Part III

France

In numbers of men killed, in economic dislocation, and in psychological damage, France suffered more from World War I than almost any country, except possibly Russia. The French estimated that, between August 1914 and February 1917, one Frenchman was killed every minute, or more than two million killed or permanently disabled in all.[1] Great damage was done to homes and factories. Widespread disillusionment, despair and fear characterized the French afterwards; they embraced a foreign policy bent on punishing Germany and otherwise followed the strictest isolation. Paris became once again the artist and writer's haven for the intellectuals of the world, a flame drawing flutterings of talent, but known above all for the carefree hedonism and despair of the generation of F. Scott Fitzgerald and others like him.

In 1923 Germany was not paying reparations, and France and Belgium invaded the Ruhr, the great German industrial area, to collect. The Germans did not resist, but they also did not pay, at least then. The French left the Ruhr in 1925, and with the bad state of their economy were forced to devalue the franc. This ruined thousands of Frenchmen, especially in the middle class, who lost four-fifths of the money they had loaned the government. They did not suffer the catastrophic inflation and dislocation of Germany, but they suffered badly nonetheless, and more extremist political parties flourished there than in either England or the United States. However, on the far left the Communists and Socialists were split and were not nearly as threatening as in Germany, when they actually seized power briefly. The far right--the Action Française, the Camelots du Roi, and the Croix de Feu were also unsuccessful. In 1934 a scandal erupted involving a dubious promoter and swindler named Stavisky, who numbered many important politicians among his friends. He committed suicide, or more likely, was murdered, before he could name anyone prominent. A suspicious judge was also murdered before the affair was hushed up. The far right took this as their issue, and rioted against the government. All the political parties loyal to the Third Republic rallied round, and as in the time of Dreyfus, kept the enemies on the right from success. In 1936 a government was brought in called the Popular Front, joining together the Radical Socialist, Socialist and Communist parties. After their success in the elections the first socialist premier was nominated, Leon Blum, representing the wishes of millions of Frenchmen who hoped to have something similar to the New Deal, i.e., a more equitable distribution of income and benefits in France. Blum began an ambitious program of benefits and also took action against the far right political groups; but the country was divided on his program and neither able nor willing to pay the taxes necessary to implement the new services. When the Popular Front fell, France remained divided between the working class which demanded benefits, and the wealthy, who were partly angry, partly fearful. However, this issue died with the new premier, Radical Socialist Daladier, for he was drawn increasingly into the foreign policy crisis of Munich in 1938.

---

[1] David Thomson, World History From 1914 to 1961 (N.Y.: Oxford University Press, 1964)

There was a certain malaise in France in 1939, and on the other hand a kind of whistling-in-the-dark overconfidence. The French had a belief that their overseas empire gave them great power, and that the Maginot Line which they had built on the German border gave them great protection. They were wrong about both. Parts of the empire were particularly ripe for independence, as evidenced by the war which began in Indochina as soon as World War II ended, followed swiftly by the war in Algeria. And the Maginot Line was an illusion. The main enemy of France was an insidious defeatism which was gnawing at them from within, which led to their surrender to Germany in less than two weeks.

Part IV

The Far East

India

Even as giant empires were still forming in the 18th and 19th century, the colonials began to demand freedom from the mother country. First with Americans, later with Latin Americans, the people who lived in the empires asserted their rights to independence. This process commenced first with European settlers, but by World War I had begun to spread to native inhabitants who were opposed not only to Europe, but also to the descendants of Europeans who had settled their countries. One manifestation of this occurred in the Mexican Revolution of 1911, when the Indians and Mestizos constituted a force opposing the pure-blooded Spanish.

In India, opposition to the colonial rule of Great Britain appeared early. In the 1850's there were riots and violence, temporarily assuaged by compromises granted from the home office, including the end of power of the East India Company. The British made concessions toward representative government in 1861 in the India Councils Act, and again in 1909. However, in 1866, the Congress Party was formed; and by the turn of the century there was a faction in India demanding complete independence. World War I enormously contributed to this feeling, partly because of the important Indian role in helping England win the war, but more likely, from exceptional Indian leadership. Upper class Indians were routinely educated in England, and although this often cemented loyalty to the British forever, such was not always the case. Mohandas Gandhi (1869-1949) was born into a fairly high caste in India, and sent to England for a law degree at Oxford. His excellent education and knowledge of British law subsequently led to his success in leading the Indian people to a brilliant and innovative way of opposing that same law. Gandhi was not politically active until he went to live in South Africa, where he encountered the worst kind of racial injustice. He was accosted in his first class seat on a South African train and thrown off the train because of his color, an outrage that changed his life: he led the Indians of South Africa on a campaign to demand their basic rights. He was partially successful in South Africa, and became enormously famous; but rather than continue to struggle there, he returned to his native land to try and win independence from England. Gandhi developed the concept of nonviolent resistance as a direct outgrowth of Hindu teachings on the illusion of force, and the influence of Henry David Thoreau--"On Civil Disobedience". He cast aside his Saville Row suits and elegant British ways, and began to live as the simplest Hindu peasant; in homespun clothes, walking rather than riding, eating only the simplest of foods. Most other Indian leaders were disdainful at first, and thought that only through power politics and force could they ever win against Great Britain. But Gandhi became increasingly popular with his people. He travelled all over the country, and developed great sympathy for the hardships Indian cottage industry was suffering from the textile competition of England. He took to spinning his own cloth as an example to his people, and urged them to stop buying British goods. He led a march to the sea against the salt tax. The British were angry and baffled. They arrested Gandhi and put him in prison, and opposed his followers defying the salt tax by clubbing and arresting thousands of them. In 1919, in their most infamous moment of violence, British troops fired on demonstrators at Amritsar, massacring hundreds of them. Every time the British used force against the Indian people, or arrested Gandhi, there was a world outcry, and by World War II, the Indian independence movement was close to succeeding. In retrospect, the amount of violence which occurred between the Indians and the British was remarkably slight, and the only reason Gandhi's techniques worked in the first place was because of British respect for the law. Such a technique would never have worked against an authoritarian regime or a dictatorship. The way in which the British finally signed the act of independence contrasts vividly with other independence movements which followed after World War II in Algeria and the Belgian Congo and elsewhere. In fact, the number of people killed in India over the religious conflict between Moslems and Hindus (more than a million) makes the British and Gandhi's achievments look even better. Ironically Gandhi suffered a violent death at the hands of a fanatically anti-Moslem Hindu in 1948, thus scotching any possibility of compromise or unity between the newly independent Moslem commonwealth of Pakistan and Hindu India.

Gandhi had an impact on the world long after his death. The American civil rights leader, Martin Luther King, was profoundly influenced by his passive, non-violent movement, so that many of the same techniques were used in the American South to gain rights for the black minority. On the other hand, as one of the great leaders of the 20th century, Gandhi also made mistakes. By standing for a primitive agrarian life and fighting the Industrial Revolution, Gandhi did the impoverished people of India a serious disservice. His political goals were impressive; his understanding of economics decidedly limited.

The leader of the new independent India was Jawaharlal Nehru, an outstanding leader, who stood for parliamentary democracy and humanitarian principles. Nehra died in 1964, and his eventual succession was his own daughter, Indira Gandhi.

China

In 1911 Sun Yat-sen, the leader of the Kuomintang and the hero of the Chinese Revolution, tried unsuccessfully to establish his control over the defiant warlords of China. When he died in 1925, he was succeeded by his brother-in-law, Chiang Kai-shek, who remained a major Chinese leader for more than 40 years. China numbered about 500,000,000 souls in the 1920's, a country which was both poor and primitive, where the peasant felt no sense of identity or even interest in the national government. Yet they became the pawns in a mighty struggle at that time between the nationalists and the communists. Sun Yat-sen had desperately needed foreign aid, and had turned to Russia in 1923. The Russians hoped to convert China to communism, and a communist party was founded in China in 1921. With Russian aid, the Kuomintang became a mass movement. Chiang Kai-shek at first cooperated with the communists and Russia, but broke with them in 1927, particularly with the young communist leader, Mao Tse-tung, who was then trying to organize landless peasants in the south. A more or less continuous civil war prevailed for the next twenty years, between communists in the south, warlords in the west and north, and the Nationalist government of Chiang, mostly confined to the lower Yangtze. However in the 1930's the Nationalists and communists fought together against a more dangerous common enemy, Japan.

Japan had long had designs on China. In 1915 they secretly presented China with Twenty-One Demands, which would have turned China virtually into a Japanese protectorate. China entered World War I at that point, in order to gain British and French protection, but at war's end, Japan kept German possession in China, Kiaochow and parts of the Shantung peninsula. In 1922 at the Washington Conference the other powers forced Japan to sign the Nine-Power Treaty, guaranteeing China's independence. This was only a sham, for in 1931 the Japanese moved again: they invaded Manchuria, with unerring instinct making their attack at a time when the other powers were reluctant to take action. The League of Nations protested in the Lytton Report, but Japan waged more or less continuous war against the Chinese from that point until the end of World War II.

Chiang Kai-Shek. (The Granger Collection)

QUESTIONS FOR REFLECTION

1. Sum up the attitude about foreign policy of all three major democracies. List three efforts to avoid future wars. How do those efforts differ from efforts today?

2. What is the difference in the atttitude about the presidency of Republicans versus Democrats? How did Roosevelt effect a political revolution? What were some of the reasons for Roosevelt's success?

3. Sum up the situation in France between the wars. How did it differ from the United States? What was the role of Winston Churchill in England between the wars?

4. What was happening in India and China between the wars?

SUGGESTED BIBLIOGRAPHY

F. L. Allen, Only Yesterday (1940)
D. W. Brogan, The Era of Franklin D. Roosevelt (1951)
J. M. Burns, Roosevelt: The Lion and the Fox (1956)
E. H. Carr, International Relations Between the Two World Wars, 1919-1939 (1947)
E. H. Carr, The Twenty Years' Crisis, 1919-1939 (1946)
M. K. Gandhi, Autobiography (1948)
E. F. Goldman, Rendevous with Destiny: A History of American Reform (1952)
R. Gould, China in the Sun (1946)
R. Hofstadter, The Age of Reform (1955)
A. Iriye, After Imperialism: The Search for a New Order in the Far East, 1921-1931 (1965)
S. Marks, The Illusion of Peace: International Relations, 1918-1933 (1976)
C. L. Mowat, Britain Between the Wars (1955)
H. Mukerjee, India Struggles for Freedom (1948)
H. Nicolson, Diaries and Letters, 3 vols. (1966-68)
K. Robinson, The Dilemma of Trusteeship: Aspects of British Colonial Policy Between the Wars (1965)
E A. Rosen, Hoover, Roosevelt, and the Brains Trust: From Depression to New Deal (1977)
A. M. Schlesinger, Jr., The Coming of the New Deal (1959)
A. M. Schlesinger, Jr., The Crisis of the Old Order 1919-1933 (1957)
A. M. Schlesinger, Jr., The Politics of Upheaval (1960)
A. J. P. Taylor, English History, 1914-1945 (1965)
D. Thomson, Democracy in France (1964)
A. Werth, The Twilight of France, 1933-1940 (1942)

Part I

The Events Leading Up to War

In the years preceding World War II, the three Axis powers engaged in a series of violent acts which, in retrospect, gave a clear indication of their ultimate ambitions. In every case the League of Nations was incapable of effectively opposing them, and the democracies floundered around in the confusion trying to pretend that nothing was really happening. In 1931 when the Japanese invaded Manchuria the Earl of Lytton condemned them in his report to the League of Nations; but the only clear result was not that Japanese aggression was stopped, but that the Japanese withdrew from the League (in 1933).

The second factor leading to the war was the rearmament of Germany, already begun in the twenties, now carried out openly by Hitler. In 1935 the League condemned Germany for violating the Treaty of Versailles, but with no effect. In 1936, Hitler performed his first overt act of aggression by sending his army into the Rhineland. His troops had orders to turn tail and run "like dogs with their tails between their legs" if the French forces resisted; but as the French did not resist, the Germans prevailed. Meanwhile,

Henrich Himmler, who was head of the Nazi secret police. (The Granger Collection)

147

THE DEFEAT OF THE AXIS 1942-45

AXIS POWERS AT THE OUTBREAK OF THE WAR

GREATEST AREA OF AXIS MILITARY POWER

ALLIES

HEAVIEST ALLIED BOMBING

INSIDE LIMIT OF U-BOAT OPERATIONS

RUSSIA

BLACK SEA

TURKEY

SYRIA

TRANS-JORDAN

PALESTINE

CYPRUS

FINLAND

ESTONIA

LATVIA

LITHUANIA

EAST PRUSSIA

POLAND

SWEDEN

NORWAY

DENMARK

BALTIC SEA

GERMANY

CZECHOSLOVAKIA

HUNGARY

AUSTRIA

RUMANIA

BULGARIA

YUGOSLAVIA

ALBANIA

GREECE

CRETE

ITALY

MEDITERRANEAN SEA

SWITZ.

CORSICA

SARDINIA

SICILY

TUNISIA

NORTH SEA

NETH.

FRANCE

GREAT BRITAIN

IRELAND

ALGERIA

SPAIN

PORTUGAL

FRENCH MOROCCO

SINKING OF THE "BISMARCK"

in 1935 Mussolini seized Ethiopia, no extraordinary feat for advanced industrial Italy over a backward African nation, but heady stuff for the Italians, who had been rather ignominiously defeated there by the Ethiopians in the Battle of Adowa in 1896. Again the League objected, and even went so far as to invoke Article 16 of their convenant, which provided for economic santions against a member resorting to war. The sanctions in no way inconvenienced Italy, for they did not include necessities for warfare (such as oil), and also did not involve the United States (who did not belong to the League). The Italians also withdrew from the League, so that by 1937, Japan, Italy and Germany had all left.

In 1936 the Spanish Civil War broke out, with the ominous participation of three totalitarian countries, and the stubborn isolation of the three leading democracies. Meanwhile, Mussolini and Hitler signed the Rome-Berlin "Axis", a formal pact committing the two nations to help each other. In retrospect Mussolini appears to have been a saner ruler than Hitler, his fascism notwithstanding. Compared to Germany, Italy had no serious antisemitism, and certainly not the drive and rather rabid fervor for conquering the world which could be seen among the Nazis. In view of their rather modest military triumphs (mostly they had defeats), the Italians seemed a far cry from the Germans. Yet ironically, Hitler was awed by Mussolini, who had come to power in 1922; and felt thoroughly intimidated on his first trip to Italy by the grandeur of the Italian uniforms and Italian pageantry (according to Speer). He was afraid Mussolini would not approve of him or support him. From Hitler's point of view, the Rome-Berlin Axis was a triumph. Only later did he realize that in power and military force Germany was several times stronger than Italy.

In 1938 Hitler annexed Austria, in all likelihood a move he had envisioned since boyhood, when as a frustrated German-speaking Austrian he had loathed the other "races" of the Hapsburg Empire. He had one Austrian chancellor assassinated (Dolfuss), and thoroughly intimidated a second (Schuschnigg); so that Austria was no match for the German army when it marched in. Next he set his sights on Czechoslovakia. That country had been artifically created in 1918 with a majority of Czech inhabitants, and also three and a half million Germans who inhabited a mountainous area known as the Sudetenland. Hitler launched his campaign with the help of Goebbels, who spread stories about the Czechs brutalizing pregnant German women. In the ensuing crisis he intimidated the English prime minister Neville Chamberlain, and the hapless French minister, Daladier, in a series of conferences. At the crucial meeting at Munich, in September 1938, the rabbit-faced and wooly-minded Chamberlain felt pleased to turn the Sudetenland over to Hitler, convinced as he was that Hitler was basically a good fellow who meant the English no harm. Chamberlain returned to London with his homburg hat and umbrella, waving the document, proclaiming before the little knot of British who gathered in the rain to greet him that he had found "peace in our time". He was disconcerted but not really annoyed when Hitler's army moved the following March to seize all of Czechoslovakia. Even when Hitler and Stalin signed their mutual non-aggression pact in August of 1939, Chamberlain refused to take active steps to organize England's defense, and at the invasion of Poland on September 1, tried to find a way to avoid honoring his promise to help them against Germany.

THE BRITISH EMPIRE AND COMMONWEALTH
ON THE EVE OF WORLD WAR II

THE UNITED KINGDOM AND THE SELF-GOVERNING DOMINIONS

Joseph Goebbels, who
headed the Nazi
propoganda machine.
(The Granger Collection)

Part II

The First Phase

The first phase of World War II was called Blitzkrieg, lightening war, for
the German army and airforce (Luftwaffe) moved against Poland with the speed
of lightening. Poland had had one of the largest armies in Europe, but they
were no match for the advanced technology of the Nazis, tragically illustrated
when their cavalry tried to stand up against modern tanks. Germany invaded
from the west, Russia from the east, and Poland was devoured by the two of
them. The Russians were cannier than the Germans: they got half of Poland
without losing a drop of blood. Afterwards, the Russians invaded Finland.

For several months there was a lull in the action, labeled the "phoney
war", but in May of 1940 the Germans abruptly invaded the Low Countries, and
moving with devastating and unprecedented speed, overcame Denmark, Holland and
Belgium. France had one of the largest armies in the world, and more tanks
than the Germans; but the events of May 1940 broke their resistence. After
World War I the French fear of another German invasion had prompted them to
build a buffer zone called the Maginot Line, composed of large concrete
obstacles and an underground labyrinth of fortifications and supply depots.
Not only could airplanes fly over it, but even more embarrassing, tanks could

151

go around it. The Ardennes, a hilly, forested area in Belgium, had been considered an obstacle to attacking France, but the Germans made short work of it, and after fighting less than two weeks, and despite the urgent pleas of Winston Churchill, England's new prime minister, France capitulated.

The English were particularly alarmed at the speed of the German victory, because trapped at the seaport of Dunkirk was the entire British army and a large portion of the French army, surrounded on three sides by German troops. Had the German general von Rundstedt been ordered to press home his advantage, World War II might have had a different outcome. But for reasons never fully understood, Hitler sent orders for his troops to hold back. Possibly he hoped to persuade the British to surrender or perhaps even to ally with him. Hitler made scathing comments on the Russians, the French and the Americans, but he admired the British as the one race almost as admirable as the Aryans. If he thought he could win the British over, he was very much on the wrong track, for they were led by the indomitable Churchill, who was determined never to surrender. Winston Churchill was short and enormously fat, with a cheerful cherubic face, always smoking a massive cigar. The British loved him. Churchill conceived of a brilliant madcap scheme to rescue the troops from Dunkirk by rounding up every available ship and fishing boat in Britain, and sending them across the Channel to collect as many men as they could carry. They rescued more than 300,000 French and British soldiers, a feat of bravado which shored up British pride, and gave them the determination to carry them through the terrible events which lay ahead during the Battle of Britain. France surrendered on June 22, 1940, leaving England entirely alone in the fight. Angry at the "Miracle of Dunkirk," which had humiliated him, Hitler now proposed Operation Sea Lion, the code name for the invasion of Great Britain. It was to consist largely of an attack by sea, but first Goering and his Luftwaffe were to knock out the Royal Air Force.

The Battle of Britain began in the fall of 1940, when the relatively tiny RAF tried to defend England from the vastly stronger Luftwaffe which had brought all of Europe to its knees. In this they were aided by a number of secret advantages. The first of these was radar, a British invention, then still in its early stages, which informed them of the whereabouts of German planes flying over for an attack. The second was ingenuity, the kind of audacious cleverness which led the English to plant giant telephone poles in the ground up and down the coastline, aimed at the Channel, painted gunmetal grey, which effectively fooled Goering into believing they had better defense than they did. The third was the British possession of the greatest secret of the war, appropriately named the Ultra Secret: two Poles had smuggled to England information and equipment on Germany's secret code, known as the Enigma Machine. The Enigma Machine resembled a typewriter, with a series of revolving drums inside, which permitted a person to type messages which were absolutely undecipherable without the key. The Germans never learned that their code had been broken. In the early days of the war, the British had to scramble to decipher the first messages which they received, and they always had to take pains to keep the Nazis from guessing they had broken the code. There is controversy even now about the bombing of Coventry: some scholars claimed Winston Churchill knew of the attack in advance, but he was afraid to warn the inhabitants for fear the Germans would know the code had been broken, so thousands of lives were lost. However, forty years later, Churchill experts denied that he knew about Coventry.[1] Other information they did have in advance, such as knowledge of convoys on their way to Africa with supplies for Rommel.[2]

Radar, the ultra secret and the extraordinary skill of the RAF saved Britain from the Luftwaffe. Just when all seemed lost, the RAF made a daring raid on Berlin, and bombed the city Hitler had guaranteed would never be bombed. Hitler was outraged, and shifted the focus of his attack from the RAF to the city of London. With courage from the royal family, brilliant leadership from Churchill, and a magnificent attitude in the people, London became a symbol of heroism, and survived. As for the RAF, this intrepid group of nineteen-year-old pilots had a life expectancy of only three months once they joined up. Speaking of their heroism, Churchill said, "Never have so many owed so much to so few."

In the spring of 1941 Hitler attacked the Balkans, and in June he invaded Russia, in what may have been his biggest single mistake. It is conceivable that even without assistance, Russia might have survived, for she had defeated that other great conqueror of modern times, Napoleon. As it was, when Hitler turned on his ally, both Churchill and Roosevelt decided immediately to go to Stalin's aid. The United States still was not in the war, but they sent millions of dollars in food and supplies in the next four years. At first the German armies looked invincible, and by 1942 had penetrated Russia to a line running roughly from Leningrad to just outside Moscow and southeastward to Stalingrad, and the Black Sea. The besieged Leningrad suffered over one million killed in that city alone, but Russian resilience, aided by the worst winter since 1812, blunted the German advance. Nazi tanks froze in their tracks and German soldiers froze barefooted in the snow. The Russians were used to the cold, and had warm clothes, ski patrols, Siberian ponies, and an attitude about outwitting the enemy which went back to the Scythians in 500 B.C. The Battle of Stalingrad, 1943, was the turning point of the war.

The role of the United States up until this point had been isolationist. After World I Americans had persisted in their belief that they could lead a happy-go-lucky existence without involvement in European political troubles, even as economically they became more and more inextricably interwoven. It was American money which produced the economic recovery in Weimar, and it was the American stock market crash which sent Germany wheeling into its next depression. As Hitler rose to power, outspoken conservatives in both Britain and the United States insisted on a policy first of ignoring him, then appeasing him. Often it seemed that the only two individuals truly aware of the menace were Franklin Roosevelt and Winston Churchill. Yet Roosevelt was hampered by the isolationism of congress; and Churchill wasn't even in office until the war actually began.

One example of the attitude which prevailed in those days can be seen in the popular hero, Charles Lindberg, "Lucky Lindy", the lanky and naive aviator

---

[1]William Manchester, The Last Lion, Winston Spencer Churchill: Vision of Glory, 1874-1932 (Boston: Little, Brown, 1983)

[2]F. W. Winterbotham, The Ultra Secret, (Dell, 1982)

who was very good at flying planes but not very good at understanding politics. Lindberg visited Hitler and dined with Goering, and returned to America awestruck at the brilliance of Germany's airplanes. In widely publicized speeches he told Americans that Germany was the wave of the future, and that the United States could never hope to duplicate their airforce. Roosevelt tried to counter this and arouse the American public to the real dangers which faced them, but to no avail; in 1940 he ran for an unprecedented third term on the platform that he would not send American boys overseas to fight. He won the election, at least in part because of his antiwar stand; but as England stood alone against Hitler, like the Dutchboy holding back the dyke, Roosevelt was secretly determined to do everything short of war to help them hold the line. In March of 1941, he persuaded Congress to pass the Lend-Lease Act, which enabled the United States to provide material to aid any country whose defense was vital to the United States. The United States also gave England fifty "overage" destroyers, ostensibly in return for the loan of fifty bases. Roosevelt justified these plans in a speech comparing the United States to a family lending a garden hose to a neighbor whose house was burning down. The homely metaphor made it seem urgent to help out, and not to worry about the cost until after the "fire" was put out. At one stroke the United States thus avoided some of the worst problems of World War I, including the earlier methods of lending money to the allies, which created such serious problems after the first war. In this way, the United States channeled millions of dollars in aid to Communist Russia. Because of the subterfuge, neither the American public nor Hitler was alarmed.

Soon after, on December 7, 1941, Japan brought the United States openly into the war by a surprise attack on Pearl Harbor, in which most of the the American Pacific Fleet was sunk or disabled. The Japanese had conquered an empire in the Far East, and were poised to strike at the colonies of France, the Netherlands, and England. The Japanese realized that the United States would not permit them to continue unopposed; but they were confused by the American press, which was strongly against war; the Japanese apparently believed the American people would not fight. Furthermore, they expected the attack on the American fleet to cripple U.S. efforts in the Pacific from then on. Both ideas were wrong: and the American response was overwhelming. A myth sprang up that Roosevelt had actually planned Pearl Harbor, or at least had known about the attack in advance, but had done nothing about it because he wanted to get into the war. Logic alone would refute such a claim; for it was hardly necessary to have the American fleet so thoroughly disabled in order to anger the American public. That fateful day only three aircraft carriers were out at sea; six out of eight battleships, three destroyers, and four other ships were sunk; three cruisers damaged; and 2,400 men were killed. One ship, the Maine, brought the United States into the Spanish-American War; one ship, the Lusitania brought them into World War I. In 1941 probably one ship would also have sufficed to bring them into World War II. In any case, the secret information about the attack was among thousand of messages so far not deciphered by American intelligence.[1] The American nation rose up as one to avenge this outrage, and declared war on Japan immediately. Germany and Italy honored their own obligations by declaring war on the United States on December 11, so that the conflict became worldwide.

---

[1] W.M. Stevenson, A Man Called Intrepid (N.Y.: Harcourt Brace Jonovich, 1976).

Pearl Harbor, Dec. 7, 1941. (United Press International)

The next three months were grim for the Americans without their seapower. Japan seized Guam, Wake Island and the Philippines (General Douglas MacArthur left only under duress, defiantly claiming, "I shall return!") They also seized Malaya, Indonesia, Siam and Burma, and seemed about to attack Australia. Yet the United States began to win a victory within their own nation, a victory of technology and industry, as they threw all their energies into the production of new ships and planes (eventually producing one ship a week). Only a few months after Pearl Harbor came the Battle of Midway, usually claimed as the turning point in the Pacific, although the war continued for three more years.

In the fall of 1942 the Americans landed at North Africa. General George Patton and General Dwight Eisenhower went to the aid of the British officer, General George Montgomery, against the brilliant German "Desert Fox", Erwin Rommel. With the help of the ultra secret the allies were able to cut off most German supplies to Rommel, and after a series of spectacular battles, including El Alamein, they were victorious. In July 1943, they moved on to a landing on Sicily, preparatory to a push up through Italy from the South. Under Montgomery and the brilliant but controversial Patton, the armies were at first successful; but the rugged terrain of the Apenines made the fighting in 1944 extremely costly and bitter.

Meanwhile, the final decisive campaign was planned, an invasion of France in June of 1944, at Normandy. On June 6 an army of English, Canadians, Australians, French and Americans landed on the beaches of Normandy, and despite initial losses began to push the Nazis back. At the insistence of General Charles De Gaulle, the hero of the French Resistance, the invasion force paused in its pursuit to reconquer Paris, a city which Hitler in a last outburst of mania, tried to burn to the ground. The final winter of 1944-45, the Americans and English suffered a serious final setback from Germany in the murderous Battle of the Bulge; but with Russia attacking from the East, the joint armies were victorious by April. Hitler spent the last few weeks of the war hidden in his Bunker underneath Berlin, along with advisors, secretaries and friends, including his mistress, Eva Braun, and the Goebbels family. On April 30, 1945, Hitler married Eva Braun, then shot her and also himself. Goebbels was instructed to burn the bodies in order to make identification and desecration by the Russians impossible. The effort was in vain, for the Russians did identify the bodies (although they kept this a secret for twenty years). Goebbels shot his own wife, his six children and himself, and efforts to cremate Goebbels also failed. The war in the west was over.

Part III

The End of the War

The Allied command had two important steps remaining: initiate plans for peace and a postwar settlement, and terminate the war in the Pacific.

Roosevelt and Churchill had been in close contact with each other by telephone before 1939, and continued to confer frequently, even when only one of the countries was in the war, and only one of the men was in power. They met off the coast of Newfoundland and issued the Atlantic Charter on August 14, 1941, in which they called for freedom of the seas, equal access to economic opportunity, abandonment of aggression, and the restoration of rights to conquered nations. They also met at Casablanca in January of 1943, and at Quebec in August of 1943. Roosevelt, Churchill and Stalin met twice, the first time at Teheran, in December of 1943; and the second and last time, at Yalta, in February, 1945. In the summer of 1945 Roosevelt was replaced by Truman (Roosevelt died in April), and Churchill by Clement Atlee, when the three powers conferred at Potsdam.

The subjects discussed at these meetings included details on coordinating the war effort, and political issues on the lands occupied by Hitler. The former was an unusual success story, for Britain and the United States cooperated to an unprecedented degree during the war, sharing commands at all levels, including the highest. There were occasional incidents of jealousy, but the armies fought extremely well together. No such effort was made with the Russians, where differences in language, heritage and political attitudes were altogether too great. The English and the Americans did have disagreements on occupied countries, particularly in regard to France. Charles De Gaulle who became the leader of the French resistance in June of 1940, was a thorn in their side. Churchill found him to be an arrogant man, but indispensible; while Roosevelt distrusted him as a potential dictator. Roosevelt did not want De Gaulle to play a very large role in the Normandy landings, nor did he intend to turn France over to him when it was liberated. This clash of personalities was unfortunate, for the French people felt that in a war of tragic disappointments and failures (and worse), De Gaulle was the one man who had shown great leadership. The Gaullists did take over the newly liberated government. De Gaulle never forgave Roosevelt, and long after Roosevelt's death, when he became President of the 5th Republic, De Gaulle continued to take out his resentment on the United States. Had France been still a giant in world power, this vendetta could have been serious, and it did cause problems. But with Russia, which was a superpower, some of the misunderstandings of the wartime conferences were fatal.

Both Roosevelt and Churchill, but especially Roosevelt, have been blamed for disregarding the threat of Russia to the freedom of eastern Europe. Some of the most important decisions of the war have been labeled foolish and even criminal. Why did Churchill and Roosevelt rush to Stalin's aid? Wouldn't it have been better to let the two totalitarian dictators destroy each other? Why did the United States let Russia take Berlin? Why did Roosevelt and Churchill believe Stalin at Yalta when he guaranteed free elections in the eastern countries? Did Roosevelt, as he has so often been accused, "sell out" to Stalin?

These questions cannot be understood without imagining oneself in the war, knowing what Churchill and Roosevelt knew about Hitler at the time. Since Hitler was ultimately defeated, it is easy to forget how very close he came to winning. In 1941, when he invaded Russia, the United States was not even in the war, and gave every indication that it would never join. Churchill knew that with their limited resources, England could not stand up against Hitler for long. It seemed clear to him at the time that the fight against Russia could be England's salvation, and that every effort should be made to help Russia win. Secondly, even when the United States entered the war at the end of that year, no one dared predict victory. The Germans had a vastly superior technology, and various weapons which if properly deployed, might still have won the war: they invented the jet plane, the rocket, and were very close to the atomic bomb. To take the rockets, for example, if the V-2's which were ready for firing in the summer of 1944, had been directed at the invasion force gathered in England for the assault on Normandy (more than a million men), they could have changed the outcome of the war. Instead, Hitler continued to attack London, and both the V-1's (nicknamed "buzz bombs") and the V-2's were aimed at the civilian population of that city, where they killed more than 60,000 people, but did not materially affect the war.

A second argument in defense of Churchill and Roosevelt's view of Stalin is that all the countries of eastern Europe except for Czechoslovakia, had been leaning toward fascism before the war. They had never had experience with democracy, and there was never any guarantee that Allied intervention could turn them into democracies. The reasoning behind giving the Russians the right to take Berlin was rather clearcut: the Allies, and especially the Americans, wanted to risk no more American soldiers than absolutely necessary. At this point they were hardly concerned about the political well-being of the German people after the war. Also, except for the intervention in Spain, Russian foreign policy before World War II cannot be compared to what it became afterward: Russia had not intervened on a large scale in other countries before the war. Russia had been concerned with domestic issues--the purges, the five year plans, the consolidation of communist rule. There was little to suggest how aggressive their foreign policy would later become.

Churchill, Roosevelt and Stalin at the Yalta Conference, February 1945.
(United Press International)

In February of 1945 perhaps the main reason why Roosevelt and Churchill continued to court Stalin was that after a very hard winter of fighting the Battle of the Bulge, the Allies still faced a hard struggle to defeat Japan. They were persuaded that it was crucial for Russia to join them in the Far East, and a few concessions in Europe would be worth the cost. In his books afterwards, Churchill wrote that he saw Stalin as a wily manipulator, while Roosevelt was the one really taken in by his Byzantine charm. That may be; it is also true that at Yalta Roosevelt was extremely ill, and with only a few weeks to live, his judgment could not have been at its best.

Because of the Yalta agreement, Patton and Eisenhower stopped more or less at the Rhine (to Patton's great annoyance), and permitted the Russians to take Berlin. By that spring of 1945, there were already indications that Stalin had no intention of fulfilling his commitment to honor free elections in the territories of eastern Europe. Nevertheless when the powers met again at Potsdam the overriding concern was still Japan, and how to defeat her unconditionally. This set the scene for the last event of the war: the dropping of the atomic bomb.

The atomic bomb was a secret even to Harry Truman until the day Roosevelt died. Two billion dollars had been spent developing it, and events of the summer of 1945 persuaded Truman to drop it on Japan. One reason was the amount of money which had gone into the project. Another reason was that the Japanese would not surrender unconditionally, which the Americans insisted on. Furthermore, in the last few months of the war the Japanese revealed a streak of fanaticism which was alien to the American temperament: they began to commit suicide rather than surrender to the United States. Some of the suicides were civilians on islands the Americans recaptured in the Pacific, who threw themselves off cliffs; others were commanding officers who would not accept defeat. The most famous group were the Kamikaze pilots, who crashed their planes onto American battleships hoping to sink them. At Okinawa there were 1,500 Kamikaze attacks, which sank 34 naval craft and damaged 368.[1] Although far more Japanese surrendered at Okinawa (7,400) than committed suicide, the idea was widely circulated that the Japanese would defend Japan to the death, and that capturing it might cost as many as one million American lives. Still, the main reason for dropping the bomb was probably to make an impression on Russia. The Russians had encroached steadily on Eastern Europe since Yalta back in February, and although they did not help fight the Japanese when the Americans wanted them to, now it looked as if they would enter the war against Japan to get in on the spoils.

Persuasive arguments could be made against dropping the bomb, the most telling being that it would be an inhuman massacre of women and children, a terrible new weapon which ill accorded with American morality and ideals. There were alternative ways to warn the Japanese of its devastation without actually dropping it on a civilian population. There were indications from various European embassies that the Japanese were ready to surrender that summer without the use of such a barbaric weapon. Most important of all, it is clear today and should have been clear then that the Japanese had already

---

[1] B. H. Liddel Hart, _History of the Second War_, (N.Y.: Perigee Books, 1971), p. 686

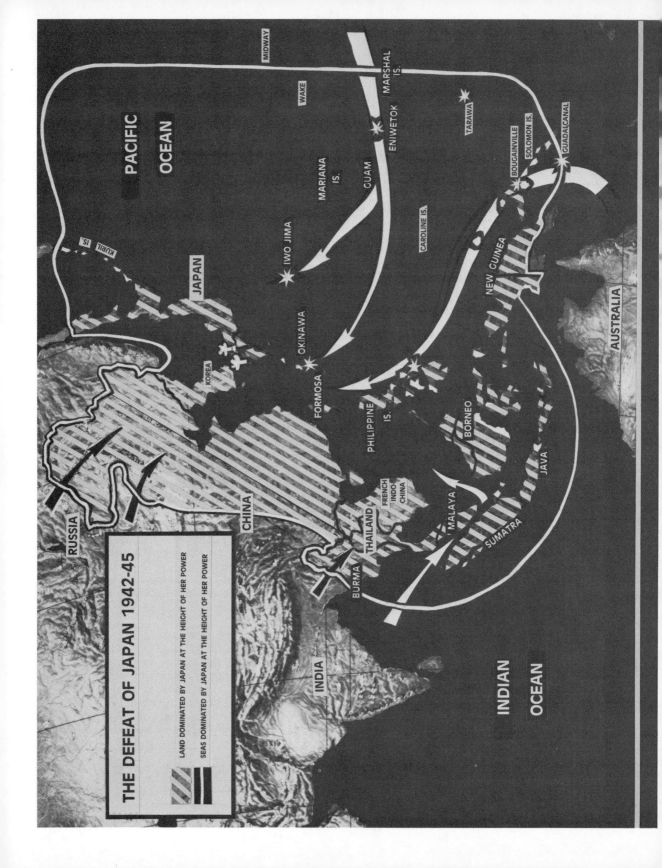

THE DEFEAT OF JAPAN 1942-45

LAND DOMINATED BY JAPAN AT THE HEIGHT OF HER POWER

SEAS DOMINATED BY JAPAN AT THE HEIGHT OF HER POWER

MIDWAY

WAKE

MARSHAL IS.

PACIFIC

OCEAN

ENIWETOK

TARAWA

GUAM

MARIANA IS.

BOUGAINVILLE

SOLOMON IS.

GUADALCANAL

KURIL IS.

CAROLINE IS.

IWO JIMA

JAPAN

NEW GUINEA

OKINAWA

KOREA

AUSTRALIA

FORMOSA

PHILIPPINE IS.

CHINA

BORNEO

JAVA

SUMATRA

FRENCH INDO-CHINA

MALAYA

THAILAND

RUSSIA

BURMA

INDIA

INDIAN

OCEAN

lost the war. In 1944 they were virtually defeated in the air--they lost 480 planes and most of their crews in the battle over the Marianas alone; their planes were rebuilt, but the lost pilots were irreplaceable. Even more serious was the damage Americans did to Japanese shipping. The Japanese empire was a sea empire, dependent upon overseas supplies for much of her food, and such key war material as oil, iron and rubber. Her merchant marine had been 6 million tons at the outset of the war, less than one third that of Britain. American submarines sank 1,355,000 gross tons in 1943; and in 1944, in one month (October) alone they sank 321,000 tons of shipping. Their merchant marine had been for all practical purposes eliminated by 1945, and a blockade would have obliged them to surrender.

Nevertheless, on August 6, 1945, the Americans dropped the first atomic bomb on Hiroshima, killing 80,000 people. Two days later Russia entered the war against Japan. Japan still did not surrender, and on August 9 the Americans dropped the second bomb on Nagasaki. The two bombs caused unprecedented devastation and threw the world into a new and terrifying nuclear age.

Part IV

Results of World War II

Future generations looking back on the 20th century may well decide that World Wars I and II were not two distinct conflicts, but actually one and the same, separated only by a twenty-year break. Certainly, World War I seemed to lead directly to World War II, as if there were unfinished business which had to be taken care of--specifically, Germany had to be defeated a second time more thoroughly than the first time. However, this may be a simplistic way of looking at it; the two wars in fact were quite different. The first one began as an isolated political incident in the Balkans, where the other participants fell almost accidentally into the fray, like pedestrians caught on a collapsing bridge. But the 1939 war began as a calculated act of conquest by two powers, Russia and Germany, and continued in the same vein, with Hitler attacking one nation after the other, eventually even Russia herself; and meanwhile in the Far East the Japanese were undertaking a like conquest. As one looks back over the centuries seldom does one see an event where the participants were so clearly defined as good versus evil as in World War II. Not since tiny Greece held off the Empire of Persia, or not since Athens tried to withstand Sparta, had there been such a clear-cut demarcation. It is for this reason that a generation later World War II became a very popular subject for novels, books, films, and studies of every description: in a world where aggravating little wars were constantly breaking out, and the "good" side turned out to be just as dubious as the "bad" side, it was very satisfying to rerun the events caused by the worst dictator the world had ever seen.

World War I ended with the Treaty of Versailles, which was a vindictive effort to punish Germany for the war. By the war guilt clause, loss of territory, exhorbitant reparations, and the reduction in armed force, Germany was punished. New nations were created; old empires were dismantled. The victors rather hypocritically pursued the idealistic 14 Points, but at the same time gave themselves mandates, which were thinly disguised colonies. The postwar period was characterized by disillusionment on all sides, and the determination widely shared by the allies to avoid future entanglements, and above all, future wars. A League of Nations was created, but was rather ineffective from the start, as neither the United States, Germany or Russia belonged to it.

At the close of World War II there was no peace treaty with Germany at all; there was no bitter determination to punish entire nations. Ironically, in view of Hitler's genuine evil deeds, the German nation was not punished as a nation; individual Nazis were put on trial at Nuremberg, but the longterm impression is not that the Nazis were particularly punished for their murders, but rather, that too many of them escaped punishment altogether. When Klaus Barbie, "the butcher of Lyons", was finally captured in South America in 1982, after forty years of freedom, people were angry that so many top Nazis (including Mengele, the "angel of death") had gone free.

Rather than punishing Germany, the victorious nations and the United States in particular, supervised the construction of a new democratic government, and then left it entirely in German hands: and spent billions of dollars rebuilding the devastated country. The same process took place in Japan under an American team headed by General Douglas MacArthur. The Japanese were guided in the first steps of creating a democracy, and then given full control; and again, Japan was rebuilt with American money. Forty years later the positive results of these actions were clear to all: both Germany and Japan had exceptionally well-running democracies, with high citizen participation; both had strong economies; and both were consistent allies of the United States.

This is not to say that Germany came out of the war unscathed and unchanged. On the contrary, the victorious powers were in serious disagreement on the subject. At Yalta, Russia had insisted on receiving territory from Poland, in return for which at Potsdam, Poland demanded compensation from Germany, and continued to occupy all of Germany east of the Oder and Neisse rivers. When Germany was first occupied in 1945, it was divided into four parts, one part each to Russia, the United States, England and France; and Berlin, the capital, was also divided. The three democratic powers could not reach an agreement with Russia satisfactory to all concerned, either on the political format Germany should have, or on its economic life. In 1946 the democracies merged their zones economically, and the area was given American economic aid, with excellent results. By 1950, West Germany had reached its 1936 level of industrial production, and continued to prosper in the years after that. The new government of the Federal Republic was put into operation in 1949, not based on a constitution but on a general law, with a new capital at Bonn, and Konrad Adenauer as their first chancellor.

East Germany, meanwhile, remained under Communist control, and was known as the German Democratic Republic. Soviet forces created a state controlled by secret police, with a single party, the Socialist Unity (Communist) Party. The Russians appropriated large supplies of machinery and equipment to help restore their own ravaged industry, leaving East Germany without the wherewithal to effect its own economic recovery, a circumstance evident even forty years later in the difference in prosperity between the two halves of

Germany. East Germany acquired a centralized constitution in 1949, whereupon Russia dissolved its occupation zone; but Russian troops remained. In 1953 the Soviet Union transferred control from the military to a civilian commissioner. But the central issue that the two halves of Germany were disunited continued to be a serious and pressing problem.

The most important difference between Japan and Germany, after the war was that Japan was not split into sections and a subject of dispute, but was administered solely by the United States. General Douglas MacArthur was in charge of Japan from the end of the war until the inauguration of a new democratic government there in May 1947. Although their new constitution was drafted by MacArthur and his staff, it was not modeled on the United States, but on the government of Britain, with which the Japanese were more familiar. The emperor remained theoretically in power, but the power rested with the Diet and the prime minister, who was responsible to the House of Representatives. The constitution guaranteed human rights, gave women the vote, and renounced forever the right to make war. Many other reforms were soon carried out, including a sweeping land reform and a revision of the education system. Today the Japanese are among the most democratic people in the world, with the world's highest rate of literacy, one of the lowest crime rates, and probably the most impressive economy. Thus the two "enemy" powers in World War II had a vastly different and primarily positive experience after that war.

Another important result was the creation of the United Nations. The idea of a union among nations to maintain the peace was not new: after the Congress of Vienna the Quadruple Alliance had been the forerunner of such a plan. The ambitious creation of the League of Nations after World War I was another, much broader effort at national cooperation. Now after World War II the great powers were more ambitious still, and created the United Nations. In the spring of 1945 they held a conference in San Francisco in order to draw up a new charter, proclaiming as their goals the maintenance of peace and helping to solve social, economic and cultural problems among nations. Any peace-loving nation could join the organization, and any state violating the charter might be expelled. The U.N., like the League, was dominated by the big powers. It had a Security Council of five permanent members--the United States, the Soviet Union, Great Britain, France, and China (first Nationalist China; after 1972 the seat was given to Communist China), each with an absolute veto. The veto has hampered every effort to deal with serious problems. The first time the U.N. acted in a crisis despite the veto occured in 1950, when Russia walked out of the Security Council during the debate on the Korean War, thus permitting the remaining members to vote for U.N. intervention. This was the only time the U.N. actually fought a war, though in later years they had repeatedly sent peace keeping missions to Africa and the Middle East. In 1983 there were one hundred and fifty-seven members of the United Nations, and only eleven countries which were not members. The organization is still faced with serious problems. One handicap is the disputatious behavior of so many disparate countries in the General Assembly (the main body of the U.N.). The other is financial: the organization is still not supported by equitable payments from all its members.

Other important results of World War II were the emergence of two new superpowers, the United States and Russia; and the comparative decline of the power of Europe. Great Britain, in particular, was high in prestige after the war, but had abruptly lost her power. She was transformed from a creditor nation to a debtor nation, and owed the United States $3,750,000,000. The Commonwealth as a whole had also declined in power since before the war.

Important new developments would be the spread of communism to Eastern Europe and to the Far East, where China became a communist state in 1949. Secondly, in Europe there was an attempt to offset the reduction of power through the creation of a European political union. This European Community did not become politically powerful, but economically it was a great success. Thirdly, immediately after the war the trend continued toward national self-consciousness on the part of colonial populations of Asia, the Middle East and Africa, and in quick succession new nations won their independence. In some cases this process was comparatively peaceful; but most of the time there was violence. Many of the newly independent countries attempted to establish democratic government, but this proved to be exceedingly difficult, and by the 1980's there were only one or two functioning democracies among them--the most notable were India and Israel. Others, such as Nigeria, were struggling in that direction; but many had gone the way of Pakistan or Libya, with virtual dictatorships.

QUESTIONS FOR REFLECTION

1. Of all the steps leading up to World War II, which ones made the war truly inevitable? For example, Britain was trying to sign a pact with Russia in the summer of 1939, but lost out when Hitler signed one himself. Without Stalin's friendship, would Hitler still have invaded Poland? That is, if England and Russia had made an alliance then, would that have stopped him? Hitler's secret alliance with Russians has been called a brilliant coup, but it may have been a foolish mistake. Can you think why the Germans themselves later called this a bad blunder?

2. Why did France fall so fast? Could anything have persuaded them to hold on?

3. What mistakes did Hitler make in the war? How close did he come to defeating England? Why did he decide to invade Russia?

4. What would have happened if the United States had not entered the war? Should the United States have entered sooner? How could Roosevelt have accomplished that? (How have we gotten into wars since then?)

5. Was the defeat of Japan by the Americans inevitable? How could they have won?

6. Evaluate the weapons developed by England, Germany, the United States and Japan.

7. What would have happened if England hadn't gotten the Ultra Secret

8. What should have been the role of England and the "~'
Russia, after Hitler invaded them? Were Churchill and Roosevelt right or

wrong? Were the decisions at Yalta wicked, foolish or reasonable, considering the circumstances at the time?

9. List all the arguments for and against dropping the atomic bomb, then evaluate the decision.

10. What were the main differences in the world wars? Compare the number of people killed, the number of great powers destroyed, the number of new countries created at war's end. How did the U.N. compare with the League of Nations?

11. What happened to Germany and Japan at the end of the war? What happened to Eastern Europe? To India?

12. How had the balance of power shifted? Did the atomic bomb affect the postwar settlement?

Special Project:

In 1983 an accusation was made that the Rudolph Hess imprisoned at Spandau prison in West Germany, was not the same Hess who flew to England during the war, and landed in Scotland. He has been said to be a double, because both Russia and England wanted the real Hess killed because he knew too much about pro-Nazi Englishmen in the war. Find out what you can about the Hess flight, and this remarkable accusation.

SUGGESTED BIBLIOGRAPHY

W. S. Churchill, The Second World War, 6 vols. (1948-53)
W. S. Churchill, Triumph and Tragedy (1953)
Liddell Hart, History of the Second World War (1970)
J. Hersey, Hiroshima (1946)
G. Jackson, The Spanish Republic and the Civil War, 1931-1939 (1965)
F. C. Jones, Japan's New Order in East Asia: Its Rise and Fall, 1937-1945
    (1954)
W. L. Neumann, Making the Peace, 1941-1945 (1950)
L. Poliakov, Harvest of Hate (1954)
G. Reitlinger, The Final Solution (1953)
A. J. P. Taylor, The Origins of the Second World War (1961)
H. S. Truman, Memoirs, Vol I: Year of Decisions (1955)
G. Weinberg, The Foreign Policy of Hitler's Germany: Diplomatic Revolution in
    Europe, 1933-1936 (1971)
T. A. Wilson, The First Summit: Roosevelt and Churchill at Placentia Bay, 1941
    (1970)
D. Young, Rommel: The Desert Fox (1950)

Part I

The United States

For many years the United States was so strikingly influenced by the Puritan thinking of early New England that Americans seemed to be a living embodiment of Max Weber's Protestant Ethic. Today the Protestant Ethic may be on the wane, as the nation increasingly shows a fondness for the material pleasures of a hedonistic life. But for a considerable time Americans seemed determined to work hard and save their money. A corollary of the Protestant Ethic was the Doctrine of Stewardship, another Puritanical belief (though by no means limited to Puritans or even to Christians), that the wealthy and fortunate who have been blessed by God must share their affluence with their less fortunate neighbors. This credo was particularly evident in the United States after the Civil War, when a new generation of millionaires amassed vast wealth through the new industrialization. John D. Rockefeller was a curious example of the new entrepreneur, a wizened old skinflint, a hard-nosed Baptist who read the Bible every day and then (so one imagines) ruined a few widows and orphans before lunch. Yet Rockefeller gave millions of dollars to the nation, endowed the University of Chicago, one of the great universities of the world, and passed on this conviction of dispensing his largesse to his offspring, who in turn gave a parcel of priceless land in Manhatten to the world for the U.N. building in 1945. The Vanderbilts, Carnegies, Fords and other millionaires shared this attitude about their wealth, and after World War II, the nation itself embarked on a foreign policy inspired by the same philosophy.

Thus World War II was a war with an unprecedented outcome. Unlike other wars in which the defeated nations were despoiled, annexed, enslaved or sown with salt, the leading victorious power, the United States, gave them money to rebuild. In 1947 this was expanded in the Truman Doctrine, which gave millions to Greece and Turkey; and the Marshall Plan, which gave money to Europe as a whole. The motivation was not pure altruiusm; rather, it was an altruistic way of accomplishing a political goal--which, after World War II, consisted of fending off the communist influence of Russia. The reasoning was that countries which were socially and economically comfortable would not be open to communist persuasion or to communist force--an assumption which time seemed to bear out. No country with a free government, which has been prosperous and stable, has become communist in this century. From the Truman Doctrine and the Marshall Plan, the United States expanded its concept to encompass foreign aid in general, sharing its wealth with the rest of the world for the next two generations ($75 billion in the first 15 years). The rule of thumb seemed to be that any nation opposed to communism, and especially if threatened with communism, would receive U.S. aid. This overall policy of various programs and actions to blunt the spread of communism was characterized as the policy of "Containment." One exception was Yugoslavia, a communist regime which got American support because Marshall Tito was maintaining an independent stand against Russia. However, certainly the criteria never seemed to include threats from the far right. In the period after World War I, the democracies and especially Germany tolerated the far right because it was not an international ideology which they considered a menace to their own safety, and communism was. This same thinking persisted after World War II. The sympathy of the United States toward rightest governments, even if fascist, is also due to the economic practices of communist states: American capital is often invested in such countries. Right-wing and military dictators tend to protect it; but in leftist states, even when the governments call for humanitarian social change, they support policies of confiscating property and companies, contrary to American interests.

One result of the American foreign aid program was that Russia almost immediately began such a program of its own, the "Molotov Plan"; and the two superpowers have been competing since then in the matter of aid. In Egypt in the 1950's the United States refused to finance the Aswan Dam because of the hostile behavior of President Nasser, whereupon he turned to Russia and got the dam from them. Eventually most industrialized nations began foreign aid programs, and now provide assistance to many Third World countries.

Truman

Two important events during the Truman administration were the McCarthy hearings and the Korean War, interrelated in that both were wars of a sort against communism. Joseph McCarthy, Republican Senator from Wisconsin, created a 20th century witchhunt when he began to make speeches warning against high level communistic infiltration in the United States. For four years fear and paranoia swept the country; hundreds of people were arrested, and thousands accused, the vast majority innocent. McCarthy used slander and innuendo against such people as General George C. Marshall, General Dwight D. Eisenhower, Secretary of State Dean Acheson, and President Truman. However, he met his downfall when he began attacking the U.S. Army for covering up subversive activities, for the army hearings were televised, thus giving the people a chance to see his shabby tactics. McCarthy was condemned by the Senate in 1954, and faded quickly from view.

One reason the fear of communism was so pervasive was that in less than five years all of Eastern Europe and all of China had become communist states, and a new war began when Communist North Korea invaded South Korea. Truman wanted to keep the Korean war as limited as possible, and when General Douglas MacArthur, the U.S. Commander-in-Chief in Korea, wanted to carry the war into China, there was a major crisis. Truman fired MacArthur. But the McCarthy scandals of the war and the general fear of communism combined to influence the election of 1952. The people wanted reassurance; they voted less for the party than for the man: Dwight D. Eisenhower was the one authentic American hero of his generation, the man who had "won" World War II. Superficially simple-hearted and smiling, he was actually politically astute and as tough as nails.

Eisenhower

As president, Eisenhower returned to the Republican philosophy of twenty years before, of doing as little as possible and letting the country run

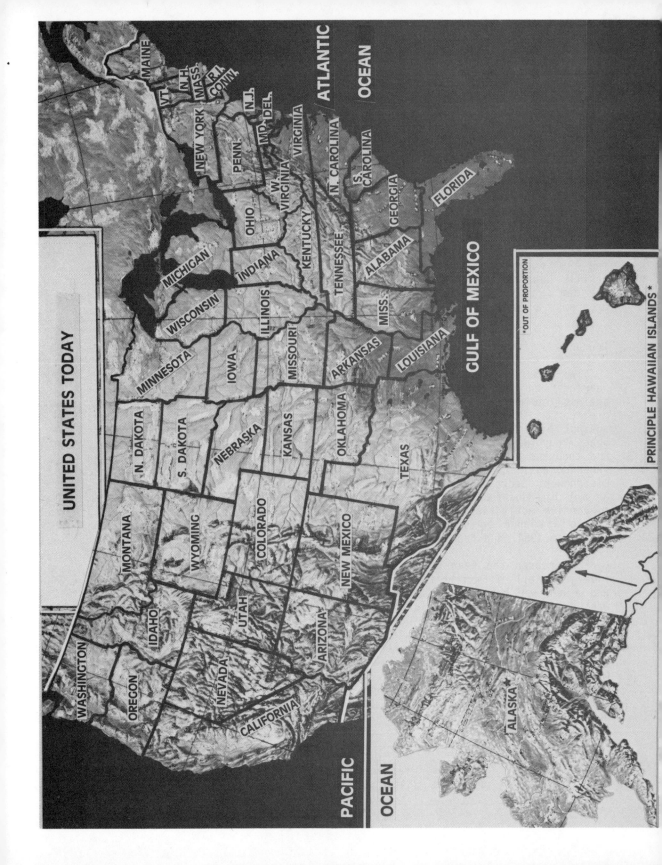

UNITED STATES TODAY

PACIFIC OCEAN

ATLANTIC OCEAN

GULF OF MEXICO

WASHINGTON
OREGON
IDAHO
MONTANA
N. DAKOTA
S. DAKOTA
MINNESOTA
WISCONSIN
MICHIGAN
MAINE
VT
N.H.
MASS.
R.I.
CONN.
NEW YORK
PENN.
N.J.
DEL.
MD.
OHIO
INDIANA
ILLINOIS
IOWA
NEBRASKA
WYOMING
NEVADA
CALIFORNIA
UTAH
ARIZONA
COLORADO
NEW MEXICO
KANSAS
MISSOURI
KENTUCKY
W. VIRGINIA
VIRGINIA
N. CAROLINA
S. CAROLINA
TENNESSEE
ARKANSAS
OKLAHOMA
TEXAS
LOUISIANA
MISS.
ALABAMA
GEORGIA
FLORIDA

ALASKA ★

PRINCIPLE HAWAIIAN ISLANDS *

*OUT OF PROPORTION

ıtself; or as Secretary of Defense Wilson put it, "The business of the United States is business," and business flourished.

There were a number of international crises during Eisenhower's eight years in office, and he avoided involvement in almost all of them: the French asked for American assistance in Indochina and were turned down; Castro asked for U.S. recognition of his government when he overthrew Batista and was turned down. In the Suez crises when Nasser of Egypt seized the canal from England and France, the United States also refused to participate. The 1950's was a period of great self-confidence and prosperity in the United States; Americans were supremely convinced of the greatness of their nation, and seemed to be increasingly complacent and even apathetic about politics and world responsibility. Several events conspired to shake them loose from this comfortable fantasy, for perhaps never again could they assume that they were the greatest power in the world. In 1957 the Russians sent the first satellite into space, Sputnik, an accomplishment which left Americans shattered. Secondly, the Russians shot down an American spy plane, a U-2, flown by Francis Gary Powers, and put him on trial in full view of the world. This latter incident was important for several reasons: many Americans still assumed that the government in Washington was the same simple, down-home, friendly government that they had in their small towns in America. They believed the United States could do no wrong, and certainly didn't endulge in spying or international intrigue. Furthermore, Eisenhower was a hero, and all presidents were honest and upright men and would never lie. Both these assumptions turned out to be false, creating a national embarrassment. The discovery that a hero such as Eisenhower would lie to the people was a serious blow against the presidency. Americans expected their cowboys, their daughters and their presidents to be pure: the national outcry and loathing which erupted later against Richard Nixon would never have happened in the more jaded and realistic European nations.

Civil Rights

The most important domestic event to take place after World War II was the Civil Rights Movement, a concerted effort to improve the lot of the American black people which spanned several presidencies, beginning with Harry Truman, the man who integrated the armed forces. The Civil Rights movement got its first impetus from the Supreme Court decision of 1954, Brown v. Board of Education of Topeka which overturned a decision of 1896, Plessy v. Ferguson. In the earlier decision the court had ruled that separate but equal facilities for the races were constitutional; in the later decision, they ruled that they were not. This was a milestone, and a rare time in history when the usually lethargic Supreme Court was actually ahead of public opinion.

Life for black people in the United States had continued to be grim and dangerous after the Civil War. In the South the Reconstruction era had left a defensive attitude in the white population, and societies such as Red Shirts Remembered (S.C.), and the better known Ku Klux Klan were created to keep black people in their place, which meant keeping them out of job competition and out of politics. Black men had gained the right to vote in 1870; but in many parts of the United States poll taxes, literacy tests and threats from the Klan kept them from enjoying their right. In case of trouble, a black person faced genuine danger: black people were lynched in the United States every year, up until the 1950's. The murder of the boy Emmet Till in 1955 for purportedly whistling at a white woman in Mississippi got national attention: such inhumanity would no longer be tolerated.

On December 1, 1955 a woman named Rosa Parks was ordered to stand up on a bus in Montgomery, Alabama, and give her seat to a white man. She refused, and was arrested. A pullman car porter named R. D. Nixon persuaded her to sue the city, and persuaded the people of the town to boycott all buses until black people were treated equally. He also persuaded a young minister, Dr. Martin Luther King, gifted with real eloquence, to take on the leadership of the boycott. That year all the black people of Montgomery walked, for as one old lady put it, "My feets is tired but my soul is rested."[1] The white people were confused and angry and someone bombed Martin Luther King's house. But two important things happened: the black people won their case against the city of Montgomery; and King refined a philosophy borrowed from Plato, Christ, Thoreau and Gandhi, of peaceful, nonviolent resistence.

The movement spread. Soon black people were sitting in on lunch counters in Greensboro, N.C.; defying southern governors like Wallace of Alabama and Faubus of Arkansas and sending their children to universities. In October, 1960, Martin Luther King was arrested for trying to eat lunch at Rich's Department Store in Atlanta, Georgia. He was sentenced to four months of hard labor.[2] His followers contacted the candidates running in the 1960 presidential race--Richard Nixon and John F. Kennedy. Nixon did not respond, but Kennedy and his brother Bobby acted at once to release King from jail, and promised support for civil rights if he were elected. A few days later Kennedy barely won the presidency: he was a Catholic, and millions of fundamentalist white Protestants had voted against him. It was the election where Mayor Daley of Chicago purportedly told his people, "Vote early and often;" where even the cemetaries of Chicago turned out for Kennedy. In that exceedingly close race, it was probably the black vote which made the difference for Kennedy. And afterwards, during his three years in office he pushed the movement forward.

After 1960, television every night showed scenes from cities such as Birmingham, Alabama, where the black citizens tried to peacefully march to register to vote and were turned back by policemen with clubs, German shepherds and fire hoses. The nation was horrified at the violence in its midst, the bigotry and hatred. Decent white Southerners were especially chagrined to see their dirty linen made public. The United States government passed the Civil Rights Act in 1964, outlawed the poll tax in constitutional Amendment XXIV, and began to integrate schools, neighborhoods, parks and restaurants all over the nation. The Civil Rights Movement had not won even half its goals when the Vietnam War drew the nation's attention away from it. This other cause of injustice affected black men disproportionately, for larger numbers of them were drafted. Martin Luther King and Bobby Kennedy both spoke strongly against the war in 1968, an election year. King was killed in March, and Bobby Kennedy was killed in June.

---

[1] See the book by this name, by Howell Raines (N.Y.: G.P. Putman, 1977)
[2] For details, see ibid., p. 74

Martin Luther King and his wife, Coretta, during the March of Selma to Montgomery. (United Press International)

John Kennedy's support of civil rights led to a mass exodus of Southern white Democrats from the party, led by Senator Strom Thurmond of S.C., who in 1948 had run for president as a Dixiecrat. Thurmond was reelected as a Republican, but even he eventually acquiesced in the tide of public opinion for civil rights.

In his short three years in office, Kennedy brought a wave of idealism and enthusiasm to the nation for fighting just causes, ending racism and poverty. He established the Peace Corps and inspired thousands of young Americans to go overseas and endure great hardships in order to help Third World countries. Kennedy was imaginative in foreign policy. One reason for his vast appeal was that he was tall, youthful and fit, with a brilliant smile, easily the handsomest head of state in the entire world at the time. He suffered a serious defeat at the Bay of Pigs fiasco shortly after taking office; but rallied with vigor the following year, and stood up to Russia during the Cuban Missile Crisis. He captured the affections of Germans when he went to Berlin and stood by the wall, saying, "Ich bin ein Berliner." But it took his death in November of 1963 to reveal how widely admired he had been by people all over the world. His assassination was a crude and bitter shock; his funeral was witnessed by millions of people on television; his death marked the beginning of a decade of bitter disillusionment.

Johnson

Lyndon B. Johnson succeeded Kennedy as president, an experienced legislator, a Texan; a man who accomplished more with Congress than any president in history, but who was singularly inept in foreign policy. Johnson put through the Civil Rights Bill and the Poverty Bill. But he had no luck with the American people: the black people had gotten high expectations and now they responded bitterly. Even before the murders of Bobby Kennedy and Martin Luther King, the black communities in Los Angeles (Watts) and Detroit rioted. Of all issues bringing anger and frustration to Americans, Vietnam was the worst. Kennedy had sent American advisors and money to Vietnam beginning in 1961; but Johnson sent troops and eventually broadened the conflict to a war. Never in American History has there been such an unpopular war. the young people of the sixties had alrady begun to revolt against their elders in unprecedented ways. Boys grew long hair and beards. Boys and girls alike wore disreputable, foul-smelling clothes, stopped taking baths, fought the "Establishment", took drugs, and in thousands of cases "dropped out" altogether, becoming hippies, or "flower children", moving to communes, joining radical religious communities, becoming vegetarians. For the first time in two hundred years, American youth became really radical in politics, demonstrating and rioting. College students demanded the right to take over their universities; sat-in at the University of Chicago, brandished guns at Cornell; blew up a building at the University of Wisconsin;got shot at Kent State. The civil rights movement had hardened into a black power movement, which was tangled up with anti-war feelings, anti-establishment feelings, and pro-communism. The actual number of radicals was minute; the weathermen, the terrorists who became the most famous, numbered only a handful. But to the average citizen they seemed quite numerous. At the Democratic National Convention in Chicago in 1968, riots broke out between radical young people against the war and the Chicago police. Mayor Daly, who as a tough machine mayor had nevertheless supported liberal policies for the poor and the blacks, mouthed obsenities and symbolized for millions watching on television all the innate corruption of American politics. The escalating war and the escalating violence within American society frightened the middle class, who brought in Repulican Richard Nixon.

Nixon

Nixon ended the war in Vietnam and recognized Red China, two acts which would have won him longlasting fame if he had left office at that point. The war ended in bitter failure: 55,000 American men had apparently been killed for nothing, and American behavior in the war seemed to be a disgrace: bombing towns and villages, massacring women and children (My Lai), defoliating forests with deadly chemicals, all for a dubious cause. One result: the nation reacted against the leftist furor of the sixties by becoming increasingly conservative in the seventies, with a new generation of college students who eschewed politics altogether, and resembled increasingly the apathetic generation of the 1950's.

On the eve of his second election, Nixon was a popular man. Yet in a curious way he himself was as troubled and paranoid as the nation itself; he felt threatened by outspoken Democrats and compiled an "enemies list" of people such as Jane Fonda and Paul Newman whom he considered "dangerous". His people broke into Democratic Party headquarters at the Watergate Hotel in Washington in June 1972, in order to spy on Democratic plans for the election. The criminals were caught, and ripples of the ensuing scandal swelled into a tidal wave which wrecked the Nixon presidency.

President and Mrs. Nixon at the Great Wall of China.
(United Press International)

173

Part II

France

The Third Republic fell when the Nazis invaded France in 1940, and was succeeded by an authoritarian regime of aged Marshal Pétain, and the notorious Pierre Laval, who was a collaborator of the Nazis. This government, located at Vichy, was a puppet of Germany, and governed France until the Allied invasion of 1944.

During this time many French collaborated with the Germans during the occupation, a sad fact documented thirty years later in a searing three-hour film, Le Chagrin et la Pitié (The Sorrow and the Pity). The French Resistance during the war consisted of only a few hundred people, but as time passed the numbers were greatly exaggerated out of wishful thinking. The real story was shown in the film: The French helped the Germans round up their own Jews for concentration campus. In one part of the film a typical threesome of French Resistence farmers were shown, who had performed heroic acts for the Allies in their small occupied village; but their French neighbors turned them in to the gestapo and they were sent to Auschwitz. Twenty years later, farmers again, they only wanted to forget it, shrugging their shoulders in the perennial gallic gesture of philosophy toward life. Not everyone could forgive as easily.

One of the most important world developments after World War II was the dissolution of the world's great empires. The French did not accept this development with good grace. After the war, they were weighted down with sour memories, and also with a leaky economy which sputtered and stalled. As the English and Germans began to prosper again, their own plight was particularly hard to bear. In the circumstances it was particularly galling to have the empire begin to break up: their one tenuous hold on the glories of the past. The first to go was Indochina, lost by 1954, after a bloody and vainglorious struggle. They also lost in rapid succession Syria, Lebanon, Morocco and Tunisia. But the bitterest loss for them was Algeria. The Fourth Republic fell over this issue: it had been a rather unstable government and unsuccessful in most of its dealings, not only with the colonies, but with the nation's economy. De Gaulle had served briefly as president in 1945, then had retired. In 1958 he was called back in a dramatic appeal to solve the national crisis over Algeria, and this he did, by lending his prestige to the bitter solution of Algerian independence (settled in 1962).

For the next seven years De Gaulle tried to recapture French glory, largely by acting difficult with England and the United States. He kept England out of the Common Market; followed a separate, nationalistic nuclear policy; he sold arms to Arab states who used them against Israel; he opposed the United States in Vietnam; and on a trip to Canada he caused a furor by approving of the independence of Quebec. (He shouted, "Vive le Quebec libre!") Although the French did begin to prosper in the 1960's and did recover pride in their country as a great power, De Gaulle alienated many other countries, and also many of his own people, especially the young generation who had not followed his career in the war. To them he was practically a dictator. In May 1968 the leftist students of the University of

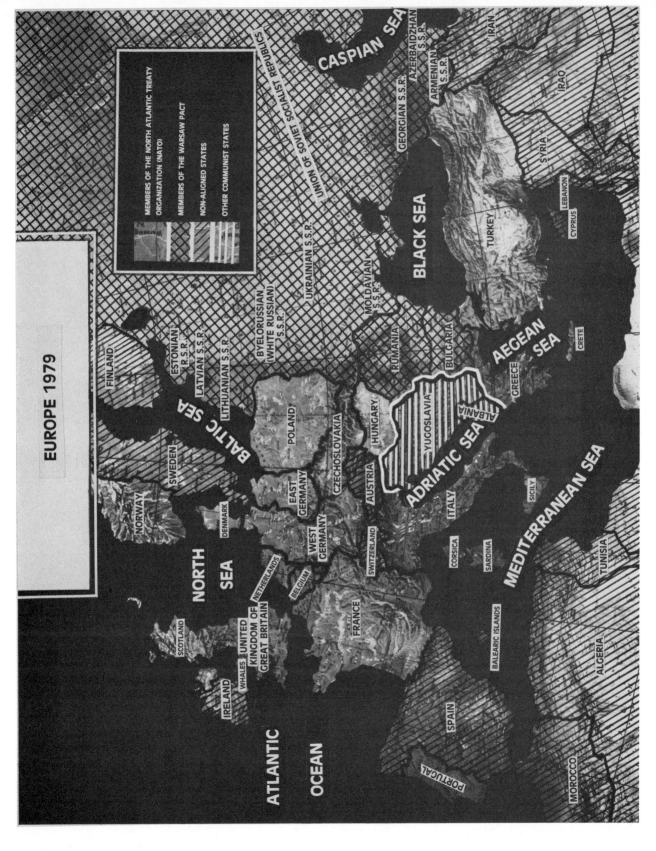

EUROPE 1979

MEMBERS OF THE NORTH ATLANTIC TREATY
ORGANIZATION (NATO)

MEMBERS OF THE WARSAW PACT

NON-ALIGNED STATES

OTHER COMMUNIST STATES

ATLANTIC

OCEAN

NORTH
SEA

BALTIC SEA

CASPIAN SEA

BLACK SEA

AEGEAN
SEA

ADRIATIC SEA

MEDITERRANEAN SEA

UNION OF SOVIET SOCIALIST REPUBLICS

IRELAND

SCOTLAND

WHALES

UNITED
KINGDOM OF
GREAT BRITAIN

NETHERLANDS

BELGIUM

FRANCE

SWITZERLAND

SPAIN

PORTUGAL

BALEARIC ISLANDS

CORSICA

SARDINA

ALGERIA

MOROCCO

TUNISIA

SICILY

ITALY

AUSTRIA

HUNGARY

YUGOSLAVIA

ALBANIA

GREECE

CRETE

BULGARIA

RUMANIA

MOLDAVIAN
S.S.R.

UKRAINIAN S.S.R.

CZECHOSLOVAKIA

POLAND

EAST
GERMANY

WEST
GERMANY

DENMARK

NORWAY

SWEDEN

FINLAND

ESTONIAN
S.S.R.

LATVIAN S.S.R.

LITHUANIAN S.S.R.

BYELORUSSIAN
(WHITE RUSSIAN)
S.S.R.

TURKEY

GEORGIAN S.S.R.

AZERBAIDZHAN
S.S.R.

ARMENIAN
S.S.R.

IRAN

IRAQ

SYRIA

LEBANON

CYPRUS

Paris began a revolt against De Gaulle. They poured out onto the Boulevard St. Michel in a series of demonstrations that won the sympathy of almost everyone in France; trains, buses and planes all ceased to run; Parisians gaily walked to work. But the students went too far and turned ugly, burning cars and cutting down trees along the Seine. In June the reaction against them was almost complete--in the first election since the revolt, De Gaulle won. But the people were called to vote again the following spring. De Gaulle arrogantly asked them to vote one word, "Yes", to him; but the people decided it would be much more amusing to vote "No". He was gone. He died a short time later at his country estate.

De Gaulle was followed initially by a series of conservative presidents who continued to govern France much as he had done, except for quite a change in foreign policy: to a large extent they continued the nationalism, but not the anti-British and anti-American attitude. The biggest change took place in 1980 when the Socialist François Mitterand was elected president. He began to nationalize French industries, including banks. The Baron de Rothschild and many other rich bankers and industrial leaders left the country. Viewed from practically any angle the policies of nationalization were not a success: by 1983 France was in great difficulty economically, and the franc was devalued.

Part III

The Decline of Great Britain

World War II hadn't properly ended when the British public voted Winston Churchill and his Conservative government out of office, replacing them with the Labour Party and Clement Atlee. Atlee's government followed socialistic policies for the next three years, which brought important changes in British society: the government assumed ownership of the Bank of England, public transportation, coal, steel and electricity. It undertook socialized medicine, and began a more comprehensive program of welfare legislation, including unemployment assistance, and old-age pensions. The rapid loss of overseas colonies such as India and Pakistan indicated that at the very time the government was taking on expensive new programs for its people, it was losing power and wealth on the world scene. Within twenty years the once great empire had dwindled to only token outposts, and the British economy never recovered its old strength. Economic recovery from the war was much slower than anticipated, and revenues could not adequately pay for the new programs, so that the government was obliged to suspend further changes after 1948. Nevertheless, the socialism was not undone. A Conservative governent came to office in 1951 and stayed until 1964, with Churchill back in as a prime minister. They set themselves up as distinct from Labour, but in fact they retained Labour's programs (returning only steel to private ownership). The British system of partial socialization became a matter of great pride with them; twenty years later even staunch Conservatives praised their socialized medicine, particularly when compared to the quality of medicine available to the average person in the United States.

The loss of the Suez Canal in 1956 was a blow to British pride, and an unmistakable sign of their declining power in the world. They suffered another blow when De Gaulle kept them out of the Common Market in the 1960's. One serious problem in post-war Britain was the attitude of people in different sectors of the economy. The workers were less productive than their counterparts in booming economies like Germany and Japan; the unions were old-fashioned; management was timid; no one seemed to have the drive or imagination to modernize British industry. The Labour Party returned to office in 1964 under Harold Wilson, but had little success in improving the economy. The Conservatives were back again under Edward Heath in 1970, and did manage to enter the Common Market in 1973. But devaluation of the pound, a serious coal strike, and soaring inflation showed the depth of their problems. Margaret Thatcher became Conservative Prime Minister in 1975, the first woman to hold that post. She began a program of high interest rates, tax cuts, and reduced government spending, with only moderate success. During her administration a problem which had been festering for years erupted in an ugly series of racial clashes. As the British Empire had diminished in size, ironically, the number of colonial non-whites who wanted to move to England increased. Thousands upon thousands of immigrants poured into Heathrow from India, the Middle East and Africa; so that on any given day, that airport was a jostling melee of hundreds of dialects, native costumes, crying babies, and crudely printed welcome signs. These people poured into London. The crowded ghettoes chock-a-block with different cultures erupted in riots in 1981. The violence temporily died down, but the government made no move to address the causes.

Another long-standing problem was Ireland. By the treaty of 1921 the Ulster counties remained a part of the United Kingdom, although Ulster governed itself to a considerable extent. The Protestant majority systematically suppressed the Catholic minority, and in 1968 the Catholics began to fight for independence. Militant Protestant groups on the one hand, and Catholics on the other hand, particularly the Provisional Wing of the Irish Republican Army, became increasing violent. In fifteen years some 1,500 people were killed, either in combat, by starving themselves to death in protest, or through terror by the IRA. The queen's uncle, Lord Mountbatten, was killed by the IRA, as were several of the queen's guards and a dozen tourists in the center of London in 1982. The British army moved into Ireland in 1970, and in 1972 the British suspended the Northern Irish Parliament. Ten years later nothing had changed.

Part IV

Germany

Germany was only half its former size after the war, and began its new existence with the separation from East Germany as a constant reminder of the menaces of Russia. Problems arose immediately over Berlin, an island inside the communist-bloc, itself divided between the free western half, and the communist half. From 1948 to 1949 Russia tried to force the western powers out of Berlin by imposing a blockade. They were foiled by an airlift of over three hundred thousand flights of food and supplies.

The new government began in 1949 with Konrad Adenauer as Chancellor. He remained in power until 1963, a conservative and very able politician, who presided over an economic and political miracle. West Germany developed from

177

a wasteland after the war to one of the three great economic powers of the world in just fifteen years. Even more remarkable in view of their past, they shifted from a totalitarian Nazi regime to one of the most effective democracies in the world, with extremely high citizen participation. East Germany was also rebuilt, and was intended to be a sort of communist show place to the world. But the contrast between the two states was startling, for the vigorous pulsating thriving West Berlin always seemed to defy the clean, stark and lifeless East Berlin. Thousands of easterners fled to the other side, apparently some two million people between 1949 and 1961. Khrushchev decided to force the western countries out of Berlin, and to crack down on escapees. In 1961 he erected an ugly massive wall in Berlin, topped with barbed wire. It embarrassed the United States, partly because there was no way they could object to it. The number of refugees had been a thousand a day, and was reduced to a tiny trickle, many of whom were caught and killed. The wall remained as an ugly symbol of the two different lifestyles it separated.

During the Adenauer era Germany was governed by the Christian Democrats, a fairly conservative party which called for a democratic and economically stable Germany, and which was especially anticommunist. For a while the Federal Republic refused to have diplomatic ties with any nation (other than Russia) which recognized East Germany. Adenauer's anticommunism may have done more harm than good in the cold war in keeping emotions at a fervor pitch against Russia. In 1966 the Social Democratic Party (SPD) won enough seats to form a coalition, with their leader, Willy Brandt, as head of the goverment. The SPD was a socialist party which had been very important before Germany's deviation with Hitler. Now it became increasingly popular, in part by playing down socialism and for the workers, emphasizing economic reforms which appealed also to the middle class. In foreign policy under Brandt there was a major shift toward accepting the inevitable, and improving relations with Eastern Europe.

The SPD continued in power first under Brandt, then under Helmut Schmidt, through the 1970's. In 1982 a conservative government came in under Kohl, with implications which were not immediately clear. Desite the success of Kohl, one longterm trend was evident for Western Europe from about 1960 on: the steady success of socialist parties and doctrines in virtually every country. Scandinavia had "cradle to grave" security for its people before any other western democracies, but Britain was also early on the scene with national ownership of transportation, mines, and medicine which was retained even under staunch conservative Margaret Thatcher. By 1983 France, Spain and Portugal had all elected socialist governments, and Italy, which had fluctuated for years, and had been dominated by the Catholic Christian Democrats, looked forward to an election which might bring socialism to them as well.

Part V

European Unity

World War II was a turning point in history of world power, as the two most powerful nations after 1945 were no longer European nations, but the

United States and Russia. England, France, Italy and Germany (not to mention the Netherlands and Spain) which had once been the greatest nations in the world, were great no longer, and at at first blush, seemed unlikely ever to compete seriously with the two new giants. A plan to unite the diminished countries of Europe into some sort of supranational unity gathered popularity after the war. Some enthusiasts envisaged a government of Europe and even an army of Europe; but national pride stood in the way of their realization. The creation of the Council of Europe in 1949 at Strasbourg, France, was the first step toward a political state, but it never became more than an advisory body; likewise, up until 1954 there was talk of a European Defense Community, a plan vetoed that year by France. Leading advocates of economic unity were Jean Monnet and Robert Schuman of France, and Konrad Adenauer of West Germany.

In 1951 Schuman persuaded France, West Germany, Italy, the Netherlands, Belgium and Luxembourg to form the European Coal and Steel Community. The union was a success, for by 1955 coal production had increased 23 percent; and iron and steel by 150 percent. In 1957 the six nations involved signed the Treaty of Rome, which created the European Economic Community, known as the Common Market, or the EEC. This called for free trade among its members, free flow of capital and labor, and equal wages and social benefits for all six countries. The Common Market was a great success and other countries began to imitate it and also to try to enter its union. However, when France single-handedly kept Britain out of the Common Market in 1963 and 1967, one weakness of the organization was apparent to all. De Gaulle also arrogantly pushed his own policies on other issues. After he left office, England was admitted in 1973, as well as Denmark and Ireland; and later Spain, Portugal and Greece applied for membership. But the impossibility of defying another egocentric in the future was a source of concern.

QUESTIONS FOR REFLECTION

1. What were some of the main problems plaguing the United States in the first fifteen years after the war? How did these differ from problems suffered by England, France and Germany?

2. Read extra material on the McCarthy hearings, the Civil Rights movement, the Cuban Missile crisis, and the Vietnam War. How serious was each of these problems for the American nation? What mistakes did the American government make? How did the American public react in each case; was public opinion "right" or "wrong"?

3. How democratic is Germany today? How does it compare with England or France? How prosperous have those countries been since the war?

4. What are the prospects for a united Europe? What are the successes and what are the failures of the European Community?

SUGGESTED BIBLIOGRAPHY

G. A. Almond (ed.), The Struggle for Democracy in Germany (1949)
M. Balfour, West Germany (1968)

C. N. Degler, Alluence and Anxiety: The United States Since 1945 (1968)
H. Feis, Churchill, Roosevelt, Stalin: The War They Wages and the Peace They
  Sought (1957)
J. H. Franklin, From Freedom to Slavery (1947, 1967)
W. B. Hamilton (ed.), A Decade of the Commonwealth, 1955-1964 (1966)
M. F. Hertz, Beginnings of the Cold War (1966)
A. Meir and E. M. Rudwick, From Plantation to Ghetto (1966)
G. E. Mowry, The Urban Nation, 1920 - 1960 (1965)
A. Werth, France, 1940-1955 (1956)
A. Werth, The de Gaulle Revolultion (1960)
C. Wilmot, The Struggle for Europe (1952)
G. Wright, The Reshaping of French Democracy (1948)

CHAPTER 13: AFTER 1945: THE COMMUNIST BLOC

Part I

Eastern Europe After Stalin

Stalin died in January 1953, and it was widely assumed that this would mean a lessening of autocracy within the Soviet Union. In the East European Soviet satellite countries there was a widespread hope for relaxation of police power, more national diversity and perhaps a measure of political freedom. A wave of uprisings took place, sparked by a new optimism that things could change. In East Germany a wave of strikes began in 1953, set off by a raise in work norms. The strikers attacked Russian troops and government buildings, but were put down when Russia sent three armored division to East Berlin. In 1956 in Poznan, Poland, factory workers rioted, and over a hundred people were killed and hundreds arrested. Here the outcome was a political change: Wladislaw Gomulka became the new head of the government, who introduced some liberal policies. The most serious outburst occurred in Hungary. There, in October 1956, workers and students staged an uprising with molotov cocktails and rifles. They attacked the police and some communist officials, and even shied rocks at Russian tanks. There was a temporary victory of sorts under a popular leader, Imre Nagy; but Russian troops moved in in November, seized the government, and put in Janos Kadar as premier. Nagy was executed, and some 200,000 Hungarians fled to safety, many of them to the United States.

Sometimes genuinely liberal changes took place, as in Rumania. After 1958 the Rumanian leader Gheorghiu-Dej took a stand against economic demands of the Russians, and pursued a rather successful policy of independent industrialization with aid and loans from the West. Russian control was relaxed. Russian troops left the country in 1958, and the Russian language was dropped from the schools. Nicolae Ceausecu, who followed as premier, was even more nationalistic but managed to hold his own. In Czechoslavakia, in contrast, a more aggressive stand for nationalism and independence from Russian control was pursued by Alexander Dubcek in 1968, with tragic results. The Czechs were becoming very liberal and industrial, and making a mark in intellectual work, particularly filmmaking, with greater bonds being formed with the West. The Russians invaded the country in August 1968, and immediately reversed all of Dubcek's liberal policies.

No other meaningful tests of socialist independence from Soviet domination were made for more than fifteen years, then once again Poland became the center of certain limited demands against Russia. Under Gomulka, in the late fifties and early sixties, the Polish Community Party made peace with the Catholic Church, halted collectivization of land, and established greater· trade and cultural contacts with the West. They suffered from economic mismanagement and food shortages, however. In 1970 a series of strikes broke out over food shortages, attracting particular attention at the shipyards at Gdansk. The strikes were put down violently, with a number of deaths. For ten years there was a hiatus, during which time the economy continued to falter and food remained in scarce supply. In 1980 the government of Edward

Gierek raised meat prices, and was faced with more strikes, and a charismatic new leader of the Polish Solidarity Movement, Lech Walesa. The workers demanded increased wages and family subsidies, and a memorial to the victims of 1970. Gierek was dismissed as head of the Polish party and replaced by Stanislaw Kania, who in 1981 was in turn replaced by General Wojciech Jaruzelski. At first the Polish Communist Party made real changes; then in 1981 Jaruzelski imposed martial law, eventually arrested Walesa, and kept him imprisoned for a year. The United States imposed economic sanctions against Russia and against Poland, without any marked success in forcing a change for the better. There was a moderation of tone in 1983. But the prospect was confusing--Walesa was out of prison and restored to his former job, but constantly subjected to detention and interrogation.

Part II

Russia After Stalin

After Stalin's death no new leader at first emerged. Lavrenti Beria, the much feared and hated head of the secret police was dismissed and then executed. Georgi Malenkov became premier for two years, but by 1955 Nikita Khrushchev used his power to have Malenkov removed and Nikolai Bulganin placed as premier; then in 1958 Khrushchev himself became premier. Khrushchev led an attack on Stalin's memory, to such effect that by 1958 all strong supporters of Stalin's policies had been removed. However, they were not executed, as enemies might have been in Stalin's day. There was a slight easing up of repression at this time: intellectuals enjoyed more freedom than they had before but there were always distinct limits. Aleksandr Solzhenitsyn was allowed to publish One Day in the Life of Denisovitch, but Boris Pasternak was not allowed to accept the Nobel Prize for literature in 1958 for Dr. Zhivago.

Khrushchev made a number of mistakes, both in foreign policy and in economic policy. He tried to keep up the defense budget (Sputnik was launched in 1957), yet he also tried to decentralize economic planning and to provide more consumer goods. In agriculture he tried to bring virgin land under cultivation, determined to feed his own people; this increased wheat production initially, but all too soon the land had eroded and the problem of inadequate grain remained a serious one. When added to this aggressive but unsuccessful foreign policy, by 1964 Khrushchev was in serious trouble and had to resign. He was replaced by Alexei Kosygin as premier and Leonid Brezhnev as party secretary. Brezhnev in 1977 became president and head of state as well as head of party, with more personal power than anyone since Stalin. Under his leadership the regime became substantially more repressive, with freedom for intelectuals and harassment of Jews. Two of the most visible intellectuals, Solzhenitsyn and the physicist, Andrei Sakharov, both won Nobel prizes, and suffered from varying degrees of harassment, until Solzhenitzyn was actually expelled (he now lives in the United States). There is still no place for intellectual freedom in the Soviet Union, much less for open criticism of the governemnt.

In foreign policy, the Brezhnev period was less threatening than the Khrushchev years, although the Russians did put down the Czech uprising with force, supplied weapons and expertise to Third World countries in Africa, Latin America and Asia, and also invaded Afghanistan in 1979. The Afghanistan invasion was the most openly aggressive act in twenty years, and produced a grain embargo from the United States and a American boycott of the 1980 Moscow Olympic Games. However, the invasion was not a success. The Afghanistani people resisted obdurately and by 1983 the Russians had suffered 30,000 casualties and low morale in their army. For the first time Russian television acknowledged difficulties with the invasion. The Soviets did not play a large role in Vietnam, or openly interfere in Poland. The arms race between the two superpowers continued, but the Soviets seemed unlikely to project any radical moves in the near future.

QUESTIONS FOR REFLECTION

1. How repressive has Russia been since the war in Eastern Europe? What successes have the various countries had in self-determination? How does their life today compare with the situation there before World War I?

2. How has the Soviet Union changed since the war? Is their foreign policy still basically the same? Are they as "dangerous" to the United States today as they were in 1960?

3. Do you find evidence that the Soviet Union will change in the future? If you lived in Eastern Europe, how would you behave?

CHAPTER 14 - AFTER 1945: THE EAST

Part I

The Middle East

The area of the world which has seen the most bitter conflict since World War II has been the Middle East, and forty years later passions and hatred still run rampant. There are many threads running through the story, but the two most dominant themes and the two main sources of distrust have been religion and oil--sometimes, but not always related. Of the two, oil has been a recent phenomenon. But religious conflict in the region goes back five thousand years.

Religious Background

Of the three great religions competing for the holy places of Jerusalem, the oldest is Judaism. In ancient times when most of the people of the world were polytheistic, the Jews had two striking new concepts: they were monotheistic, believing in only one God; and they were moral and ethical, believing that their God (Yahweh) demanded righteous behavior from them. In contrast, the ancient Egyptians and Mesopotamians, and later also the Greeks and Romans, believed in numerous of gods and godesses, and endowed them with any number of immoral and capricious characteristics. The goddess of love, to take one example, was called Ishtar in Mesopotamia, Aphrodite in Greece, and Venus in Rome. In the Epic of Gilgamesh (around 3000 B.C.), Ishtar is a willful, jealous and murderous creature, one of Gilgamesh's most deadly enemies. In Greece, two thousand years later in The Iliad, Aphrodite is less poisonous and deadly, but still rather nasty and capricous, in many ways more deceitful and immature than the human beings in the story.

Judaism was unique in that it was the only religion in ancient times which had a modern concept of one God, and a code of moral and ethical behavior demanded of all its believers. Jews survived without too much trouble in those times because in the days of polytheism, societies tended to be rather hospitable about religions. This was true in Rome, where there was a plethora of religions all more or less accepted: the familiar paganism (Venus, Jupiter, Mars and other deities of Mount Olympus), Isis from Egypt, Zoroaster from Persia, Mithra, beloved of the Roman soldiers (for men only), and of course the cult of the emperor himself, Caeser. The Jews were different, but they did not proselytize, and kept to themselves. They ran into conflict with Rome at the siege of Masada, a tragic episode where some Jews committed suicide rather than give in to Rome; but Masada was unusual.

Things were different with Christianity. The Christians took many of their beliefs from Judaism, including monotheism and the concept of a rigorous moral code. However, they differed not only in the fact that they followed Jesus Christ, but also because they proselytized from the start. In some ways Jesus Christ was crucified because he was a threat to law and order in the Roman Empire; he and his followers were not harmless to the Romans--Christians

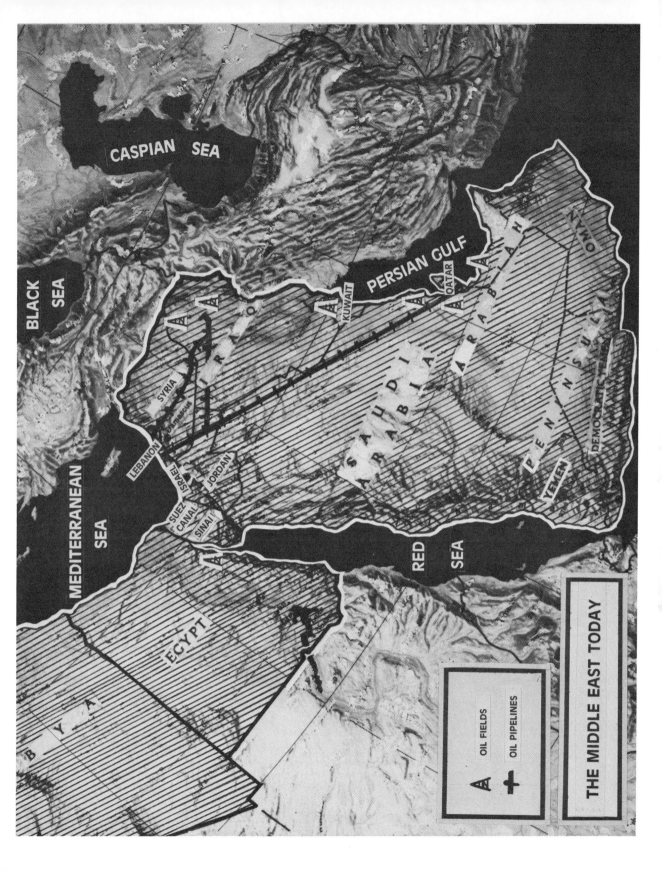

CASPIAN SEA

BLACK SEA

MEDITERRANEAN SEA

PERSIAN GULF

SYRIA

Damascus

LEBANON

ISRAEL

JORDAN

SUEZ CANAL

SINAI

EGYPT

LIBYA

RED SEA

SAUDI ARABIA

ARABIAN PENINSULA

KUWAIT

QATAR

OMAN

YEMEN

DEMOCRATIC

IRAQ

OIL FIELDS

OIL PIPELINES

A

THE MIDDLE EAST TODAY

were a threat because they defied the worship of the emperor, and undercut his authority. The bloody saga of Christianity is a direct result of such beliefs, including the important idea constantly reaffirmed in the centuries to follow (especially during the Crusades), that a Christian killed while battling to spread the faith would go directly to heaven. Once Christians agreed on a pope and an oracle of truth for their faith, deviations from the conventional faith were punishable by death. Since there were more than eighty varieties of Christianity within the first two centuries after Christ, this meant a constant bloodbath among Christian themselves, whereby heretics such as the Albigensians or Antinomians were put to death. Later there were rivers of blood when the Protestant Reformation divided all of Christendom between Catholics and Protestants. There was appalling devastation; and in the 20th century this religious struggle continues in Northern Ireland.

Islam began with Mohammed, who was born in what is now Saudia Arabia, in 570. Also monotheistic and highly moral, Islam is based on revelations made to Mohammed by God through the angel Gabriel, which Mohammed wrote down as the Koran. Unlike Jesus Christ, Mohammed was never supposed to be a deity himself, but rather, an intermediary. The faithful were enjoined to believe that there was no other God but Allah, to pray to Allah five times a day facing the holy city of Mecca, to visit Mecca once in their lifetime, read the Koran, give alms to the poor, and fast from sunup to sundown during the month of Ramadan (which corresponds more or less with the month of August). There was a wrathful God who would fiercely punish anyone breaking their moral code, or refusing to believe in the true faith.

One difficulty is that Jews, Christians and Moslems have always differed on their moral code: only the Moslems have always forbidden alcoholic beverages (a very small number of Christians do also, but it was never a tenet of the original faith). More important, Jews and Christians have strictly insisted on monogamy, while Moslems have always permitted polygamy, and Mohammed himself had numerous wives. Moslems are extremely puritanical and especially strict with women. These differences were important, for Christians and Moslems believed that anyone breaking their moral law should be put to death. In fact, Moslems accepted the Christian premise that a person dying in defense of faith was dispatched instantly to heaven; and in the centuries after Mohammed died (in 632) both groups conveyed thousands of the faithful to the pearly gates in just that fashion.

Mohammed's death created a crisis in the faith, for his followers disagreed on the method of choosing a successor. The larger group known today as the Sunni Moslem have agreed that religious leaders may be chosen in each generation from the wise and reputable men on hand; while a smaller number, the Shiites, insisted that only a direct heir of Mohammed could lead the faithful. Most of Mohammed's descendants were hacked to bits in the desert after his death. Shiites believe that there was a miraculous escape, and that the twelth, or "hidden imam", Mohammed al-Muntazar (Mohammed's last descendant who disappeared in 878), lives on among the people, and will return on the last day to bring an era of peace and prosperity. Governments until then are only provisional. Shiites have stricter rules than Sunnis, and also more religious holidays. They commemorate one of the massacres of Mohammed's heirs by a day of atonement and flagellation. In Shiite countries there is no difference between church and state; the ayatollah is the highest religious leader in the faith, and crimes against the faith may be punished by the state executioner. One of the main differences between Jews and Christians on the one hand, and Moslems, particularly Shiite Moslems, on the other hand, is the marked disparity in law codes. In the 1980's adultery was still punishable in Iran, the leading Shiite country, by death by stoning; and other moral deviations were punishable by beheading or by whipping.

In the first hundred years after Mohammed's death, the Moslems carved out an empire which included most of the Middle East, North Africa, Portugal and Spain. They were held back in Tours, France, in the year 733 by Charles Martel; but they remained in Spain until 1492. They also swept up through the Byzantine Empire into Eastern Europe and there rose as far as Vienna, where they were defeated in the 17th century. In between those years, there were numerous conflicts between Moslems and European Christians, particularly at the time of the Crusades. In the 20th century two faiths continue to habor irreconcilable differences, and have quite opposing views philosophically and politically.

The Creation of Israel

Jews were scattered throughout Europe after the advent of Christianity, and tended to be persecuted everywhere at some time or other; but a new wave of antisemitism was engulging central Europe in the late 19th century. In response to this, Jews became persuaded that their best hope was to return to Palestine, which they considered their ancient homeland, to found a Zionist state. At the instigation of Theodore Herzl (who was shocked over the Dreyfus case in France) several thousand families settled there by World War I. Although the native Palestinians were not pleased, as only a small part of the Ottoman Empire, they had no say in the matter. The English issued the Balfour Declaration in 1917 promising their support for a Jewish homeland in Palestine, providing non-Jews were given civil and religious rights. After World War I the area was a British mandate, and thousands of Jews moved there, bought land and put down roots. By 1922 there were 85,000 Jews to 650,000 Palestinians. By the mid-thirties the numbers were greater and tension increased accordingly; so despite the vastly increased numbers of Jews now fleeing Hitler's Europe, in 1939 the British limited the number who could enter Palestine to 75,000 per year. During World War II some fled to England, some to Argentina, and some to the United States; and thousands more continued to try and enter Palestine, despite the fact that the British troops stationed there were under orders to prevent ships from docking once the quota was filled. Many people in desperation entered the area secretly; some scuttled their ships in order to force the British to take them. By 1946 the Jewish population was 678,000 to 1,269,000 Palestinians. The Jewish extremist groups Stern and Irgun Zvai Leumi (the latter included Menachem Begin) committed a number of atrocities at this time, killing several people in an explosion at the King David Hotel in Jerusalem, and 254 Arabs in the village of Deir Yassin.

In 1947 the British asked the U.N. for a solution, and they proposed a partition plan which would have given about half the land area to the Jews and the other half to the Palestinians. The Jews accepted the partition plan but the Palestinians did not, and there was soon a civil war. The British withdrew on May 14, 1948, and the same day the state of Israel was created.

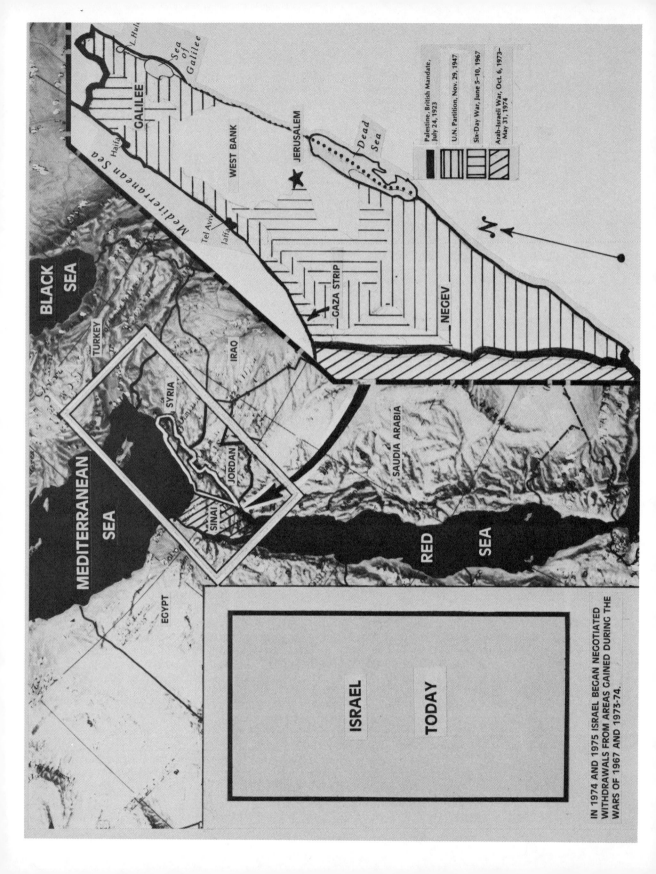

BLACK SEA

MEDITERRANEAN SEA

TURKEY

IRAQ

SYRIA

JORDAN

SINAI

EGYPT

RED SEA

SAUDIA ARABIA

Mediterranean Sea

L. Hula

Sea of Galilee

GALILEE

Haifa

WEST BANK

Tel Aviv

Jaffa

JERUSALEM

Dead Sea

GAZA STRIP

NEGEV

Palestine, British Mandate, July 24, 1923

U.N. Partition, Nov. 29, 1947

Six-Day War, June 5–10, 1967

Arab-Israeli War, Oct. 6, 1973– May 31, 1974

N

ISRAEL

TODAY

IN 1974 AND 1975 ISRAEL BEGAN NEGOTIATED WITHDRAWALS FROM AREAS GAINED DURING THE WARS OF 1967 AND 1973-74.

On May 15, Egypt, Jordan, Lebanon and Syria declared war. Meanwhile, King Farouk of Egypt and King Abdullah of Jordan (grandfather of current King Hussein) suggested to the Palestinian people that they might want to leave for the duration of the war, which was expected to be brief. Some 500,000 Palestinians followed this advice, and moved to Jordan and Lebanon. But they lost the war and did not return as planned; instead they continued to live on in refugee camps. The Jews were vastly outnumbered by the Arabs in the first war, but were superior in weapons and expertise, as many of them were European-educated and had fought in World War II. Israel gained fifty percent more territory than they had before.

King Farouk was overthrown in 1952, and the following year Gamal Abdel Nasser emerged as the Egyptian president, the most charismatic man of the Middle East in modern times. Nasser had a swarthy, handsome face, with heavy black eyebrows and flashing teeth. He was a man of great personal charm and far-ranging plans for his people, with unremitting hatred for Israel. He was hostile to the west for their colonialism and their pro-Israeli attitude, and began a flirtation with the Soviet Union. Egypt began planning to dam the Nile River at Aswan, and when the United States refused to finance it, Nasser went to the Kremlin. He also seized the Suez Canal, which had been built and run by France and England. A war broke out between Egypt on the one hand, and France, England and Israel on the other. The U.N. denounced France, England and Israel as aggressors, and ended the war by sending a peace-keeping force to the area. The United States stayed out. At the end of the war, the Suez Canal was purchased by Nasser and was opened to all traffic, but problems continued: France and England felt let down by the United States, and Nasser had been humiliated by Israel.

In 1958 Nasser created the short-lived United Arab Republic of Egypt and Syria. In 1967 he persuaded the U.N. peacekeeping force in the Sinai to depart, and he moved Egyptian troops into the location. Israel, persuaded that Egypt was about to invade, attacked Egypt first, starting the third war. The Israelis destroyed many Egyptian planes (Russian made) on the ground, and defeated them in six days. The Israelis occupied the Sinai; all of Palestine west of the Jordan River, including Jerusalem; and the Golan Heights, from where Syria had been attacking them. It was a humiliating defeat for Nasser personally, and he was planning yet another war when he died of a heart attack in 1970.

Nasser was succeeded by Anwar el-Sadat, another man of great charm and sophistication, although not the popular idol Nasser had been. Sadat broke with Russia and expelled their advisors in 1972; and in 1973, hoping to regain the lost territory, he began the fourth war against Israel by attacking on the Israeli holy day, Yom Kippur. This war lasted longer, but the Israelis occupied even more territory than before, including the Sinai; and Sadat then followed a policy which angered the Arab world, although it gladdened the hearts of the West: he agreed to pursue a plan for peace with Prime Minister Begin of Israeli, under the auspices of American President Jimmy Carter. The Camp David accord was signed in 1979, and included a complicated timetable whereby the Israelis would evacuate the Sinai and the West Bank, while Egypt would become the first Arabic state to recognize the existence of Israel. The treaty in no way ended the bloodshed; on the contrary, violence in the Middle East continued to be a daily theme, and even increased. Sadat was assassinated in October of 1981 by right-wing religious fanatics. And the fifth war began.

The PLO

In 1948 when the Palestinians left Israel, most ended up in refugee camps in Jordan, Lebanon and Syria. In 1964 when it became clear that there was no united Arab front to press their claims, some of their number created the Palestine Liberation Organization, or PLO, whose purpose was to destroy Israel. After the 1967 war, the Al Fatah wing of the organization, led by Yasser Arafat, assumed the leadership. For a few years more radical spinter groups of the PLO, the Popular Front for the Liberation of Palestine and the Black September movement, pursued a policy of terrorism. Planes were hijacked, tourists were shot at airports and bloody raids were made across the Israeli border. Two of the most notorious acts of terrorism were the massacre of eleven Israeli atheletes during the 1972 Munich Olympic Games; and the 1976 hijacking of an Air France plane to Entebbe, Uganda, where the 103 passengers were rescued by an Israeli commando raid. The PLO also directed hostilities toward King Hussein of Jordan in 1970, so that the king ordered the several hundred thousand Palestinians to leave his country and resettle in Lebanon. By 1982 they numbered almost 700,000 people in Lebanon.

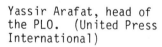
Yassir Arafat, head of the PLO. (United Press International)

Lebanon

Lebanon was the site of ancient Phoenicia, the sailing wonder of the ancient world, and a center of finance and tourism after World War II. Lebanon had been a mandate of France, and became independent in 1941, with a charming blend of French and Arabic cultures unique in the Middle East. Lebanon was also unique in that it had a large number of Christians in its population, and a democratic government which provided for equal representation of Moslems and Christians in the administration. This compromise began to crack as early as 1958, when a civil war broke out between Christians and Moslems. Things were patched up (American marines landed), but in the 1970's the war was renewed. The Christian-Moslem conflict was enormously complicated by the PLO attacks on Israel, for they brought retaliation from Israel in the form of bombings and harassment. Thus the civil war broadened to include foreign intervention. This took a serious turn in 1976 when Syria invaded, ostensibly to restore peace, and Syrian troops were still present seven years later. In the mid-seventies more than 40,000 people were killed, and Lebanon was divided between Moslem, Christian, PLO and Syrian areas. In 1978 Israel invaded briefly, then turned the area over to the U.N. force, UNIFIL. But hostilities between the PLO and the Israelis never ceased, and in June 1982 Israel invaded a second time, killing thousands of Lebanese and virtually destroying Beirut. The PLO and many Palestinians left, and were now dispersed through eleven countries in the Middle East. But Lebanon continued in a state of almost total anarchy. The new president Bashir Gemayel, elected in August 1982, was immediately murdered. With Israeli forces looking on, the Lebanese Christian Phalangists then massacred several hundred Palestinians in a refugee camp. Other western troops were brought in to restore order, including American marines; but as of 1983 Lebanon was still a violent and troubled nation. When the U.S. embassy was bombed that April, one of the most ominous developments was that the first group to claim responsibility was a fanatical Shiite organization which had been sent by the Ayatollah Khomeini of Iran to southern Lebanon to stir up trouble. In discussions over the latest outrage, some observers felt that Lebanon was not a viable country and would never successfully be united again, a bleak prospect to say the least.

The 1982 Lebanese invasion by Israel was the cause of serious forebodings. For forty years many westerners and especially Americans had supported Israel through thick and thin. As the one successful democratic state in the Middle East, as the one state which purported to conduct itself in an ethical and moral way (much like the United States), both Israelis themselves and Americans who supported them were horrified at Israel's militant new role. There were noisy demonstrations through Israel against Prime Minister Begin, not only because of Lebanon, but also because of his repressive policies toward Arabs in the West Bank of the Jordan. A former terrorist, Begin was a hardnosed conservative and a great favorite among Sephardic Jews, who constituted the majority in Israel. Unlike the Ashkenazi Jews, who immigrated from Europe and tended to be liberal and well-educated, the Sephardim were an impoverished group who had lived in the Middle East for centuries, who had suffered under Arabic regimes, and who were the most anti-Arab members of the population. This group rejoiced when Begin bombed a nuclear plant in Iraq, annexed all of Jerusalem, annexed the Golan Heights, and invaded Lebanon. But the Ashkenazi majority and many observers elsewhere in the world shuddered.

Oil

Apart from and in addition to religious differences, one of the other sources of tension in the Middle East was oil. The first oil in the area was discovered in Iran before World War I, and exploited by the Anglo-Iranian Oil Company. Between the wars, other western nations began to exploit the oil of Iraq; but most important of all was the opening up of the oil of Saudia Arabia in the 1930's by the Arabian-American Oil Company (Aramco). Saudia Arabian production grew rapidly, from 165,000 barrels a day in 1945 to over a million in 1955. In 1979 they produced 476 million metric tons a year. Oil was also found in vast new quantities in Kuwait, Qatar and Bahrein. The period of initial development of the oil reserves coincided with a period of nationalistic feeling in the Middle East, followed quickly by the conviction that they were being exploited by western companies.

This resentment came to a head in Iran, and is still a factor in Iranian politics. In 1951 the Iranian government of Dr. Mohammed Mossadeq nationalized the Anglo-Iranian Oil Company. The shah, Mohammed Reza Pahlavi, dismissed Mossadeq in 1953, then fled the country himself when rioting broke out. The United States gave him the support necessary to return to power, and for the next twenty years he ruled Iran while closely aligned to the United States. Under the shah, Iran was thrown into a cultural revolution. Schools, hospitals, factories and roads were built. Land was distributed to the peasants, and a form of parliamentary government was established. But the government was still rigidly autocratic, with a notorious secret police, the Savak. And corruption which was rampant at every level, was particularly conspicuous at the top, where the shah and his numerous family amassed gigantic fortunes from the oil revenues of the country.

Despite their close ties to the United States, in 1976 Iran led nine other members of OPEC (an international organization of oil-producing countries) in raising oil prices. The efforts to control oil prices of OPEC caused a serious energy crisis in the West; but they also brought serious problems to the countries involved. In 1976 Saudia Arabia and the United Arab Emirates refused to cooperate, so that Iranian oil exports dropped by 38 percent. This created a serious economic crisis in Iran and brought anti-shah forces into prominence.

The Ayatollah Khomeini, living in exile, inspired a religious Shiite uprising against the shah, which proceeded as a social and political upheaval at the same time. The puritanical Shiites protested the crude western materialism which was taking over Iran, the loose behavior of their women, the public drinking of the shah and his entourage. The government toppled in a few days, and the royal family fled overseas, where the shah eventually died. Khomeini threatened to export the Shiite fervor throughout the Middle East, and did send troublemakers to Lebanon in 1982, and began a war with Iraq. The shah had tried to move Iran forward too quickly; Khomeini tried to move backward too fast. The shah had been widely criticized for his repressive government and secret police; Khomeini was if anything, even more repressive.

The anti-western hostility of Syria and Iraq, the Russian invasion of Afghanistan, and the megalomania of Muammar el-Qaddafi of Libya were all additional reasons for alarm over the Middle East in the 1980's.

Part II

China

In 1931 Japan began an expansionary thrust into Manchuria, setting up and occupying a separate entity named Manchukuo under Japanese hegemony. Then in 1937 China was subjected to a full-scale invasion by Japan. The Japanese made a string of coastal conquests, and set up two puppet governments. The Nationalists under Chiang Kai-shek therefore retired to the remote western area of Chungking, for the duration of the war, where they seemed to stagnate and grow even more corrupt, certainly failing to win any lasting affection or loyalty from the 500,000,000 Chinese people. It was a different story with the Communists. They were based in Yenan in the north, from where they fanned out in all directions, creating a network of armies and loyal councils through the North China countryside. During the ensuing war, Mao's forces offered more resistence to the Japanese invasion than did the Nationalists. They organized more effective cooperation and control over the people in the non-occupied areas and came to exemplify a restored Chinese "nationalism".

In 1945 when the war ended the Chinese were in desperate straits from disease and malnutrition, with hundreds of thousands of refugees and widespread devastation, despite a billion dollars in aid they had received from the United States. When the Nationlists tried to resume control of the country they were faced with a civil war; it lasted from 1946 until 1949. Chiang's regime had deteriorated badly. His army and government were corrupt; his bureaucrats venal; his troops cruel and repacious toward the people; and politically they had become increasingly dictatorial. Mao Tse-t'ung and his communists were a striking contrast. Puritanical and severe, his troops were well disciplined and trained. The years of work in he countryside had paid off with loyalty from the peasants. They were won over by Mao's ideology of a peasant revolution, particularly as communist troops had shared in the agricultural work in the villages. In 1949 Chiang Kai-shek fled to Taiwan, and Mao established the People's Republic of China.

During the first three years Mao consolidated his power. The communist party extended its reach down into the smallest villages, with mass meetings and massive political indoctrination. Landlords were punished and even executed; land was redistributed. Many value changes were made: women's rights were promoted, divorce was accepted, and the party began trying to transfer the traditional loyalty of the Chinese from the family to the state. As this was happening, Mao received substantial quantities of aid and hundreds of advisors from Soviet Russia. In 1953 he issued his first Five Year Plan. Farm property was collectivized and peasants began to work as laborers on the farms. China also began to industrialize at a furious pace, building new railroads, steel factories, dams, irrigation projects, and for the first time tapping their oil.

China was going through the same transformation which Stalin had produced in Russia, a radical break with the past and metamorphosis into an advanced industrial nation. The Mao regime never suffered the disastrous human slaughter Russia saw in the 1920's, but there were serious problems just the same: by 1958 many people were frustrated at the loss of freedom and privacy, and angry over food shortages. To cope with the crisis Mao began The Great Leap Forward, which entailed a break with the Soviet model of communism, and the consolidation of collective farms into large communes of four or five thousand families, with communal meals. An important change forced local communes to undertake everything from their own government to the production of steel. By 1960 the move was acknowledged to be a failure, and the country was in trouble from lack of food. Now the policy was reversed, and the communes were broken down again. There was an economic recovery of sorts. In 1966 Mao became occupied with a new problem--he was disillusioned with the direction of the Chinese Communist Party. To reorient the country he launched the Great Proletarian Cultural Revolution, which was an effort to revive revolutionay fervor, combat the elitism of the Soviets, and foster proletarian culture. This movement was spearheaded principally by young people in the Red Guards. Released from schools, which were virtually shut down, and other tasks, they were free to roam the countryside on a violent campagin against old ideas and customs, and against decadent influences from the West (such as Beethoven). Many professors, white-collar workers and other professionals were forced to work with the peasants in agricultural experiments during this period. The Movement soon lapsed into senseless violence and caused a national crisis. A deep split in the party occurred, although Mao, his defense minister Lin Piao, and Mao's wife, Chiang Chi'ing, won for the time being, and hounded their enemies out of office. During this time China had broken completely with the Soviet Union, and had backed Albania against them. They had supported dissident groups in Asia, fought a border war with India in 1962, and in 1964 exploded their first atomic bomb. Certainly the break with Russia was welcome news to the West. The United States had supported Chiang Kai-shek for years, and after 1949 had recognized his regime in Taiwan as the official China, a policy many Americans considered ludicrous. Now the time seemed propitious to make a change. President Nixon seized the opportunity, and after numerous overtures and offers of promising trade relations, Nixon went to China and posed pretentiously by the Great Wall in 1972. The two powers began a policy of trade and cultural exchanges and established full diplomatic relations in 1979.

Mao's second in command from 1949 on had been Chou En-lai, prime minister at the time of the accord with the United States. However, both men died in 1976. The new leader to emerge was Teng Hsiao-p'ing, who, in much the same way Khrushchev had turned on Stalin in Russia, now turned on Mao and all he had done in the sixties. The excesses of Mao's cultural revolution were categorically denounced, and Mao's widow, Chiang Ch'ing and her "Gang of Four" were arrested; she was sentenced to death, although the sentence was not carried out. Teng called for many changes, above all modernization in China of industry, agriculture and defense. He began obtaining loans from the West, sent students abroad, and signed trade treaties with Japan, the United States and European powers. Within the country factories were now allowed to sell goods above their quotas at a profit, and peasants were permitted to cultivate more private land.

THE FAR EAST SINCE THE SECOND WORLD WAR

U.S.S.R.

SAKHALIN

KURILE
ISLANDS

MONGOLIA

MANCHURIA

JAPAN

N. KOREA

S. KOREA

PAKISTAN

KASHMIR

NEPAL

CHINA

BANGLADESH

INDIA

BURMA

LAOS

MACAO

N. VIETNAM

S. VIETNAM

CAMBODIA

RYUKYU ISLANDS

FORMOSA\TAIWAN

PHILIPPINES

PACIFIC
OCEAN

TERRITORY OF THE
PACIFIC ISLANDS

CEYLON

INDIAN
OCEAN

MALAYSIA

SINGAPORE

BRUNEI

SABAH

INDONESIA

TIMOR

WEST
IRIAN

TERR. OF
NEW GUINEA

PAPUA

AUSTRALIA

COUNTRIES GAINING INDEPENDENCE AFTER THE SECOND WORLD WAR

After his death Mao was denounced and many of his policies reversed, but as the great leader of the Chinese Revolution his reputation remained intact, even as his book, "The Thought of Mao Tse-tung" remained the ideological bible. His contribution had been impressive. China had doubled in population, to about one billion people in 1980, yet with food and shelter for all of them. The per capita income remained low, estimated at $300 to $460 per year; but there was equitable distribution. A new industrial base had been created, foreign trade was soaring, literacy had improved to 90%; health care was available to all. Russia entered the 1980's with problems of crime and alcoholism, dissatisfied religious minority groups, and a society plagued with a new elite almost as untouchable as the aristocrats under the czar. China seemed to fit the ideological mold of communism more closely. They had a regime which maintained strict control over their daily lives and even dictated the size of their families, so that there was no freedom to speak of, and no privacy. On the other hand, their society was scrupulously honest and well disciplined, and enjoyed a degree of prosperity and distribution of benefits never before seen in that country.

Part III

Vietnam

France had colonized Indochina, including Laos, Cambodia and Vietnam, between 1857 and 1883. Although Indochinese troops fought on the French side in World War I, already they shared with other colonials a desire for independence. A young intellectual by the name of Ho Chi Minh, emerged as the leader of this movement and called for self-determination of Indochina at the Versailles Peace Conference, without success. Ho Chi Minh was a communist. He travelled to Russia in the 1920's and joined the French Communist Party, but his first real opportunity came only in World War II. France had fallen to the Nazis, and when the Japanese invaded Indochina, the French regime there collaborated with the enemy. By helping the Japanese, at one stroke, the French gave Ho Chi Minh and his nationalists the loyalty of anyone who was against them. In 1945 he declared Vietnam independent under the Viet Minh. This claim was disputed not only by France, but by religious groups and all anticommunist nationalists. The French reacted by fighting a war from 1946 until their disastrous defeat at Dien Bien Phu in 1954. The United States refused to intervene to help France, although they did contribute $4 billion in aid. After the defeat of Dien Bien Phu, The Geneva Agreements of July 1954 provided for the withdrawal of French and Vietminh troops to either side of a demarcation zone (DMZ), until such time as elections were held to determine reunification. However, the elections were never held. Meanwhile, the United States created the Southeast Asia Treaty Organization (SEATO), a collective security agreement which included the United States, Britain, France, Australia, New Zealand, Thailand, Pakistan and the Philippines.

By 1955 the Americans were convinced that Vietnam was only another version of Korea, a puppet state of the communists in the north. Washington began to support the south Vietnamese government of Ngo Dinh Diem with advisors, military supplies and money. Diem postponed elections and became increasingly repressive. He alienated peasants by restoring rents to landlords, and abolished elected village councils. Since the United States was publicly identified with sympathy to the French, or colonial side, there was automatic resistence to anyone they supported. But Diem alienated many of the Vietnam people in his own right. By 1960 a new anticolonial, nationalist and Communist group was formed, the National Liberation Front, with a military wing called the Viet Cong. The Viet Cong took over much of the countryside and established an informal government which received widespread support, partly out of respect, partly out of fear. Other opponents of Diem were anticommunist, including the Buddhists, some of whom horrified the world by immolating themselves.

Between 1961 and 1963 the United States increased its military presence from 600 to 16,000 troops, and exerted continuous but unsuccessful pressure on Diem to reform. Finally, in 1963 Diem was overthrown in a military coup, with American connivance, and murdered. The Americans then threw their support to the new government of Nguyen Van Thieu. Kennedy was killed on November 22, 1963, and his successor Lyndon Johnson vastly increased U.S. committment to Vietnam. American bombing of North Vietnam began in 1964, with a major, scarcely interrupted barrage lasting from 1965 until 1973. The number of American troops grew to 500,000, though President Nixon began a gradual withdrawal in 1969. Meanwhile, in 1968 peace talks were held in Paris, and after five years, in 1973, a ceasefire was finally arranged and prisoners of war exchanged. Violations of the ceasefire occurred on both sides. In 1975 as South Vietnam was withdrawing its troops from the north, they were attacked and put to rout; the same year Saigon fell to military forces of the north and the Viet Cong. The war was over.

The United States had been mistaken in thinking Vietnam was another version of the conflict in Korea. Vietnam was not only much larger and with an altogether different terrain, they had a long colonial history which was of consummate importance. Because of anger against the French, there was a predisposition for the Vietnamese to distrust all western powers. The war egendered a bitter controversy, not only within the United States, but also in Europe. Europeans who had admired the United States after World War II, now grew contemptuous of American goals and methods, not to mention American expertise. It was difficult to reconcile American bombing of civilians and American massacres with the ideals Americans purported to be serving. American prestige fell throughout the world, and within the United States an entire generation of young people was alienated from their government.

QUESTIONS FOR REFLECTION

1. What would have been the best way to handle the desire of Jews to establish a homeland in the Middle East? (At World War I) At the end of World War II, what would have been an alternative solution? Should the U.N. partition plan have been imposed by force?

2. What solutions are there to the Palestinian problem today? Should there be, for example, a new partition plan?

3. Is Lebanon a viable country today? Some scholars argue that there is too big a gulf between the Shiite Moslems in the south and the Maronite Christians ever to have agreement on a common government. Others say that if Lebanon is further divided, it will become even easier to prey to the Israelis and Syrians. What do you think?

4. How should the West handle relations with a government like that of Khomeini in Iran? Is it likely that Shiism will spread? Experts say the time may be ripe for a new religious revival in the Middle East; if so, what should the West do about it?

5. How has China fared under communism compared to their circumstances since 1850? How does communism in China differ from that in Russia and Eastern Europe?

6. As China increases its contacts with Americans and other Westerners, is it likely that their people will become materialistic? What are the longterm possibilities for such contact?

7. Today, practically everyone believes that the situation in Vietnam was handled wrong ever since 1945. What would have been a better way? Compare Vietnam to Korea and also to El Salvador.

8. Make a list of U.S. interventions in foreign governments since 1945. What tends to make us intervene? Should we intervene in the future?

SUGGESTED BIBLIOGRAPHY

Z. K. Brzezinski, The Soviet Bloc: Unity and Conflict (1960), rev., 1967)
H. Feis, From Trust to Terror: The Onset of the Cold War, 1945-1950 (1970)
G. F. Kennan, American Diplomacy, 1900-1950 (1951)
S. Mikolajczyk, The Rape of Poland (1950)
F. Nagy, The Struggle Behind the Iron Curtain (1948)
H. Ripka, Czechoslavakia Enslaved (1950)
H. Seton-Watson, The East-European Revolution (1950, 1956)
D. Yergin, Shattered Peace: The Origins of the Cold War and the National Security State (1977)

Part I

Latin America

One of the major regions of the Third World is Latin America. It differs from Africa and the Middle East in that most Latin American countries gained their independence a hundred and fifty years ago, while independence came to Africa and the Middle East for the most part since World War II. Yet the longer experience as independent nations has not endowed these nations with stability, democracy, or economic security. On the contrary, for most of their recent history they have been characterized by military coups, rightest dictatorships and economic crises. The stability of the area was particularly threatened when Cuba became a communist country in 1959, and subsequently attempted to export the revolution to the rest of Latin America. The United States has consistently interfered in these countries, first in the 19th century after they issued the Monroe Doctrine. That document was a warning to Europe to stay away from the area, and for the most part they did, although European nations frequently complained when Latin American governments failed to pay their debts. The United States intervened repeatedly. In 1898 they fought a war in Cuba. In 1903 they intervened in Columbia; they helped part of it break away and become an independent Panama, and the United States then built the Panama Canal there. They landed the navy in Nicaragua in 1909, and kept a force there from 1912 to 1925. They sent an army into Mexico in 1916 under General Pershing. These and other incidents created a widespread resentment against Americans and American interference.

The United States pursued a foreign policy known as "Dollar Diplomacy", which meant that Americans investing millions of dollars in Latin America expected the U.S. government to come to their aid if their interests were threatened. American property has been seized on several occasions. In Mexico, in 1938 President Cardenas seized American oil wells; but President Franklin Roosevelt was pursuing his innovative "Good Neighbor Policy", to improve relations with Latin America, and Mexico compensated American oil owners. In 1958 Argentina seized American oil companies; the United States complained to Argentina, but did not actively intervene. Then in 1972 President Salvador Allende of Chile threatened American copper mines with seizure. Allende, a communist, was legally elected, but on the eve of the next election the American CIA helped bring about a coup, during which Allende was killed, and a right-wing military dictatorship was established under Augusto Pinochet.

To many observers, one of the most disturbing features of American intervention was the consistent way in which the U.S. government seemed to support fascist right-wing regimes, such as that of Fulgencio Batista of Cuba, while taking active steps to overthrow Leftist governments, such as those of Allende, or Fidel Castro.

Cuba was an area of great concern after World War II. In 1934 the United States abrogated the Platt Amendment, which ever since the Spanish-American

War had given them the right to intervene in Cuban affairs whenever democracy seemed threatened. There was a coup soon after, and then a succession of presidents. In 1952 Batista seized power, and became one of the most ruthless dictators in the world. Cuba was the richest of all Latin American countries, with lucrative tobacco and sugar exports, and a flourishing tourist industry, which catered to Americans who like to gamble in Havana. This came to an end when Fidel Castro overthrew Batista with a handful of guerilla fighters, in 1959. Batista fled to Florida with some $200 million dollars. Castro established an authoritarian regime, executed opponents, and seized U.S. property. In 1961 the United States broke off relations with Cuba, and Castro revealed his alliance with the Soviet Union. Thousands of Cubans had fled to the United States, and on April 17, 1961, some of their number landed at the Bay of Pigs in an attempt to overthrow Castro. The American government had assisted the expedition in some ways, though they withheld air support. But the expedition was a complete failure, and devastating not only to the Cubans who ended up imprisoned by Castro, but also to the American government. A year later, in October 1962 President Kennedy learned that the Soviet Union was building missile sites in Cuba, and gave notice of a blockade until such time as the missiles were removed. Nikita Khrushchev tried to weather the crisis with bluff threats, but capitulated, ending the deadliest crisis the two superpowers endured after World War II. Kruschev fell from power soon after, while Kennedy had just one year to enjoy his success before he was assassinated. In the meantime, Castro released 1,113 Bay of Pigs prisoners, and relations between Cuba and the United States began to thaw. Twenty years later, Castro was still in power, still anti-American, still attempting to spread the revolution, even though his lieutenant, Che Guevara had been killed years earlier. Trade relations with the United States never really resumed, but the open hostility had now given way to toleration.

One of the countries most synonymous with military dictorship after World War II was Argentina. They had several dictatorships after their independence from Spain, and a new period of authoritarianism began when Juan D. Peron came to power in 1946. Peron was a charismatic leader who appealed particularly to the working class; and his wife, Evita, was even more appealing than he. Originally a very poor girl, she fell in with Peron, bleached her hair blond, acquired a patina of glamour, and began a love affair with the poor Argentine people, who identified with her success and literally worshipped her. Under the Perons, Argentina was a police state, with spies, prisons, military parades and regular harranging of the crowds from the Casa Rosada. Evita dedicated swimming pools to the poor and gave out free bicycles, all the while draped in mink and diamonds. Gestures such as this were a substitute for any real social programs, and in the meantime, the Perons acquired a vast fortune. However, it must be said that Argentina prospered at that time in a way it ceased to do afterward, and Buenos Aires was a gleaming, elegant city, the "Paris" of South America. All this came to an end when Evita died of cancer at the age of thirty-three, in 1953. Peron was unable to keep power without her, and was overthrown in 1955. He was followed by a string of military regimes until 1973 when he was called back from exile. He returned with his third wife, Isabel, at his side; and also his first wife, in a glass casket. The Argentines began a process of deification for the deceased Evita.

The second Peron regime was brief, for Peron himself died July 1, 1974; and although Isabel tried to govern alone, she fell from power in 1976. A

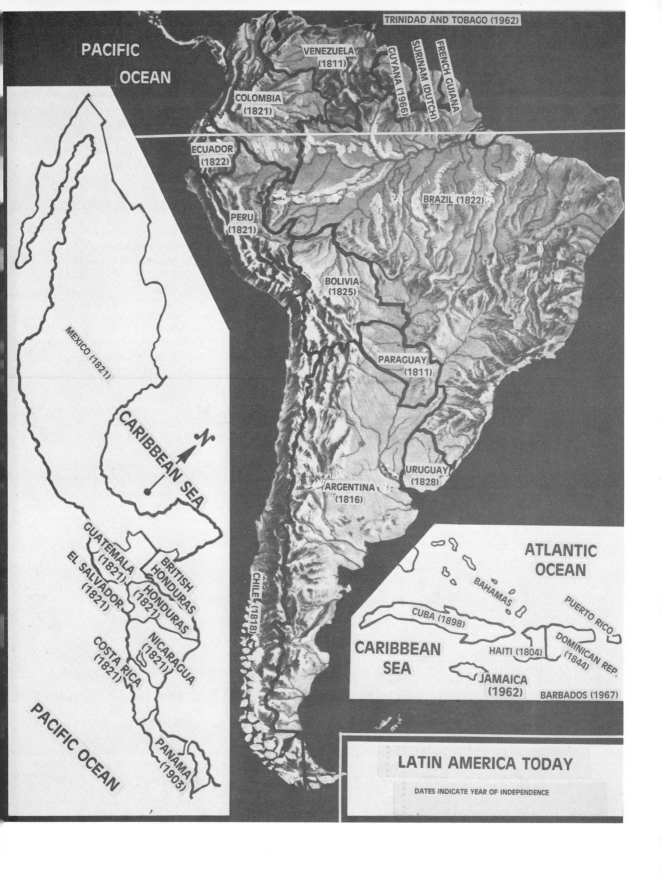

PACIFIC

OCEAN

TRINIDAD AND TOBAGO (1962)

VENEZUELA
(1811)

GUYANA
(1966)

SURINAM (DUTCH)

FRENCH GUIANA

COLOMBIA
(1821)

ECUADOR
(1822)

BRAZIL (1822)

PERU
(1821)

BOLIVIA
(1825)

PARAGUAY
(1811)

URUGUAY
(1828)

ARGENTINA
(1816)

CHILE (1818)

MEXICO (1821)

CARIBBEAN SEA

N

GUATEMALA
(1821)

EL SALVADOR
(1821)

BRITISH
HONDURAS

HONDURAS
(1821)

NICARAGUA
(1821)

COSTA RICA
(1821)

PANAMA
(1903)

PACIFIC OCEAN

ATLANTIC
OCEAN

BAHAMAS

PUERTO RICO

CUBA (1898)

CARIBBEAN
SEA

HAITI (1804)

DOMINICAN REP.
(1844)

JAMAICA
(1962)

BARBADOS (1967)

LATIN AMERICA TODAY

DATES INDICATE YEAR OF INDEPENDENCE

military junta thereupon seized control, and Argentina became a byword for terrorism and political murder. One of the richest countries in Latin America, with some of the world's best beef hoofing it about the pampas with the gauchos, Argentina has been plagued with meatless days, rampant inflation and unemployment. In 1982 they were humiliated when their then-dictator Leopoldo Galtieri tried to seize the Falkland Islands from Great Britain. A farcical little war ensued, which brought fanfare without glory to England, and disaster to Argentina. Galtieri fell from power, and once again the people were promised a return to democratic ways.

In the 1980's Latin America had mixed prospects. Two countries which had been democratic in the past were no longer--Uruguay and Chile. Two which were trying to be democratic, Mexico and Colombia, had very serious problems. Mexico, with only one political party, the PRI, had a limited democracy at best, but did have political stability. They had vast reserves of oil, but in 1982 their new president, Madrid, had an unprecedented economic crisis due to falling oil prices and a large debt. Columbia on the other hand, was plagued with banditry and turmoil from 1946 until 1958, when a military junta brought stability at the cost of represssion. By the 1980's they had settled down to regular elections, and enjoyed fair prosperity. One source of wealth was the coca plant, bringing in millions of dollars in revenue from the illegal sale of cocaine to the United States. The most stable government of all probably, was Venezuela, whose oil revenues gave them the highest per capita income in Latin America, $3,630 per year in 1982.

The most serious Latin American problems were those of Central America: as of 1983 El Salvador had been in a state of civil war for several years. Leftists supplied with Soviet arms via Cuba and Nicaragua were waging a persistent guerilla attack on the repressive rightest government. American aid to the government was increasing despite evidence of the government's corruption and inefficiency. As Congress was refusing to vote an increase in aid, the news media reported CIA involvement in trying to overthrow the leftist Sandanista government of Nicaragua, and Libyan involvement trying to keep it in power. Many Americans were alarmed at the continued interference of their government in Latin America, despite congressional efforts to curb the president's powers to send troops of military force secretly. Since the Vietnam War many Americans were determined to avoid any future conflicts.

Part II

Africa

One of the most important developments in the period following World War II was the break-up of colonial empires and the emergence of new nations in what is now known as the "Third World". The first such step came with the independence movement of India under Mahatma Gandhi. This was a unique development in that the Indians were non-violent, and the mother country, in this case England, granted independence without resorting to war. As a rule of thumb, one of the ways to differentiate between the political experience of the Third World countries is to first distinguish the mother countries: when the empires were English, the English way of doing government (the

202

"Westminster System"), English attitudes about law and justice, generally were conveyed to the colonials, with the result that in many cases democratic governments were created as the new nations came into being. The French, on the other hand, fought two wars to prevent the dissolution of their empire--the first in Indochina, the second in Algeria, with tragic results still apparent many years later. The French were also substantially less successful in transplanting a republican form of government overseas, perhaps because they had been less successful than the English in creating democratic stability at home. The Spanish not only fought to keep their empire, they never had a democratic government themselves, and endowed their colonies with an authoritarian political system. The results of this heritage were apparent in the 1980's, when democracy was only just beginning in Spain itself, and there was little in the way of democracy in Latin America (only Venezuela, Columbia and Mexico), but many examples of militarism and authoritarianism.

In Africa, the British had held the Gold Cost, Nigeria, Egypt, Rhodesia, Kenya, and South Africa by World War I. The Boer War had broken out in South Africa in the 1890's between the British and the Dutch settlers there, the Boers, over gold and diamonds. The English won the war, and in 1910 the Union of South Africa was created, with four provinces and a democratic government. The English, more liberal than the Boers, had originally alienated them by freeing the slaves, and after World War I created more disharmony by advocating liberal racial policies, including black participation in the government. Although there were fifty different native tribes, the Boers under the Afrikaner Nationalist Party, called for withdrawal from the Commonwealth, and racial separation. By World War II the Boers were getting the upper hand in the government, as they outnumbered the English in the population. They refused to sign the Universal Declaration of Human Rights at the founding of the United Nations in 1945. They won independence from Great Britain in 1961, and under Prime Minister H. F. Verwoerd rigorously began to restrict the freedom of the vast black population (21 million by 1981, or 68% of the population). Blacks were required to carry identity cards, and were subjected to laws restricting their marriages, their jobs and their place of residence. The black population several times expressed anger and frustration over this treatment in the next twenty years, more than once erupting in riots which led to death and imprisonment. Violence affected both sides: Verwoerd was assassinated. In 1977 the leading black leader in South Africa, Steve Biko, was murdered by the police. The government began to establish homelands for the black population in an effort to continue their policy of separation of the races (apartheid). There were ten of these "bantustans" or satellite states by 1983, none recognized internationally, and all of them a subject of bitter dispute because of their obvious role in keeping the black people out of power. Prime Minister P. W. Botha proposed a compromise of sorts in the 1980's, which was intended to deflate some of the foreign criticism of the racist regime. By his proposal, political power would be extended to two non-white groups, the Indians and the people of mixed race. He was heartily condemned for this on the one hand, by white supremacists, who opposed sharing any power whatsoever; but also by the spokesman for the majority population of the country--the black people who make up 72% of the 32 million people living there.

In Kenya, Rhodesia and Nigeria there was violence as independence arrived, but only in the first case was this due to a conflict between England and the

203

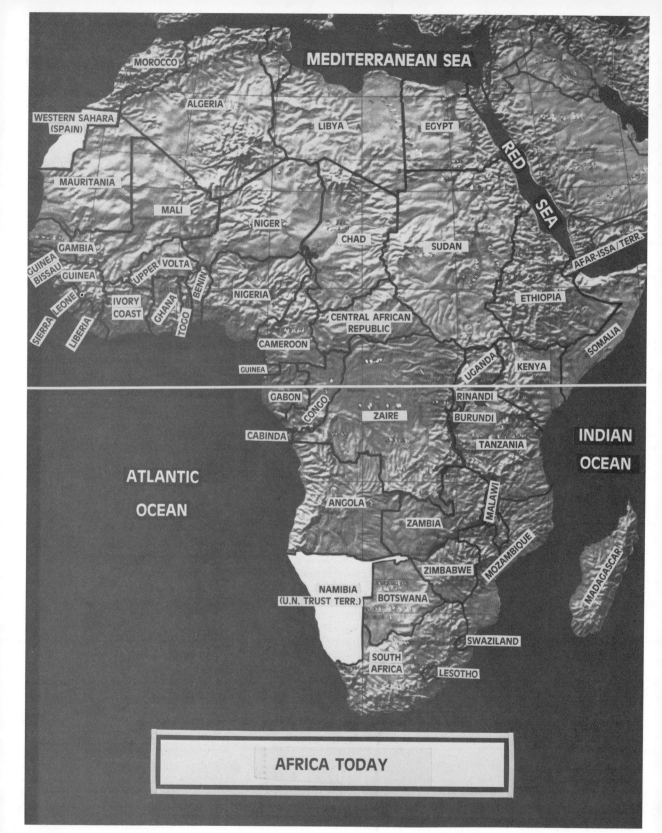

MEDITERRANEAN SEA

MOROCCO

ALGERIA

WESTERN SAHARA
(SPAIN)

LIBYA

EGYPT

RED SEA

MAURITANIA

MALI

NIGER

CHAD

SUDAN

AFAR-ISSA/TERR.

GAMBIA

GUINEA
BISSAU

GUINEA

UPPER VOLTA

BENIN

NIGERIA

ETHIOPIA

SIERRA LEONE

IVORY
COAST

GHANA

TOGO

CENTRAL AFRICAN
REPUBLIC

SOMALIA

LIBERIA

CAMEROON

GUINEA

UGANDA

KENYA

GABON

CONGO

ZAIRE

RINANDI

BURUNDI

CABINDA

TANZANIA

INDIAN

OCEAN

ATLANTIC

OCEAN

ANGOLA

ZAMBIA

MALAWI

MOZAMBIQUE

MADAGASCAR

ZIMBABWE

NAMIBIA
(U.N. TRUST TERR.)

BOTSWANA

SWAZILAND

SOUTH
AFRICA

LESOTHO

AFRICA TODAY

people seeking independence; the other instances resembled the violence of India, which had to do with internal conflicts and not with the English government. Even in Kenya the violence was not in opposition to independence movements but to terrorism. In 1952 a group of native kikuyus formed a secret terrorist society known as the Mau Mau, famous for their deadly and repulsive initiation rites, who murdered the families of a number of British colonists and spread terror throughout the land. The British responded by rounding up and murdering some 20,000 kikuyus. In 1954 they also prepared the colony for its independence, ultimately granted in 1961. Jomo Kenyatta was Kenya's first president, and served until his death in 1978.

Rhodesia, now called Zimbabwe, was originally created by Cecil Rhode's British South Africa Company, and like South Africa, had a white population which insisted on white supremacy. It declared its independence from England in 1965. For eleven years, President Ian Smith led them in a policy of resisting pressure from England, the United Nations and black Africans to grant some form of political participation for the black natives. Intermittent civil war continued, though Smith capitulated in 1976, and Britain oversaw a transition period during which Rhodesian blacks struggled among themselves for power. In 1980 after a ceasefire, a new constitution, and a general election, Robert Mugabe, a Marxist and guerilla leader became prime minister. With its history of racial animosity and twenty years or so of civil war, Zimbabwe looked to be an unlikely candidate for peaceful democratic rule.

Nigeria is one of the most important democracies in the world, but after many years of civil war and military rule appeared to be rather shaky. It won its independence from Britain in 1960, but had a particularly difficult task of reconciling ethnic and religious differences among its people. Unlike Kenya, Zimbabwe and South Africa, Nigeria did not have a considerable population of British colonials to complicate their independence: here there was no question of white supremacy. But there was a question of Moslem supremacy, of power being granted to the more aristocratic Hausa over the other tribes. In 1966 the Hausas began a massacre of Ibos, a well-educated, mostly Christian group who lived in east, and a civil war broke out. The Ibos created the state of Biafra and seceded from the union. Most western powers, including the United States, refused to recognize Biafra, and in the midst of terrible starvation and warfare the people submitted. Some authorites estimate one million Biafrans were killed. For twelve years there was military rule in Nigeria, but in 1978 a democratic government was created, a federal model very much like the United States. Shehu Shagari was elected president in 1979. After a violent recent history of three military coups, presidential assassinations, civil war, tribal conflict, corruption in the government, and economic turmoil, Nigeria appeared to lose more ground during Shagari's term. The most populous and the wealthiest black African nation, with very large oil reserves, the country has suffered financial reverses because of a drop in oil prices in the early 1980's.

If black Africa's birth pangs were harrowing for former British colonies, they were often worse for areas held by other European powers. One of the worst crises over independence took place in the Belgium Congo, known afterwards as Zaire. The Congo originally belonged to the King of Belgium, but was taken over by the country after complaints about forced labor and cruelty to the natives. The Europeans in that area were said to have been the cruelist of all colonial powers, and in the 1950's a movement for independence resulted in one of the bloodiest civil wars in African history. Zaire became a free republic in 1960, but Katanga province and South Kasai province tried to secede. Belgium sent paratroopers, and the U.N. sent a peacekeeping force. President Joseph Kasavubu engineered an army coup, and turned his opponent, Premier Patrice Lumumba over to Katangan forces, whereupon Lumumba was murdered, while on a mission to bring about a resolution of the problem. The secretary general of the U.N., Dag Hammarskjold, was also murdered. In 1965 General Joseph-Desiré Mobutu seized power (now called Mobutu Sese Seko), and continues to rule the country. He often asks the United States for assistance against Cuban and Russian troops which Mobutu claims are threatening Zaire from neighboring Angola. As recently as 1978 such an attack shattered the mining operations of Kolwezi, the center of Zaire's economy, and although Cuban and Russian troops took part, apparently large numbers of Katangan rebels played an important role as well.

Angola began its independence movement also in the late 1950's. Discovered in 1492 by Portugal and directly on the route to India, Angola was one of the oldest colonies in black Africa. In its four hundred years in Portugal's possession, Angola never received any experience in democratic forms of government, for Portugal was an absolute monarchy. A bitter war broke out over the independence issue, and it took a revolution at home in 1974 for Portugal to recognize Angola's independence. Meanwhile, Soviet and Cuban troops moved into the area, and the colony became a battleground between Marxist and Western ideology. The Marxist MPLA gained power in 1976, and nationalized nineteen major industries, mostly Portuguese. The Angolan government has been blamed repeatedly by Zaire for harboring soviet and Cuban expeditions against them.

Algeria, in north Africa, was French for over a hundred years and an integral part of their empire. While retaining its Arabic identity, it had close ties with the mother country; writers like Camus lived and wrote there: La Peste, a great modern classic, takes place in Algiers. The French were determined to block independence when the colony rebelled in the 1950's, and a bloody war ensued which reached a deadlock by 1958. In France the Fourth Republic fell over this issue, and General Charles De Gaulle came to power as President of the Fifth Republic with the pledge to end the war. The liberation of Algeria was bitterly opposed by the OAS, a secret army terrorist organization; while Algerians were equally determined to succeed. For several years Algerian terrorists exploded crude home-made bombs known as "plastiques" in Paris, terrorizing residents and tourists. De Gaulle arranged independence, with the consent of the French people, in 1962. Ahmed Ben Bella, the first president, nationalized foreign holdings and alienated much of the west; he was overthrown in 1965 in a military coup by Colonel Houari Boumediene, who restored friendly relations with France and the United States. Algeria intervened in the Iranian crisis of 1980 and secured the release of the fifty-two American hostages held in the U.S. embassy there. They are part of the Arab block. They fought against Israel in 1967, but maintain close ties with France. Like so many other new African nations, they are not a democracy.

QUESTIONS FOR REFLECTION

1.   Take several prominent Latin American countries, including Mexico, Colombia, Argentina and Cuba and compare their experiences since 1945. How many Latin American countries are democratic? How many were democratic in the past and now are under dictators?

2.   Why wouldn't the United States recognize Fidel Castro at the beginning? Do you think that was correct on our part, or foolish?

3.   What has been the role of the United States in Latin America in the 20th century? What is happening now in Nicaragua and El Salvador?

4.   Which countries in Africa are struggling today to establish democratic government? Which ones have had military regimes or dictatorships? Which ones are prosperous?

5.   Why is South Africa such a trouble spot? Is there any peaceful way to incorporate their black majority into the government?

SUGGESTED BIBLIOGRAPHY

E. Berger, The Covenant and the Sword: Arab-Israeli Relations, 1946-1956 (1965)
J. Buttinger, Vietnam: A Dragon Embattled (2 vols., 1967)
A. B. Cole, Forty Years of Chinese Communism (1962)
J. K. Fairbank, The United States and China (rev., 1958)
E. J. Hammer, The Struggle for Indochina (1966)
G. Henderson, Korea: The Politics of the Vortex (1968)
C. Hurewitz, Middle East Dilemmas (1953)
F. J. Khouri, The Arab-Israeli Dilemma (1968)
D. Kimche, A Clash of Destinies: The Arab-Jewish War and the Founding of the State of Israel (1960)
G. Myrdal, Asian Drama: An Inquiry into the Poverty of Nations (3 vols., 1968)
W. R. Polk, The United States and the Arab World (1965)
V. Purcell, The Revolution in Southeast Asia (1963)
J. Strachey, The End of Empire (1960)
C. Tuan-sheng, The Government and Politics of China, 1912-1949 (1961)
A. S. Whiting, China Crosses the Yalu: The Decision to Enter the Korean War (1960)

CHAPTER 16 - INTELLECTUAL LIFE IN THE 20TH CENTURY

In science and technology, the 20th century was a marvel of human ingenuity and brilliance. Machines broke through the limits of possibility; now there were radios, televisions and computers. Images and voices were transmitted in seconds; there were rockets and landings on the moon. There were medical breakthroughs of every sort; major diseases were cured forever with miracle drugs like penicillin. Science fiction stories of heart transplants and test-tube babies were now reality. Architecture symbolized much of this, for now buildings were bursting into the sky as skyscrapers, with peaks and bubbles and fantastic towers, like fireworks captured in concrete. Yet above all things it was a century of paradox. The 20th century also found ways to destroy it all, quicker and more tragically than ever before.

There were a number of themes traceable in the intellectual life of the century--one of them inspired by disillusionment with the world wars and the atomic bomb (existentialism); a second one carrying forth the consequences of the thinking of Freud and Darwin; a third one linked to the rapidly spreading democracy.

Part I

Culture Becomes Democratic

One striking characteristic of the 20th century was the growth of democracy; men and women were enfranchised throughout the western world, and entire new countries, such as India, with 800,000,000 people, became democratic. In culture also, the masses for the first time in history were able to enjoy and participate in intellectual life. The world of culture had always been refined, and limited to an elite of wealth, taste and intellect. The common man could not read, owned no books, never saw a good painting, never attended concerts featuring classical music. In the 1800's books were not difficult to understand, unless you couldn't read; and paintings were not abstruse--but you never got to see one. All this changed in the 20th century. First, education became available for everyone; and with literacy, and the steadily increasing amounts of free time, even the lower classes had the means to read. Their new expertise coincided with a revolution in printing; for suddenly the world's greatest books were printed in millions of cheap paperbacks; the most famous paintings were turned out in posters, pictures and postcards. Next, phonographs, radios, television and tapes made all the world's great music accessible to all: records and tapes proliferated. Operas and ballets and great plays were seen on film and every night on television, and the number of such productions increased with time, even as the cost of television fell to where it was affordable by all social classes.

In another way a democratic revolution took place: through the camera. Always in history the poor had passed in and out of existence without leaving a trace. Generally only kings or the very rich could afford to hire artists to paint their image. Art was not only decoration, it was also an historical record, sometimes the only record that a person had ever lived. Within a generation of its invention photography became available to the common man. The human instinct to leave some kind of record is a strong one, and even the poor and uneducated could afford to have one picture taken in their lifetime, often a wedding picture; if not, a picture at their death. But within a hundred years photography was so very cheap that ordinary people could have hundreds or even thousands pictures of themselves; they could take their own.

Leaving a record of their thoughts also became eminently possible. Throughout history thoughts of common people were lost forever; none of them could write; paper had not been invented. Many things changed this story; mass education, the availability and cheapness of paper, ink and the penny post stamps. Even so, writing letters was time-consuming and more a habit of the middle and upper classes. The invention of the telephone made communication of thoughts open to all. Typewriters, xeroxes, tape recorders and other inventions made it possible for anyone to record an idea in writing or with his actual voice, and also to reproduce it dozens of times.

These marvels are not without irony. First of all, as the ability to keep in touch with loved ones, talk to them however far away, keep their pictures, even hear their voices after they were dead, did nothing to improve human closeness. On the contrary, the 20th century was the century of divorce and alienation. Likewise, the ability to obtain and keep forever millions of records of ordinary people suddenly changed the value of the records. A laundry list from ancient Egypt, a love letter from a Viking would be priceless treasures. Today, the sheer output of human communication is so colossal that millions of tons of letters, memos, tapes and records are destroyed every day, and if they weren't, the earth would soon be buried under them.

As the masses acquired the ability to enjoy cultural works, they in turn affected the nature of those works. This led to the pessimistic prediction that the lowest common denominator would prevail, that the comic book mentality would chase away the real works of art. This has not happened. True, comic book art became high culture with Roy Lichtenstein's paintings in the 1960's (not to mention Andy Warhols' paintings of Campbell Soup cans), but good works of art became steadily more available, not less. The good and the bad existed side by side. In music for example, the music of common people became both available and popular; black music, folk songs, country and western music all became popular worldwide. The democratic process was still working in culture, for the elite began to appreciate the talents of the people. Yet at the same time the classics proliferated.

However in the century when at last culture became available to the common man, when millions of reproductions of great works of art could be bought for a song, there was still a barrier between the common man and culture. Now the barrier was not the cost or the rarity of the object. Rather, the barrier was built into the object by the artist himself, so that it was still true that only a tiny elite could possibly enjoy many of the cultural works of the 20th century. In painting, the artists became totally abstract. Literature became incomprehensible; and music became strange and dissonant. This was particulary ironic, for in the century with all the technological marvels in communications, it was above all the century of incomprehensibility. At the time when man could communicate with unprecedented speed and accuracy, one of the great truisms seemed to be his inability to communicate, or his wish not to communicate. This feature of modern culture is related to the continued influence of Freud and Darwin.

Part II

Intellectual Impact of Darwin and Freud

The 19th century romantic movement had been an anti-intellectual movement, a rebellion against reason, a celebration of the senses and the heart. In the 20th century there was still a strongly anti-intellectual and anti-scientific attitude. This was partly an expression of "democracy", an objection to elites in society. It was also due to the continued impacts of Darwin and Freud, on thinking, for both had theories which stressed the irrational aspects of human behavior. From Darwin came ideas about the influence of the environment, and the importance of physical (as against mental) characteristics, such as brute strength. People were the victims of forces beyond their control; survival depended on physical strength, not brains. From Freud came another revelation, that people were the victims of their own subconscious. People were shaped by experiences they had when very young (also forces beyond their control); and these experiences, long forgotten, visited upon them dreams, strange impulses, phobias, hysterial behavior, or any number of adult ills. The way to cure mental disturbance was to encourage the patient to relate the dreams, or to tell in stream-of-consciousness fashion what sort of things were on their mind. The theories of both Freud and Darwin had a significant impact on intellectual and artistic creativity in the 20th century.

In the case of Freud, literature first began to show the impact of his thinking with such original works as Ulysses, by James Joyce. This stream-of-consciousness novel was a voyage through the subconscious, and possibly the most influential literacy work of the past two hundred years. Ironically, considering its irrational emphasis, only the most dedicated of scrupulous intellectuals could hope to understand it. In poety a similar path was taken, particularly some years later, in the works of Gertrude Stein, e.e. cummings and Marianne Moore. The emphasis was no longer on logical, orderly sequence of ideas, meter and much less, rhyme; but in words themselves and the images and/or emotions they evoke. "A rose is a rose is a rose", wrote Gertrude Stein--a line frequently quoted, and usually misunderstood. Indeed, if Ulysses was a difficult book, modern poetry sometimes seemed completely incomprehensable.

Something similar happened in painting. At the turn of the century when the Impressionists were at their height, Cezanne was already painting in a style which foreshadowed Cubism. Matisse, Picasso and Bracque were all experimenting with shapes in painting, trying to take an object apart and put it back together on a canvas, not necessarily in its familiar form. After World War I Cubism was a major movement; and also the German and Russian school of expressionists. Wassily Kandinsky painted grim foreboding canvasses like nightmares, of people soundlessly screaming in dark ominous shapes, a

configuration of dark colors and bizarre distortions which spelled anxiety.
These were not familiar representational paintings, but were at least
recognizable figures. The next change was to abstract expressionism, bare
emotions which were revealed by color alone. These two schools of painting
seemed to draw their inspiration directly from the work of Freud, as if the
subconscious mind of the artist with all his hidden fears and hopes, were laid
bare for all to see. One of the leading abstract expressionists after World
War II was Jackson Pollack, an American. He dribbled streams of paint
directly from the tubes onto enormous canvasses on the floor, creating an
effect of light and energy and spontaneity--but not for the average viewer.

One of the other 20th century schools of painting which baffled the common
man was Surrealism, most known from the works of Salvador Dali, or the Belgian
artist, René Magritte. Dali seemed to paint directly from his subconscious,
strange "surreal"--that is, unreal--landscapes from a world of dreams, deserts
strewn with clocks, distant figures, a large flower; the ubiquitous clocks
were sometimes distorted, like large blobs of butter which had melted in the
sun. The dreamworld of Dali was fascinating to intellectuals, and his
symbolism of time distorted by thoughts and memories seemed inspired to them.
Again, the average man could make nothing of it; nor could he understand the
whimsical work of Magritte, who liked to show large eyes with clouds and sky
in them, like windows.

Part III

Existentialism

One of the anomalies of the century was that as the common man learned to
read and had access to paintings and great music, he found that there was
still a barrier there: he couldn't understand them. Freud and Darwin
crystallized feelings that there were many things lurking beneath man's
subconscious or out in the physical world which affected his life but were
beyond his ken. Man was driven, beaten down, by alien and unknowable fears
and fantasies. This theme was reitereated in a different way by the
predominant philosophy of the century, existentialism, which was the ultimate
statement that life was unknowable, and existence imcomprehensible. Now that
man thought he could know all, he knew nothing. Life was meaningless. World
War I had been a senseless slaughter of ten million people; its tragic
insanity was summed up in T.S. Eliot's poem, The Wasteland. The futility of
existence seemed particularly pronounced in Paris, where artists and
intellectuals gathered in cafés on the left bank, and in a mist of absinthe,
tried to winnow out the sorrows of the world. Germans Martin Heidigger and
Karl Jaspers, and Frenchmen Jean-Paul Satre and Albert Camus became the
leading exponents of existentialism between the wars. They had little in
common other than a distrust of reason and science, and doubt. World War II
confirmed all their skepticism, for now mankind had the atomic bomb, and the
fascist cry, "Long live death!" seemed to have taken over man's mind. This
world of alienation and strangeness was depicted in many ways, in the years
after the war, including a spate of brilliant films (mostly from the 1960's),
including Breathless, The Four Hundred Blows and Last Year at Marienbad.
These provided sensitive images of 20th century man: he is always running but

has no destination--the running is the only meaningful thing, and that is meaningless. Reality is a mystery; appearance is an illusion. Another provocative film was Blowup, which used a story about photography to show that reality is unreal; images are fantasies; life is an illusion.

With all the astounding technological and scientific progress, man was still groping for the meaning of existence, and wondering if life was really any better than before. There seemed to be no limits to human unhappiness, or man's capacity for violence. In his novel, The Plague (La peste), Albert Camus explored human behavior during a catastrophe, and tried to provide guidelines for ethical values which would persist in an uncertain world.

One reason why this seemed to be a difficult and perhaps even impossible task, is that there had been yet another major influence on man's thinking in this century: Albert Einstein had come up with the Theory of Relativity. Like all great scientific breakthroughs, the importance of this theory for physics was beyond the comprehension of the vast majority of the people. However, practically anyone could grasp one of its implications, the fact that knowledge and even supposedly immutable laws of nature are not immutable after all: a man may believe the trees and grass around him are moving, but if he is on a train and the train is moving, the movement of the trees and grass is an illusion. Man had come full circle and was back with some of the principle puzzles to men of the Enlightenment: Descarte was concerned with sense perceptions, and so was man in the 1980's. Just because your eyes perceive that something is moving is not sufficient proof that is really is. "Everything is relative", was the conclusion, even morality. This tied in with Freud's concern with the subconscious. There was no longer a fixed definition of right and wrong; if a man acts out of subconscious fears created in him when he was an innocent child, how can he be guilty of wrong? Again, one reason for the inordinate and long-term fascination with Hitler and Nazi Germany was that that was the one development in the century which everyone could agree had been wrong, and it was terribly comforting for that reason. Every other event or deed seemed "relative"; even murderers were viewed by many people as innocent victims, and their victims as guilty.

Yet the people were uneasy with this amoral or relativistic point of view. One reason for the popularity of the enormously successful movie, "Star Wars" (apart from its witty and charming robots), was its age-old theme of good versus evil, coming to grips in an imaginative science fiction duel. The movie was comforting to an audience which was uneasy about relative attitudes on good and evil, for the comic book figures left no doubt in anyone's mind--Darth Vadar, the giant heavy-breathing figure in black armor was the most easily identifiable villain in recent memory. And the best way of tackling evil was also reassuring: once again the message was to forget science and reason, and to rely in time of trouble upon ituition, a romantic and emotional admonition, very popular among unscientific and not yet educated young people. In his moment of truth, Luke Skywalker flung aside his scientific controls and in his fight to the death relied on the Force.

QUESTIONS FOR REFLECTION

1. How many questions which have plagued mankind have been asked continuously since the 18th century? How have the answers changed? Are any of the answers of the 1980's the same as answers arrived at in earlier periods?

2. In the 1980's does man still believe in progress? Does most of the population believe in the value of science and reason? Are their anti-intellectual currents in the American population? How many kinds of evidence can you cite of people who still feel more comfortable with the Romantic solution to the world's problems--a reliance on intuition, the "heart" and not the mind?

3. How does art, literature and music in the 20th century differ from works created in previous centuries? In what ways is 20th century art, literature and music completely unique? How many possible explanations can you think of to account for this?

4. How have Freud, Darwin, and inventions in technology each had a separate and distinct impact upon culture?

5. Which works of art and literature do you feel most comfortable with? Have you ever tried to understand abstract painting or modern music?

SUGGESTED BIBLIOGRAPHY

G. Carter, Independence for Africa (1960)
P. Collaer, A History of Modern Music (1961)
M. Colum, From These Roots: The Ideas That Have Made Modern Literature (1944)
W. Haftmann, Painting in the Twentieth Century, 2 vols. (1965)
J. Hatch, A History of Postwar Africa (1965)
H. S. Hughes, Consciousness and Society: The Reorientation of European Social
   Thought, 1890-1930 (1958)
C. Mauriac, The New Literature (1959)
A. Neumeyer, The Search for Meaning in Modern Art (trans. 1964)
R. Oliver and S. D. Fage, A Short History of Africa (1962)
H. Rosenberg, The Anxious Object: Art Today and Its Audience (1964)
M. White, ed., The Age of Analysis (1955)
D. L. Wredner, A History of Africa South of the Sahara (1962)

INDEX

Braun, Eva, 156
Brest-Litovsk, Treaty of, 111
Brezhnev, Leonid, 182, 183
Briand, Aristide, 119
Brooke Farm (commune), 54
"Brown Shirts", (SA), 127
Brown vs. Board of Education,
    Topeka, Kan., (1954), 169
Burschenschaft, 31
"Butterfly Principle" (Fourier),
    54
"Buzz Bombs" (U-2 rocket), 158
Byron, Lord (poet), 31, 38

Calas, Jean, 3
Calvin, John, 3, 44
Camp David (Accord), 189
Camus, Albert, 206, 211
Canada, 100
Candide (Voltaire), 1
Carbonari, 34
Carnegie, Andrew, 47, 67, 79
"Carpet baggers", 79
Carter, President Jimmy, 189
Cartwright, Edmund, 46
Caste System (India), 102
Casto, Fidel, 81, 199, 200
Cavour, Count Camillo, 60
Ceauseseu, Nicolae, 181
Central Powers, 112
Cezanne, Paul, 91
Chamberlain, Neville, 149
Charles X, King of France, 29
Charter Act, 1833, (re: India),
    102
Chartists, 83
Chiang Chi'ung, 194
Chiang Kai-shek, 144, 193
China, 104-105
China, Nationalist, 163, 193
China, Peoples Republic Of, 163, 193
Chopin, Frederic, 39
Chou En-lai, 194
Christian Phalangists (Lebanon),
    191
Christianity, 184
Churchill, Winston, 102, 109,
    141, 152, 157, 159, 176
Civil Constitution of the
    Clergy, 13, 14
"Civil Rights", 169

Civil Rights Act (1964), 171
Clemenceau, Georges, 115
Code of Napoleon, 17
Colombia, (S.A.), 202
Committee of Public Safety, 15
Common Market, 174, 177, 179
Communism, 122, 123
Communism-Fascism (compared),
    122, 123
Communist Manifesto (1848), 56
Comte, August, 51
Concert of Europe, 25
Concordat of 1801, 17
Condorcet, Marquis de, 1
Confederacy (U.S., Civil War),
    67
Confederation of the Rhine, 21
Congress of Vienna, 25, 27
Congress Party (India), 143
Conquistadores, 44, 97
Constitution of U.S., 10-11
Consulate, 16, 17
"Containment", 166
Continental Congresses, First
    and Second, 8
Coolidge, Pres. Calvin, 138
Corvée, 12
Council of Europe (1949), 179
Crimeán War, 59
Crusades, 187
Cuba, independence acquired, 80
Cuban Missile Crisis, 172, 200
Cultural revolution, 194

Daladier, Edouard, 142
Dali, Salvadore, 211
Daly, Mayor James (Chicago), 172
Darwin, Charles, 87, 94, 210, 211
David, Jaques, 2, 41
Dawes Plan, 127
Debussey, Claude, 93
Decembrist Revolt (1825), 28
Declaration of Independence
    (1776), 8, 10
Declaration of Pillnitz, 14
Declaration of the Rights of Man
    (France), 13
Declaratory Act (1766), 8
Decline and Fall of the Roman
    Empire (Gibbon), 2
Deefield Massacre, 7

Marie Antoinette, Queen of
    France, 14
Marshall Plan, 166
Marx, Karl, 54, 55, 56, 111
Matteotti, Giacomo, 125
Mau Mau, 205
Maupassant, Guy de (French
    writer), 64, 89
Maximilian (Austria, Mexico), 74
Mayflower Compact, 4
Mazzini, Guiseppe, 34, 59
McCarthy, Sen. Joseph, 167
McKinley, Pres. William, 80, 81
Mead, Margaret, 95
Mein Kampf, 127
Mensheviks, 111
Mercantilism, 2, 51
Metternich, Prince, 27, 59
Mill, John Stuart, 52
Mir, 69, 70
Missouri Compromise (1850), 65,
    66
Mitterand, François, 176
Mobutu, Gen. Joseph O., 206
Mohammedanism, 186
Molotov Plan, 167
Monroe Doctrine (1823), 28, 65,
    81, 199
Montesquieu, 5, 6
Montgomery, George, 156
Morgan, J. P., 79
Moussorgsky, Modeste, 40, 92
Mozart, Wolfgang, 3
"Muckrakers", 82
Mugabe, Robert, 205
Mussolini, Benito, 124, 125

Nagasaki, 161
Nagy, Imre, 181
Nanking, Treaty of (1842), 104
Napoleon III (emporer, Second
    Empire, France), 60, 64, 74,
    82
Napoleon Bonaparte, 15, 16-22
Narodniki, 69
Nasser, Gamel Abdel (Egypt), 167
Nation, Carrie, 137
National Assembly, 12, 13
National Constituent Assembly,
    13
National Convention, 14, 15

Nazi Party, 127
Necker, 12
Nehru, Jawaharlal, 144
Neoclassicism, 2
NEP (New Economic Policy), 131
"New Deal", 140
New Harmony (commune), 54
Newton, Sir Isaac, 1, 51
Nicaragua, 199, 202
Nicholas I, Czar of Russia, 29
Nicholas II, Czar of Russia,
    70
Nietzche, Friedrich, 88
Nigeria, 205
Nightengale, Florence, 59
Nihilists, 69
Nixon, Pres. Richard, 169, 171,
    172, 189, 194, 197
NLF, National Liberation Front,
    197
Nobel, Alfred, 47
Non-violent Resistance, 144
Normandy Invasion, 155
North American Act of 1867
    (Brit.), 100
Northern Society, 29
Northwest Ordinance (1787), 10
Nuremburg Trials, 162

October Manifesto (1905), 70
Oedipus Complex, 93
On Civil Disobedience (Thoreau),
    144
On Liberty (J.S. Mill), 53
Oneida (commune), 54
OPEC (int'l oil cartel), 192
"Open Door" Policy (China), 105
Orange Free State, 100
Orlando, Vittorio, 115, 123-124
Orwell, George, 133, 135
Ottman Empire (Turkey), 112, 113
Ottoman Empire, 28, 29
Owen, Robert, 54

Pahlavi, Shah (Iran), 192
Pain, Thomas, 8
Palestine, 187
Panama, 199
Panama Canal, 82
Parks, Rosa, 171

Parnell, Charles Stuart, 84
Pasternak, Boris, 192
Pasteur, Louis, 50
Patton, Gen. George, 156
Pavlov, Ivan, 95
Peace Corps, 171
Pearl Harbor, Attack on, 154
Peninsular War, 19
Peron, Evita, 200
Peron, Juan D., 200
Perry, Mathew, Cmdr. U.S.N., 103
Physiocrats, 1
Picasso, Pablo, 91, 135, 210
Pinchet, (Dict., Chile), 81, 82
Pinochet, Augusto, 199
Platt Amendment, 80, 199, 200
Plessy vs. Ferguson, 79, 169
PLO, Palestine Liberation
    Organization, 190, 191
Polignac, Prince de (France),
    29
Polish Solidarity Movement, 182
Polk, Pres. James K., 65
Pollack, Jackson, 211
Portsmouth, Treaty of (1905),
    104
Potsdam, 162
Powers, Francis Gary
    (U-2 pilot), 169
Predestination (Calvin), 3
Protestant Ethic, 44, 166
Protestant Reformation, 3
Proust, Marcel, 90
Psychoanalysis, 93, 94
Psychology, 93-95
Pullman Strike, 79-80
Puritans, 4, 44, 88

Quadruple Alliance, 27
Quebec Act (1774), 7
Quesnay, François, 1

Radar, 152
Rasputin, Gregory, 70-71, 110
Ravel, Maurice, 93
"Reconstruction" (U.S. after
    Civil War), 67, 79
Reform Bill of 1832 (Eng), 8, 83
Reichstag Fire, 129
Reign of Terror (France), 14, 15
Reinsurance Treaty, 76

Remarque, Erich Maria, 109
Renoir, Pierre, 91
Reynolds, Sir Joshua, 2
Rhodes, Cecil, 100, 205
Ricardo, David, 51, 52
Rivera, Gen. Primo de, 134
"Roaring Twenties", 137, 138
Robespierre, Maximilien, 15
Rockefeller, John D., 47, 67,
    79, 166
Rococo Style, 2
Roehm, Capt., S.A., 127
Roger-Ducos, 16
Romanticism, 36-41
"Rome-Berlin Axis", 149
Rommel, Gen. Erwin, 156
Roosevelt, Pres. Franklin D.,
    81, 138, 139, 157
Roosevelt, Eleanor, 138
Roosevelt, Theodore ("Teddy"),
    vice pres., and president,
    80, 82
Rosas, Juan M. de, 99
Rosetta Stone, discovery of, 16
Rousseau, Henri, 91
Rousseau, Jean J., 2, 4, 5, 37,
    38
Rudolph (Prince of Austria), 74
Runstedt, Gen. von, 152
Russo-Japanese War, 77, 104
Rymsky-Korsakov, 92, 93

Sadat, Pres., Anwar El, 189, 190
Saint-Simon, Henri, Count of, 54
Sakharov, Andrei, 182
"Salutary Neglect", 7
San Stefano, Treaty of, 76
Sand, George, 39
Sanger, Margaret, 137
Santa Anna, Antonio L. de, 99
Sartre, Jean-Paul, 211
Sati, 102
"Scaliwags", 79
Schleswig-Holstein, 62
Schlieffen, Count, 108
Schmidt, Helmut, 178
Schuschnigg, Kurt von, 149
Scott, Sir Walter, 39
SEATO (South East Asian Treaty
    Organization), 196
"Second International", 111

Serfs (Freedom of, Russia, 1861), 69
Seurat, Georges, 91
Sexual Revolution, 94
Seven Years War (1756-63), 7, 10
Shagari, Shehu, 205
Shelley, Mary, 38
Shelley, Percy Bysshe, 38
Shiite, 186
Shuman, Robert, 179
Sibelius, Jan, 93
Siéyés, Abbé, 13, 16
Sinclair, Upton, 49, 82, 90
Sinn Fein, 141
Smith, Adam, 1, 2, 51
Smith, Ian, 205
Social Contract, 4, 5, 14
Social Darwinism, 87-88, 89
Solzhenitsyn, Aleksander, 182
Sorel, Georges, 125
South Africa, 100
Southern Society, 29
Spanish Civil War (1936), 134, 135, 149
Spanish-American War, 80
Speer, Albert, 130
Spencer, Herbert, 90
SPD (Social Democratic Party, Germ. 1875), 76, 178
Sputnik, 169
Stalin, Joseph, 70, 110, 131-33, 157
Stalingrad, Battle of, 153
Stamp Act (1765), 8
Stavisky Scandal (France), 142
Stein, Gertrude, 210
Steinbeck, John, 138
Stephenson, George, 46
Stevens, Thaddeus, 78
Stolypin, Peter, 70
Stresemann, Gustave, 119
Subjection of Women (J.S. MIll), 53
Sudetenland, 149
Suez Canal, 176
"Suffragettes" (England), 141
Sugar Act (1764), 8
Sumner, Charles, 78
Sun Yat-sen, 105, 144, 145
Sunni, 186
Syndicalism, 125

Talleyrand, 25
"Tammany Hall", 79, 81
Tannenberg, Battle of, 72
Tchaikovsky, Peter, 92-93
Teng Hsiao-P'ing, 194
Thatcher, Margaret (Prime Minister of England), 177, 178
Thermidorean Reaction, 15
Thier, Adolph, 32, 33
Thieu, Ngyen van, 197
Third French Republic, 82, 142, 174
Third Reich, 129
"Third World", 202
Thoreau, Henry David, 144
Three Emperor's League, 76
Thurmond, Sen. Strom, 172
Till, Emmet, 171
Tito, Marshal Joseph Broz, 166
Tolstoy, Leo, 90
Tom Jones (Novel, Fielding), 2
Tour, Battle of, 187
Townshend, Charles, 8
Townshend, Charles "Turnip", 48
Transvaal, 100
Treaty of Chaumont (1814), 25
Triple Alliance, 76
"Triple Entente", 77
Troppau Protocol, 28
Trotsky, Leon, 70, 110, 131
Truman, Pres. Harry S., 157, 159, 167, 169
Turgenev, Ivan, 90
Turner, Frederick Jackson, 7, 80
Twain, Mark (Samuel Clemens), 89
Twenty-Fourth Amendment, 171

U-2 Incident, 169
ULSTER, 141
Union of South Africa, 102
United Nations, 163
University of Berlin, 22
Utilitarians, 52
Utopia (T. More), 53
Utopian Socialism, 53, 54

Valera, Eamon de, 141
Van Gogh, 91
Velasques, René, 91
Versailles, Treaty of, 113-118, 119, 161